Arthur Roland, William H Ablett

Dairy-Farming

Management of Cows, etc.

Arthur Roland, William H Ablett

Dairy-Farming
Management of Cows, etc.

ISBN/EAN: 9783337198336

Printed in Europe, USA, Canada, Australia, Japan

Cover: Foto ©Lupo / pixelio.de

More available books at **www.hansebooks.com**

FARMING
FOR
PLEASURE AND PROFIT.

FARMING
FOR
PLEASURE AND PROFIT

Dairy-Farming,
Management of Cows, etc.

BY
ARTHUR ROLAND.

EDITED BY WILLIAM H. ABLETT.

New Edition.

LONDON: CHAPMAN AND HALL,
LIMITED.
1891.

CONTENTS.

CHAPTER I.

INTRODUCTORY.

PAGE

The present Work suggested by Inexperienced Friends—Being One's own Customer—Arthur Young, and a "Book of Experiments"—Jethro Tull—Circumstances which caused me to turn my first Attention to Farming—Common Error that Professional Farmers are the Best—First Experiment with Selling Turnips—Business Men and Gentlemen above Dealing with trifling Amounts—The Finer Kinds of Vegetables—Selling Shelled Peas—Carrying Vegetables up to Town—Selling "Porker" Pigs to a Pork-butcher—Skimmed Milk—Cooks and Vegetables—Contrivance for Kitchen Refuse—Conscientious Foreman often branded as a Tell-tale 3

CHAPTER II.

DAIRY FARMING.

First Attempts—Various Breeds of Cows—The Alderney—The Shorthorn—Ayrshire—Longhorns—The Herefords—The North Devons—The Suffolk Dun—West

Highland Cattle, or Kyloes—The Galloway—Points of a Good Cow—Difference in Cows—General Management—Saving One's Hay—Dairy Practice in Various Counties 27

CHAPTER III.

THE DAIRY.

Situation of the Dairy—Dairy Utensils, etc.—Produce to be aimed at—Quality of Milk—Management of Milk—Butter-making—Clotted or Clouted Cream—Butter from Clotted Cream 52

CHAPTER IV.

Cheese-making—Cheshire System—Gloucester Cheese—Egg Cheeses—Stilton Cheese—Cream Cheese—Skim-milk Cheese—New Cheese—Cheese made Abroad—Parmesan Cheese—Potato Cheese—Whole-milk Cheese—Rennet—Scotch Method of preparing Rennet 78

CHAPTER V.

Milking—Quantity of Milk yielded by Cows—Feeding—Straw, chaffed, as Food for Cows—Turnip-tasting Butter—Quantity of Meal, etc.—Quality of Butter dependent upon Feeding—The Butter Trade in Ireland—Summer Feeding—Feeding Dry Cows—Feeding with Hay on Bare Pastures 103

CHAPTER VI.

Calving—Time for Cows to Calve—Fifeshire System—
Gloucestershire System—Milk Farms—Castrating—
Cow-list—Mr. Hayward's Calculations 135

CHAPTER VII.

Rearing the Calf—Scouring in Calves—Whole-milk for
Calves—Feeding Calves in Massachusetts—Various
Methods of rearing Calves—American and Canadian
Cattle and Meat 155

CHAPTER VIII.

DISEASES OF COWS.

Abortion (Slinking, Slipping-Calf, Warping)—The Drop—
Inversion of the Uterus—Meteorisation (Hoove, Hoven,
or Blasting)—Distension of the Rumen—Choking—
Loss of Cud—Inflammation of the Rumen—Milk Fever
—Garget (Diseases of the Udder)—The Cow-pox—
Retention or Stoppage of the Urine—Sore Teats—
Moor-ill, or Wood-evil—Pleuro-pneumonia—Foot and
Mouth Disease (Epidemic)—Paralysis—Palsy or Tail-
slip—Redwater—Hepatitis—Rheumatism (Joint-felon,
Chine-felon) — Quarter-ill — Blood-striking — Black-
quarter—Fardel-bound—Blain, or Gloss Anthrax—
Foul in the Foot—Loo, or Low—The Thrush, or
Aphthæ — Mange — Lice — Diarrhœa — Catarrh—
Bronchitis 175

FARMING FOR PLEASURE & PROFIT.

DAIRY FARMING.

DAIRY FARMING.

CHAPTER I.
INTRODUCTORY.

The present Work suggested by inexperienced Friends—Being One's own Customer—Arthur Young, and a "Book of Experiments"—Jethro Tull—Circumstances which caused me to turn my first Attention to Farming—Common Error that Professional Farmers are the best—First Experiment with Selling Turnips—Business Men and Gentlemen above Dealing with trifling Amounts—The finer Kinds of Vegetables — Selling Shelled Peas — Carrying Vegetables up to Town—Selling "Porker" Pigs to a Pork-butcher—Skimmed Milk—Cooks and Vegetables—Contrivance for Kitchen Refuse—Conscientious Foreman often branded as a Tell-tale.

IT has often been suggested to me by various friends engaged in business that I should publish an account of the methods of cultivation and management which I have adopted upon my little farm, consisting of fifty-five acres, made up of forty acres of grass-land and plantations—the latter being, perhaps, five acres in extent—ten of arable, and five of hops; giving a detailed account of the technical treatment pursued in the case of each crop, and also of stock; in order that my experience may be serviceable to those who, like myself, at the period when I first turned my attention to the matter, are destitute of practical acquaintance with the subject.

Many of these, with a comical air of plaintiveness, have deplored the fact that their attachment to country pursuits and occupations, either when directed into the channel of rearing a little stock, or in growing farm produce, has alike turned out an expensive hobby; so that, instead of gaining, they have lost money by what they have undertaken.

In endeavouring to comply with the suggestion, it has occurred to me that it would be as well perhaps if I were to give a short account of all the circumstances which caused me to become a farmer upon a small scale, while carrying on a business in London; which, in my case, has resulted both in pleasure and profit.

As will be seen in the course of the details I am about to furnish, I did not jump into active operations all at once, but went to work very gradually, and felt my way from time to time in what I undertook, laying down one main principle—that, as far as possible, I would be my own customer for the produce raised. That is to say, that I would supply my household with butter, milk, bacon, fresh pork, eggs, vegetables, fruit, honey, flour for bread; oats, beans, and straw for my horses; hay, etc.; selling my surplus.

I began strictly upon this principle, and as I proceeded I found I had large quantities of produce to dispose of upon various occasions, which ultimately conferred a far greater degree of importance upon my work than at first contemplated, while a considerable amount of profit solaced me for what pains I took; which, indeed, at all times to me has been a labour of love, and never proved in the least irksome.

In the course of my experience, desirous of acquiring all the knowledge I could obtain upon agricultural subjects, I have read a great many books of one sort and another; and, amongst other authors, Arthur Young, who has done so much for British agriculture, throws out an idea to which my present attempt may perhaps form some slight resemblance.

He says: "The publication of experiments really made, faithfully related, and sufficiently authenticated, is of great and important consequence to the public good. But the very reverse is the case of those books which are published under the title of 'General Treatises and Systems,' comprehending more soils, articles of culture, etc., than any one man can experimentally have a knowledge of; consisting of the most heterogeneous parts purloined out of former books on the same subjects, without a common knowledge to discover the good from the bad. It has been said several times, and with very great justice, that what we want is a book of experiments. If any practical, intelligent husbandman, who occupied a farm, would only keep an exact register of all his business, such a collection would form, as far as it extended, a complete set of experiments. What we have are the author's reflections, instead of that which enabled him to reflect; and from which we might draw very different conclusions. The experiment is truth itself; the author's conclusions, matter of opinion which we may either agree to, or reject, according to our private notions."

The truth of Young's remarks were especially verified to me, when I came across the writings of Jethro Tull, the inventor of the drill and the horse-hoeing system of husbandry, to whom I shall again refer; and his narration of the circumstances which caused him to make certain experiments were, to me, very interesting.

The great difficulty, however, of taking as a precedent another person's experience is, that not only is modification of practice caused by difference in climate, but by variety of soil, which, while it enables, we will say, the finest carrots to be grown in the sandy soil of Surrey, will prevent them being a successful crop in the stiff clay-land of some other district; while beans, which do so admirably in a strong land of an adhesive character, answer but poorly in sandy soils.

It was the view of furnishing authentic details of every branch of rural economy, and the methods of procedure followed in each district throughout the kingdom, which induced the Government to establish a Board of Agriculture in the year 1793, under the presidency of Sir John Sinclair, with Arthur Young as secretary. The labours of this Board were chiefly directed to the arrangement of accurate agricultural surveys of every county in the kingdom, many of which were made by practical farmers and men of business—as land surveyors and others—at a time when agriculture was enjoying a period of unexampled prosperity, when particular attention had been directed to the cultivation of the soil, and abundant capital and enterprise brought to its aid, the result of the political situation of the country at that precise period. Its work having been thought completed in the year 1813, the institution was then dissolved.

It has been supposed that a great impetus to farming was given when the Bank of England, in 1797, stopped its payment of coin, and issued an unlimited paper currency, which afforded great facilities for the creation of trading capital, so that, speculation being rife, every article which was of everyday consumption was soon raised to an artificial value, and the very high price of grain in the years 1800 and 1801, and from 1809 to 1813, was the means of attracting a great deal of public attention to farming. These were the times which were spoken of by old farmers in the last generation as the "good old times," when they realised a very high price for their produce. But rents and tithes were advanced accordingly, and when the return to a metallic currency and cash payments reduced these fictitious values, the stimulus which had formerly been given to the practice of agriculture, received a corresponding check. At the season referred to, the temptation which led to the more extended growth of corn was the means of causing a vast amount of what had hitherto been permanent pasture to be broken up ; and while agriculture flourished, many important improvements were brought into use and notice.

Since that time, the abolition of the Corn Laws and the inauguration of Free Trade have taken place, and the profits of farming are now supposed to have reached their minimum, and the occupation of an agriculturist does not offer such tempting inducements as many others, to persons desirous of entering into a remunerative business.

Yet there are, without doubt, a great number of persons who would gladly supplement their incomes, if they could see their way clear to do it, by entering into rural occupations which are congenial to their tastes, but who are deterred from doing so by the want of a little practical knowledge.

There have been also many in easy circumstances who, entirely destitute of either theory or practice in agricultural matters, have engaged in them for amusement only, and the consequence has been that, not looking after details themselves, and trusting to servants who have not done them justice, they pay higher wages, and more for everything that is done for them, and get lower prices, for their stock and crops, than they ought to do ; so that, although they may sometimes grow larger crops than their neighbours, it is done at an expense which will not pay for the raising ; and these consequently say that "farming does not pay."

As the reasons which induced me to adopt the system upon which I made my first attempts may very likely influence others similarly situated, I may as well give a brief account, perhaps, of the circumstances which prompted my first endeavours as an agriculturist.

Having a large family of little children, the youngest of whom had to be brought up by hand, the little creatures were always ailing, when living in the suburbs of London, despite all the precautions which we could take.

We bargained with the milkman who used to serve us, that he would bring only the milk of one particular cow (for which we paid a higher price), as a change of milk would sometimes derange the bodily system of the infants ; but mistakes would happen at times, and we knew, from the results, that we did not always get the same cow's milk, though the dairyman, who very likely was deceived by his subordinates, stoutly maintained we did ; and my wife was always fretting about the children, and wishing that we lived in "some nice little place in the country, and kept our own cows and poultry, and all that"—a wish that I believe has been uttered by many thousands of the denizens of our large cities, whose business avocations compel them to reside in town. Our doctor also said the children would be much better in the country with plenty of fresh air and exercise in the fields, and my own inclinations also seconded the advice.

I accordingly began to look out for a place, but found it very difficult to get one with a little grass land attached, of a suitable description that came within reach of my means, which at that time were somewhat narrow; for, when living in the country, one is obliged to keep at least a pony-carriage, and extra servants; and I had taken an idea into my head that, if I went the right way about it, I could manage to save in house and other expenses the extra cost that I should necessarily be put to by my new mode of living. I had a fair knowledge of gardening, and took great interest in it as an occupation; but of the management of anything like field crops, I was utterly ignorant, as well as of keeping stock; but I had a shrewd notion that I could not do much harm with grass land, even if I took more than I wanted for my own use, as I could always sell the hay; and beyond bush-harrowing, there was really little that required to be done.

In the course of my search for a suitable house, I came across the one with the land attached which forms the subject of the present work. Of the management of hop land, I had not the most remote idea, and had only a superstitious horror of the lottery as to results which was always said to be attached to hop-growing. Nor could I then entertain the idea of the arable land, which involved, as I thought, the purchase of not only agricultural implements of various kinds, but a regular staff of labourers, which would inevitably be burdening myself wi.h a business which I did not understand. I stated my objections to the landlord, who said he could easily accommodate me to the extent of my wishes, as he had three tenants, farmers, who would gladly take any land which I did not require, his principal object being to get a good tenant for the house; but the land ought all to go together, as it had been arranged, for the hop-kiln, which was a substantial new structure, and which was a very useful building as a store-house at those seasons of the year when not being used for its legitimate purpose, would have to go with the hop land; while, for the convenience and opportunity of cultivating the arable, strangers would have to cross our meadows, so that we should not be so exclusive or private as we otherwise might be.

It was therefore definitely settled that I was to have thirty acres of the grass land only, upon which in due course I entered and settled down.

The drawback to my residence was, that it was three-and-a-half miles from the railway station, and a long journey from London for a business man to go up and down each day to the city.

I began with one cross-bred cow, for which I paid sixteen pounds to a neighbour, who wanted to get rid of it, having more animals than he had feed for—cows being somewhat cheap in our district, having been asked twenty-three pounds for a similar animal by a dealer in the neighbourhood of London—some fowls, and a couple of young pigs.

This was the list of my live-stock, with which I made my first essay, and I engaged a steady married man to look after them and the garden, and to drive me in a dog-cart to and from the station every morning and evening. There were two cottages which went with the land, which I retained in my own keeping, and the man I engaged was very glad to get the best of the two, which I allowed him to have at a nominal rent.

I was fortunate in getting an industrious man, who was somewhat clever in his way, and who understood the district—that is to say, what could be grown to the best advantage, management of cattle, etc.

I soon found out for myself as time rolled on, but at the first start off I was literally ignorant of everything; and young beginners who turn their attention to agricultural matters should make it a point of the very first consequence to obtain the services of a really competent, respectable man, even if they have to pay high wages, which was not my case, as I gave only fourteen shillings a week, with wood and vegetables, at the commencement, though I afterwards gradually rose them to a pound a week, with other little privileges, and he became a sort of working bailiff to me; the average wages of a farm labourer in the south-western counties being then twelve shillings a week.

This man at first acted as my groom, and no matter if I were detained late in town, he was invariably willing and obliging, and would never neglect his work, however late he might be; and would always see the animals made thoroughly comfortable for the night, when he had to drive me home late from the station; so that his general efficiency soon procured for him an advance of wages.

From him I learnt the best way of feeding my horse, and management of the cow, and as he showed me that two cows were necessary to calve at different times, so that when one was dry we had a supply of milk from the other, I bought another cow.

As I intend to speak of the various qualities of the different breeds of cows under a separate heading, it will be unnecessary for me to enter upon any description of the animals here, beyond saying that, for the use of a private family where only one cow is kept, an Alderney will be found to answer as well as any, as Alderneys are good butter cows; for though yielding a much smaller quantity of milk than almost any other breed, it is rich in quality; and where there are two, a good shorthorn in addition comes in well, or any other good breed of cows that give plenty of milk. For myself, I always preferred a cow between an Alderney and shorthorn, as some of the latter are disposed at times to lay on flesh, rather than yield milk; but these qualities I need not particularise here, as I have just remarked, being anxious to show merely that my beginnings were upon the very smallest scale, and that I had to find out for myself, in a great measure—which my subsequent experience will show—the best course to adopt in each particular instance.

As we progressed, certain ideas would occur to me, which we put into practice by way of experiment; and as I had no prejudices of previous education to combat with, which my man had, in the "custom of the country" in which he had been brought up, I have earned the merit of having originated several methods, and usages of procedure, which, although considered at the time great innovations, have been found to answer extremely well. In nothing more so than in the economical feeding and rearing of pigs, which no farmer near us could ever make pay till they took hints from our practice, and acted upon them. Of course, pigs are indispensable animals upon a farm, and eat up that which otherwise would become spoiled and waste; but what I mean is, that our neighbours could not keep pigs profitably where they had to buy or grow the food they consumed independently, and the profit and loss had to be estimated upon the money-value of what they ate.

There is no art in keeping pigs when a farmer thrashes out a whole stack of "tail" corn; the difficulty is to keep these animals in proper condition upon an amount of food which will leave a profit above their actual cost. And such points as these I used to make a study of.

The common idea that farming is only to be made remunerative by those who have been regularly brought up to it is a mistake. Some of the best farmers we have are men who have been brought up to quite a different class of business—Alderman Mechi, of Tiptree Hall, being a very notable example.

Marshall, who published his "Minutes of Agriculture," containing the memoranda of his operations from 1774 to 1777, and who did a great deal towards the diffusion of agricultural knowledge, was brought up to commerce. His system is not free from error, and his practice would not be much valued nowadays; but he shows himself to have made greater progress than any of his contemporaries, although he committed blunders occasionally; while in "Middleton's View of the Agriculture of Middlesex," the writer states that one of the best farmers in the county of Middlesex was a retired tailor.

The most conspicuous example of all was, perhaps, furnished by Jethro Tull, who was bred to the law; but, having a small estate in Berkshire, devoted himself to its cultivation. And although he injured his private fortune very materially, he was a decided benefactor to his country, though his merits are not even in this day generally so highly appreciated as they deserve to be; and there is something very pathetic in the account of the obloquy and opposition to which he was exposed in his lifetime, which embittered an existence tortured by pain arising from bodily disease.

In describing the steps I first made, it will be seen that I took very little risk upon myself. In the first year I got a good crop of hay, after which I let off my grass land for the after-math, which I did not require for my own two cows, to a neighbouring farmer (for I soon got a second cow), who, after his cattle had taken what they could, turned his sheep into the meadows.

I had a large stack of hay to go through the winter with, the first season; for although cows can be fed upon cheaper food than the best prime hay, after all it is their natural food, and it answered my purpose very well to give it to them, rather than take the trouble to buy roots, or fetch other food for the small number of mouths I then had to feed; and it need scarcely be said that, having reserved to myself the right of taking up the remaining grass land and the arable, and the hops, I soon saw my way clear to take the whole in hand, the only item I did not like being the valuation of the hop-poles, etc., which I thought came to a good deal of money, being mostly old poles, which I had the means of renewing without cost, beyond the labour of cutting, from my own plantations.

Two years had passed before I had taken into my own hands the whole of the land which had been originally apportioned to my house, and in the meantime I had made myself acquainted with the methods of treatment followed in hop cultivation.

The farmer who had the hop land used to complain to me of the great expense of the manure which it was necessary to put upon the land, but in the meantime I had solved the problem of being able to make pigs pay, and I had collected a large heap of manure, and knew I should be ready with plenty more by the spring, so that I should be able to dress my hop land without the outlay of a single penny for manure.

I have spoken of my surplus production which I had to dispose of. I did not get into the way of selling this to the best advantage all at once, but made mistakes in my practice at the first start off, and had to buy my experience like most others, my first venture being very instructive, which happened in this wise:

I had a very nice "piece" of white turnips, about an acre, which had grown remarkably quick and well; the rain coming just when it was wanted for their growth. They looked so white and round, and appeared such nice vegetables, that it struck me, when I saw them, that the buyers of vegetables who visited Covent Garden Market would be sure to fall in love with the turnips if they could only see them; so I procured the name of an agent who sold on commission, and determined to send a cartload up to town as an experiment

At this time I was employing three other men, besides the first man of whom I have spoken, and who was now my foreman, or working-bailiff, and he told me that he could bunch them up nicely and put them into the proper marketable shape for selling; so a large tub of water was taken into the field, and they were nicely washed, and the tops trimmed in regular technical fashion, and placed in a cart, which I hired for the occasion of a neighbouring farmer.

The men were employed the best part of a day about this job, for there was getting "withies" to tie them up, and a good deal to be done which was not quite straightforward work for the men to do, according to what they had been previously accustomed to perform, and they were duly despatched to the station, three-and-a-half miles distant, and sent up to town by railway.

Unfortunately, however, for me, the fertilising showers which had made my turnips grow so nicely, had performed the same friendly office for a number of other turnip-growers besides, and there happened to be a "glut" of turnips in the market, so that mine were sold at ninepence per dozen bunches—that is to say, three-farthings per bunch. Doubtless they got into the hands of the costermongers, who do so much good in distributing cheap vegetables in the crowded districts of London, who may have sold them for a penny or three-halfpence per bunch; and with this thought I consoled myself. But upon balancing receipts and expenditure, putting down a moderate estimate for the men's time, cart-hire to the station, and cost of carriage, I found that, after giving away the turnips for nothing, I had made a loss of a few shillings into the bargain. This experiment showed me that it would not answer to send what may be termed coarse vegetables up to town, and take the risk of the market. The case would have been different, had there been a known scarcity of any vegetable that I might have happened to have, which has fallen out so at other times.

I was tempted to make another trial in the instance of cabbages, on the recommendation of a gentleman who used to ride up and down with me to town. This person said he could not get a decent cabbage in his neighbourhood under threepence, and there was a great scarcity.

As I had a good many, which I did not quite know what to do with, beyond giving them to the pigs, I sent a cartload of the finest, with instructions to the man to sell them to the dealers at the best price he could get. But the cabbages came back, the shopkeepers stating that they were in the habit of getting vegetables down regularly by truck-loads from London—and *they would not buy them at all*. So we gained nothing by this effort, and only wasted the man's time, and employed a horse and cart for nothing. They went to the pigsties after all, and as there never was any difficulty in selling pigs, either in the shape of pork or bacon (for we used to smoke the latter ourselves), I saw clearly enough that the best I could do, would be not to trouble about the selling of inferior vegetables, but let the pigs eat them, and make an article of merchandise of the latter.

With the finer vegetables, those of a higher class, such as asparagus and green peas, the case was different, and of these I will speak again, each under its proper heading; my present allusion to these circumstances being merely for the purpose of showing that I had many little difficulties to deal with at the outset, and had my business to learn.

One thing which is against a gentleman's making a profit out of what he raises is, that he does not think it worth while to take the trouble of selling five or ten shillings' worth of anything, although he may do so every day, and in this way he is apt to overlook his profits; and although he cannot very well do this himself, or would not like to do it, he ought to have a man who will not let the advantages which are to be gained in this way slip through his fingers.

The petty huckstering of small amounts was extremely distasteful to me at first, but being very fond of growing vegetables, we used to have such large quantities of early green peas, that I spoke to the landlord of the hotel where I was in the habit of dining in the city, who agreed to take any quantity of me of *shelled* peas, for which he paid me a shilling a quart, till they got plentiful, when the price dropped down to eightpence, and I managed the huckstering work in this way: I got a couple of nice flat wicker baskets made, that would go comfortably under the seat of a first-class railway carriage. This my man would put in the dog-cart when we drove to the station, and when I got to London a porter would carry it to the cloak-room; I then sent a clerk on to my hotel with the ticket, and the landlord used to send for the peas. In this way I had not the slightest trouble, for the empty basket was put under the seat in town by my porter, which very often contained something else I had to carry home, which was slipped into the dog-cart on the return journey. By this means I never had to touch a basket with my own hands, and of course I had not any carriage to pay, and every now and then, the landlord, who was my customer, would come up to me as I was having dinner, and would lay down a paper, screwed up, containing two or three sovereigns and some silver, as the case might be, with the account made out, which was checked by that kept by my man.

It is not everybody who would like to do this, I am aware. It seemed to me at first very pettifogging sort of work, accustomed as I was to large transactions in business; but I soon got used to it, and, without any sordid feeling upon the matter, got to like the money very much.

I used to do the same with my finest early fruit. At first I was in the habit of packing it in large hampers, and consigning it by rail to a person with whom I had agreed to receive it. But fine fruit was often dreadfully damaged, and ripe pears and plums would arrive at their destination bruised and smashed, so that I received very little for it. I found out that choice fruit must be packed in small baskets, and by this means I have received twelve shillings a bushel for choice plums, where I only received four shillings perhaps, for those I had sent in large baskets; so that my man used to say he could sell them for more at home, on the spot, than what I realised by sending them away.

To have things early—to be the first in the field—is the way to make good prices. When apples have been very plentiful in our district, some of our neighbours have sent them up to town, and after paying carriage and expenses they have not got more than sixpence a bushel for them back.

I used to tell my man that, what with the trouble attending such a business, and the risk of losing one's baskets—which is always happening, more or less—it would answer the purpose better to feed the pigs upon apples, than to sell them for such miserable prices.

To me, there has always been a great amount of pleasure in growing early cucumbers, early asparagus, and other vegetable delicacies; and, as there is a certain amount of expense and trouble to be incurred, when these can be sold profitably it comes as an agreeable set-off. And the things I have mentioned are just those which are generally overlooked.

If one has eight or ten fat hogs to dispose of, the transaction comes to an amount of money, and there is no fear of anything being overlooked in this way; and the same with a quantity of corn, which will always sell at market price; but the business-man, or the gentleman, who is apt to overlook the minor profits he can make, ought, as I have before said, to keep a man who will look after them, if he is above doing it himself.

Speaking of pigs, I carried out the same principle to which I have alluded, of trying to get the best price I could, and by managing in the most advantageous manner.

Instead of sending nice young porkers, which had been fed on skimmed milk and "finished off" on good barley meal, to an agent to dispose of in Smithfield Market, to be sold side by side and with far inferior meat, I found out a good pork-butcher who did a superior trade, and wanted the best quality he could get; and he would give me nearly thirty per cent. more than I could obtain when I sold my young porkers haphazard. I, of course, had to study his convenience, and kill, and send them up as he wanted them ; but this was no trouble to me, or rather to my man, for I never had any hand in it myself. I have mentioned young porkers, but my general plan was to keep the pigs until they attained a large size ; but sometimes we had too many, and were obliged to arrange to get rid of a few of them—and my customer the pork-butcher could take eight or ten at a time of me.

I refer in a cursory manner to these details, in order to indicate, in a rough way, the various methods there are of earning a profit upon agricultural produce of different descriptions of which a man may fairly avail himself, without entering heart and soul into that wretched materialism which is too often common amongst the small trading classes, and which the pressure of circumstances compels them to adopt.

Now as I make a good deal of butter, there is a large quantity of skimmed milk. Each man in my employ has an allowance of two quarts per day for his family, and as there are a number of cottagers in the neighbourhood who have a difficulty in getting any milk, I allow it to be sold at a halfpenny per quart to them. My man has frequently said to me : " We really ought not to sell this milk, as it is worth much more to us for feeding the young calves with ; " but as it is an advantage to my poorer neighbours who have little children, and are glad to avail themselves of the privilege, the calves sometimes have to go minus, and make up with hay-tea, when we are short ; and I feel much more comfortable in letting them have it, than I should do if I were to give it to my calves and pigs, and they have to go without. The few pence secured in this way I would just as soon be without, but the independence of the cottagers is preserved while they pay for it, and the arrangement suits all parties.

It has been a great pleasure to me to have been the means indirectly of helping the families of the cottagers, through my little farming plans. Some of them earn a good deal of money by picking up acorns for my pigs, for which I pay them a shilling a bushel. Some women will go out with half-a-dozen little ones and pick up a great many, so that I have often paid eight, nine, ten, and twelve shillings—representing as many bushels—on Saturday afternoon, when we settled the weekly wages, for picking up acorns, in individual instances.

In the "acorn season" it has been quite a sight, my town friends have declared, to see the large quantity of these lying on the floor of a roomy barn I have, and they form a cheap and very important item of food for my pigs.

From these preliminary observations, the reader will be able to gather some definite outline of my method of operation, which I shall describe more in detail as I proceed with my task; but I ought to add that, being on friendly terms with my neighbours the farmers, who are co-tenants with me, I have not found it necessary to buy any farm implements, such as ploughs and harrows, but have got them to turn up my land for me, when I needed any ploughing done, the chief part of my labour being performed with the spade and fork. Yet my ten acres of arable are just enough to enable me to compute the expenses and charges for ordinary farm operations per acre, which may be fairly taken to apply in the same ratio to a larger quantity; and, where I may consider such information necessary, I will supplement my own experience with an account of the best methods of farming followed in my own and other neighbourhoods, in which I have taken a lively interest.

Some of the economical arrangements I have made, frequently bring me visitors from a distance, in order to compare my methods with their own; and I often get an idea in return from them which I put to profitable account. I ought also to add, that the bulk of what little land I have is chiefly of a light, sandy nature, though there is some clay amongst it. The hop land, which is close to the house, is for the greater part light, which has been well worked, and of course heavily manured; but in one portion, where it slopes upward to a by-road, it consists of sticky clay, which owes a good deal of its moisture to the natural surface-drainage of the adjoining land, which is covered with coppice. The ten acres of arable again are separated from us by three meadows, of from seven to nine acres each, the land altogether assuming somewhat the shape of a long strip, except near the house, which stands in park-like meadows, bounded on one side by the hop-garden, as before described.

During the two years when I had only the thirty acres of grass land to look after, I got into the way of managing poultry, and also mastered the salient features in successful pig-keeping, and in the meantime I made myself acquainted with the methods of agriculture that were carried on around me; but as far as my experience shows, the management of arable land is more troublesome, and less profitable, than grass land and stock-keeping; though the small quantity of arable I have in hand suits me remarkably well, as it is just sufficient to grow roots for my stock; and, as I have said before, a little wheat, oats, and beans, for my ordinary requirements.

In short, I have just enough land to experiment with, and fairly test matters.

Hitherto I have been speaking of my preliminary situation; henceforth I shall describe the results of my matured experience, premising that my dairying and stock-breeding operations are the most important branch; next, pig-breeding; and, lastly, the purely agricultural department, such as roots and cereals, which, although they bring me in the least results, undoubtedly cost me by far the most money in the shape of labour, that is paid for weekly.

As the kitchen-garden attached to the house was comparatively small, I laid out another in an adjoining meadow, which sloped towards the south, where we grow a large quantity of fresh vegetables. I gave orders that a liberal supply of vegetables were always to be cooked each day for the house, knowing that if they were not eaten at table, they would come in for the pigs. I was not, however, always successful in getting this done with some of the cooks I have had, for where there was plenty the servants did not care to eat them, I believe; and many times, when dining at home, there has been a short supply, much to my vexation, for a grower who takes pride in the vegetables he raises naturally does not wish to be put upon "short commons;" but the trouble in preparing them had a great deal to do with this, as sometimes, with our large family, we would consume as many green peas at a meal as would cost four or five shillings when they were realising high prices in the market.

I also had a contrivance made that, when the cook strains off her saucepans, instead of throwing the cooking refuse down the sink, it passes through a pipe to a tub outside, which is regularly emptied each time the pigs are fed; for, as my man observed, the rinsings of milk-pans, tea-slops, the fatty water in which bacon or other meat had been boiled, and the numerous odds and ends that come out of a kitchen in a liquid form, were much better than cold water to mix the pigs' food up in. By looking after these details, the profits in the course of a year are much augmented, for less has to be bought, or, if not bought, less of one's own produce is consumed, than if these economical expedients were ignored.

A business man, of course, could not spare the time to look after these details himself, nor would he like to undertake them ; but, I repeat, he ought to have a good man who will, and the better that man does his duty, the more he is sure to be disliked by negligent or wasteful servants who neglect theirs.

Many a time have I laughed in my sleeve when my foreman has come up to me, with perhaps the bones of two mutton-chops in his horny hand, with all the fat attached to them (as my children hate fat), and said with an injured air : " Look'ee here, sir, what I have just picked up off the ash-heap, these 'er nice mutton-chops, and we with hungry dogs tied up, to say nothing of pigs, as would be glad on 'em. Blest if I can keep that cook from flinging all her bacon-rind and crumbs and things under the kitchen-grate; although I speaks as perlite as maybe, and axes her to save 'em all for me."

The man of course is quite right ; but when I,

emulating my man's example, politely mentioned the circumstance to the cook's mistress, that lady, though not defending the woman's conduct, was disposed to think that our foreman was somewhat inclined to be a mischief-maker; and that, of course, is the firm conviction of his fellow-servants, when their negligence has to be reproved through his instrumentality.

Fortunate is the man who gets a good servant to look after his interests. Things go on very swimmingly when waste and idleness go on unrebuked in the absence of the master amongst servants, who are all good friends together, for which he has to stand the cost; but no sooner does a conscientious man strive to keep things as they should be, than he gets branded as a tell-tale, or sneak, or a mischief-maker, or a backbiter; and the bickering which ensues unfortunately at times causes vexation. Yet it is mainly to the waste and neglect of servants that persons are so unsuccessful in making their farming operations pay, when they are followed more for the sake of amusement and pleasure than as a help to an income. By judicious management, however, the latter is to be obtained easily enough, but one must not only have a liking for the work, but be prepared to do things systematically, and see that no point which will conduce to success is neglected.

If he acts upon a well-arranged system, things will work smoothly enough; but if matters are neglected, confusion and loss will ensue, which has caused many a man to throw up in despair what otherwise would have been a source of continual pleasure and profit to him.

CHAPTER II.

First Attempts—Various Breeds of Cows—The Alderney—The Shorthorn—The Ayrshire—Longhorns—The Herefords—The North Devons—The Suffolk Dun—West Highland Cattle, or Kyloes—The Galloway—Points of a good Cow—Difference in Cows—General Management—Saving One's Hay—Dairy Practice in various Counties.

FIRST ATTEMPTS.—The opportunity of having new milk for our delicate little children was one of the chief inducements that influenced my wife in going to live in the country; and, as the produce of one cow was quite sufficient for the family, we began our dairying operations in the most modest manner imaginable, by buying half-a-dozen blocked-tin skimming dishes, a cream pot, and an upright churn, upon the "plunging" principle, which a neighbour had to dispose of.

This churn, however, caused the butter to taste unpleasantly—perhaps from having lain by a long while unused—and we had to discard it, and procured a box-churn which turned with a handle; while we exchanged the blocked-tin skimming dishes for earthenware ones, glazed inside, which we preferred on account of being kept clean easier than the others. We had to find out the best way of doing everything for ourselves as we progressed, day by day, and experience and observation were our most effective guides, after all; for, though there were plenty who volunteered advice, much that was tendered was of little value, compared with the best methods of doing everything, which we afterwards found out; and we were not told things that we ought *not* to do. As, for example, the dairy being a nice cool place, we used to keep our meat hanging up in it, a practice that ought not for a moment to be tolerated; no food, either vegetable or animal, being allowed to enter a well-managed dairy, even the cream-jars being best away, as it is necessary to keep the air of the milk-house as pure as possible, so as to avoid the least chance of contamination.

I will, however, speak of the various matters which relate to dairy management in consecutive order; but I cannot help reverting to my first experiences now and then. I say *my* first experiences, but they were not in reality mine, but those of my wife and her servants, and the first man whom I engaged to look after our few belongings in the way of stock-keeping, which gradually forced themselves upon my notice and awakened my interest—and I draw a veil over the many accidents that happened—the churning for hours when the butter would not come—and many trials of patience which neophytes have to undergo, with which I at length got familiar, and was made a partner in; a result I never contemplated in the first instance, thinking that domestic matters would go on all very well without my taking any share in them, but in which I finally became deeply interested; and the pleasure and profit resulting from well-directed efforts offer a most agreeable contrast to the haphazard manner in which we first conducted our affairs.

The first cow I had was a capital one, that gave a good pailful of milk each time of milking, at night and morning; but, like all animals which yield a large quantity of milk, the cream was not so rich for butter-making as that of the cows I have subsequently kept, and consequently, when she approached her time of calving, and we had to allow her to get dry, I procured an Alderney cow, whose yield of milk was comparatively small, but rich in cream, which made a good quantity of butter; and I may here remark that it will be found a good plan, where a number of animals are kept, even when the aim is that of a large production of milk, to have *one* Alderney cow, at all events, amongst the herd; as the quality of the milk, as a whole, will be greatly improved thereby.

My first cow in due time brought me a fine calf; and as I was quite ignorant of the best method of management, I had to rely upon my man's advice, who really was an excellent manager after the fashion to which he had been accustomed; though, in course of time, we changed places, as I shall duly show. Said he: "As we shall now have plenty of milk, if we let the calf suck its mother for five or six weeks there will be a fine fat calf, for which the butcher will give six pounds or so." This was accordingly done; but upon calculation I found that the milk and butter produced by this cow immediately after calving was worth one pound a week. If I had given the calf away directly it had been calved, I should have been as well off as fattening it up for the butcher; though it is true the calf did not take all the cow's milk during the first few weeks. This cow could easily have brought up two calves had we so arranged it, as she had a profusion of milk, and another pair after these had been sufficiently brought forward, finishing off with a single one, or five calves altogether.

This I discovered by reading a work on farming, which gave me the necessary information; and as I had a good deal of grass land, it occurred to me, after I had acquired it, that I ought to have followed this method, as an easy way of obtaining stock which would be growing into money; but I afterwards adopted the plan of rearing my calves upon *skimmed* milk, thickened with linseed, etc., by which means we got the butter, and had the calf as well. Not indeed a fat one, but a young stock animal that was afterwards reared with comparatively little expense, all of which I shall duly speak of in the proper place; but I may as well add here that, save in exceptional circumstances, I did not rear the bull or steer calves—disposing of them after they had been five days or a week with their mothers—it being a cruel thing to both, to separate the cow and calf at once; but the heifers, or cow-calves, when they fell at convenient seasons, I have invariably reared. At one year old the male calf is commonly called a yearling, stirk, or "hog," assuming the name of bull at two years, which he retains to the day of his death, unless castrated, when he is known as a bull-stag. When castrated, the bull-calf is termed a steer, until he attains the age of four years, when he is known as an ox. The cow-calf retains the name of heifer until she is five years old, when she becomes a cow.

THE ALDERNEY.

Various Breeds of Cows.—Of the different nature and breeds of cows, like most other young beginners, I had only a very dim conception. I knew, of course, that the Alderney cow gave only a small quantity of milk, but that it was rich in butter-making properties, and recognised a few other broad distinctions ; but I had to find out for myself the various points that had to be taken into consideration, such as the breed best adapted for one's pasturage, and the nature of the soil. Many of the larger breeds require a richer pasturage than other sorts, which are equally good milkers, but are satisfied with poorer feed ; and the success of dairy farming depends very much upon the proper selection of animals for the land to carry; and of this part of the subject, perhaps, it would be better first to speak, as many breeds will give a much larger return than others in the form of milk for the food consumed.

The Alderney.—The Alderney cow is one that is highly in favour in private families, on account of the rich quality of the cream and butter produced ; but the yield of milk is small, and where a dairy farm is carried on chiefly for the sale of milk, it would not be found to answer to keep Alderney cows alone, though, as before remarked, one or two may be kept with advantage along with a greater number. The butter, however, made from the milk of a really good Alderney cow would often equal the weight of that of another giving a much larger supply of milk ; and the admixture of the cream of even one Alderney cow with that of a dozen others will sensibly improve its quality.

They, however, will do very well upon somewhat

poor pasture and inferior park land, and are very useful on a farm to cross with another breed that may possess more desirable features in the eyes of the dairy-farmer, and should thus by no means be overlooked, even when profit is the main consideration. For the purpose of the grazier they are utterly useless, as he could not deal with them profitably, and therefore it will not answer to rear the bull-calves as stock for sale. They "cut-up" badly for the butcher, though I believe they often turn out much more profitable than their appearance would seem to indicate to the purchaser. I once tried the experiment of fattening an Alderney steer for the butcher; but I lost a good deal by it, and never repeated it.

The Shorthorn.—The Shorthorn is a favourite breed on account of many good qualities which it possesses; the chief being its aptitude to fatten, and the great weight of carcase it attains in a comparatively short time. But, as dairy cows, this inclination to lay on flesh, rather than secrete milk, is an objection; and they are seldom good milkers, unless both food and climate are specially favourable to them; and under the best circumstances they consume a large amount of food, yielding no more milk than others that take far less to keep, having indeed a tendency more to produce fat than milk.

On this account they are more valuable to the grazier than to the dairy-farmer, though for dairy purposes a cross between a shorthorn and an inferior breed will often bring good milch cows. That between an Alderney and a shorthorn is generally a good one; as a rule, highly-bred animals are mostly bad milkers. It has often turned out to be the case with a number of cows, that the ugliest, most misshapen beast of the lot, whose pedigree it would be very difficult to trace, is the best milker of them all. Occasionally a shorthorn will be found to yield a good supply of milk, but for one very good one in this way there will be three found that are only indifferent, when compared with really first-class milk-producers.

Shorthorns require generous feeding, and pastures of the best quality, to develop their excellences in the most complete manner, and, after all, are better adapted for the grazier and stock-keeper than the dairy-farmer.

The Ayrshire.—One of the best Scotch breeds, amongst which good milking cows are often found, is the Ayrshire. It offers a most decided contrast to the one just named ; no breed, perhaps, being able to equal these cows in converting the produce of poor soils into so much good milk, butter, or cheese ; and for purely dairy purposes they are very difficult to beat. They are not at all suited for stock intended for beef, as the bullocks are hard to fatten, come badly to the scale, and the meat is of inferior quality ; but where an improvement is wanted, an Ayrshire cow coupled with a shorthorn bull will produce an excellent breed. They are small in size ; but great pains have been taken in developing their milking powers by breeders, their form being compact and symmetrical, with a capacious stomach, but somewhat narrow chest. They will not give so large a quantity of milk as some other cows, but it will be obtained at a relatively smaller cost.

Longhorns.—The long-horned breed of cattle has gone somewhat into the background of late years, yet at one time they were the prevailing one in most of the midland counties of England, having given way to the superior estimation in which shorthorn cattle are now generally held. The cows are fair milkers, being mostly brindled black and brown along the sides, with white along the back, their horns at times being more than a yard long, to which distinguishing characteristic they owe their name.

The Herefords.—The Herefords are a better breed for the grazier than for the dairy farmer; the cows, being generally poor milkers, do not, as a rule, make good dairy animals. They need a fertile soil, attaining a weight fully equal to that of the shorthorn breed. They are chiefly met with in Herefordshire and the south-western counties, and are generally of a red colour, with the exception of the face, the breast, the ridge of the back, and the feet, which are mostly white.

The North Devons.—These animals are admired for their colour, which is mostly red, with a little white about the udder, their elegant form, and gentle temper. Unfortunately, however, the cows are not well suited for dairy purposes, for although the milk they give is very rich, it is but small in quantity. The oxen have been extensively employed in their native country in field labour, doing the work of the farm, for which they are admirably fitted, and are altogether a hardy breed, but cannot be recommended where dairy produce is the first object in view, as the cows have a marked tendency to get dry early.

The Suffolk Dun.—This breed was originally of a mouse dun colour in most instances, and it has been surmised by some that the original stock has been crossed a good deal by the polled Galloway cattle, which find their way in good numbers to the eastern counties; but although being polled, and resembling in some respects those of Scotland, the true breed appears to be indigenous to Suffolk. They are ungainly in form, but the cows yield a large quantity of milk in proportion to the food they consume, and are consequently a desirable breed as dairy cows.

West Highland Cattle, or Kyloes.—The cows of this breed yield very rich milk, but give only a very scanty supply of it, their chief recommendation being that they will thrive on the coarsest herbage, where higher-bred animals would be scarcely able to subsist. They are symmetrical in form, the true Highland ox being especially a very handsome animal, with short muscular limbs closely covered with shaggy hair, and altogether well-fitted for the cold humid climate and coarse pasturage of the Highlands; and although unsuited for the sheltered plains and meadows of England, they are often usefully bought to eat up the inferior grass of park-land, upon which they will get in better condition than a class of animals accustomed to herbage of a superior quality.

The Galloway.—The Galloway is a polled breed, resembling otherwise the West Highland cattle, but possessing a larger frame, and being more adapted for a lower range of pastures, while their docile temperament causes them to be easy of management; but for dairy purposes, the cows are far inferior to the Ayrshire, which are the best milkers of all the Scotch breeds, of which there are several others beside those named, as the Angus, the Aberdeen, and the Fife, that are met with on the east coast of Scotland; many of which are well worthy of the notice of the stock-keeper, but not of the dairy-farmer, whose object is to produce milk or butter.

Of Irish cows, the small Kerry cow is the best for its milk-producing qualities, and the various breeds mentioned, including the Glamorgan, which is a good milker, found in that and neighbouring counties, comprise all that need any notice for dairy purposes; and the selection of animals from any of these should be guided by the circumstances affecting the farm, and the produce aimed at.

If the object be to obtain a large quantity of milk for sale, those cows naturally should be chosen which give the greatest quantity. But if the intention be to make butter and cheese, the richness of the milk must be made the principal point, for it often happens that a larger quantity of cream is to be got off the smaller yield of milk; an instance having been reported by Malcolm in his " Compendium of Modern Husbandry" of an Alderney, and Suffolk cow, the latter the best of the kind he ever saw; while the Alderney, which had dropped her first calf, was purchased out of a drove, in a miserable condition. During seven years—the milk and butter being always kept separate—it was found, year after year, that the value of the Alderney exceeded that of the Suffolk, though the latter gave more than double the quantity of milk at each meal. He adds, that he at that time had a dairy of twelve cows—two Devons, one Derby, one Lincoln, two Sussex, two Wiltshire long-horned, two Holderness, one Suffolk, and one Alderney, and the latter bore the palm clean away. The Sussex cattle, I should remark, are similar to the

Devons in colour, but larger and coarser, being mostly found in the county from which they derive their name.

In keeping a definite breed of cows, as the unprofitable animals must be weeded out of the herd from time to time, it will be found as well to keep in view a certain degree of improvement of stock, when breeding from an inferior class of cow, by crossing her with a well-bred shorthorn breed—and in most cases, where the pastures are of average quality, a cross between Alderney and shorthorn will be found to bring very useful stock—but good milkers are to be picked up amongst all breeds; the best in this respect having a worse bodily appearance than those which clothe their limbs with flesh instead of secreting milk.

A good milch cow seldom carries much flesh, and one that has a tendency to get fat should be got rid of; and as cows ought not, as a rule, to be kept when they are over nine years of age, in a large dairy it will make a considerable difference whether the animals sold are likely to be held in good estimation by the butcher. The tendency of a cow to get fat, which is an objectionable feature to the dairy-farmer, will of course constitute a recommendation when she is to be sold, and a higher price be realised for her.

Points of a good Cow.—No one likes to part with a good cow that gives a plentiful supply of milk, but the supply sometimes suddenly falls off after they have passed their ninth year, and good management will very often mainly consist in the endeavour to reconcile apparently opposite qualifications to the requirements of the owner, and the ultimate disposition of the animals. Hence with cows there will be a wide difference between the form of one meant for fattening and that intended for a milch cow; and while the former should possess as much as possible the good points of an ox, the latter should be thin and hollow in the neck, narrow in the breast and point of the shoulder, large stomach, thin head, with a brisk but placid eye, light in the fore quarter, but wide in the loins, and with but little dewlap, and not too full-fleshed along the chine, nor showing any indication of putting on too much fat. The udder should be large, round, and full, with the milk-veins boldly protruding, and, while thin-skinned, neither hanging loosely or trending far behind. The teats should stand squarely out, pointing at equal distances from one another, and being of the same size; and although neither very large nor thick close to the udder, yet long, and tapering to a point.

A cow with a large head, high backbone, small udder and teats, and drawn up in the belly, will generally be found a bad milker. Temper is also another point of importance. The cow that gave a good pailful of milk, and then kicked it over, has passed into a proverb; and kindly animals will not only give much less trouble in their management than those of an unruly disposition, but they will generally be found to have a more copious supply of milk, and will yield it up more readily. A theory has lately been broached, called the Guenon *escutcheon* theory, after the name of its suggester, who styles the slight fringe formed by the junction of the hair which points upwards with that which points downwards above the udder, the cow's *escutcheon*. The longer and wider this is, the better the cow will prove as a milker. Some people have said there is a good deal in this, while others have denied it; but, as far as I am personally concerned, the matter has not interested me very much, for beyond occasionally buying a stray cow or two out of a drove, which I have had the opportunity of getting very cheap, when animals have been passing our gates on their way to a fair, I always bring up my own calves, and am therefore not a buyer, as a rule; for sometimes there may be the seeds of disease in a strange cow. And when we have bought one, we always make a practice of isolating her from the others for a certain time, so that we may have an opportunity of assuring ourselves upon this point.

High-pedigreed, shorthorned cows are usually poor milkers, as well as unsafe breeders, and therefore they are by no means desirable as dairy cows, whatever they may be for breeding purposes, which does not concern our present business just now—the breed of a cow being of very little consequence to the dairy-farmer, as any shortcoming in this respect can be made up by the good qualities of the bull.

Difference in Cows.—There is, however, a great difference between cows, very often of the same breed; and two sisters, fed in precisely the same manner, got by the same bull, and almost the same in appearance, not only often vary in the quantity of the milk they give, but produce butter of different weights from the same amount of food. It will thus be readily seen that to make a dairy farm answer to its fullest extent, a constant supervision, and culling of the stock, should be going on, and the indifferent animals weeded out and sold. A bad cow will eat as much as a good one, and experiments should be made, by feeding the animals on the same food, and measuring the quantity of milk, and afterwards churning it into butter, which can be easily done, so as to determine their relative values; for, as in the case cited above, it is not the cow that gives the most milk that is always the best butter cow.

General Management.—A good stock of cows having been got together, the general system of management to be pursued must be decided on. In some parts of the country, especially in Gloucestershire, cows are kept out of doors a great deal. In many dairy districts they are often badly lodged, and insufficiently fed in winter.

Good warm housing in cold weather is indispensable; a certain amount of food being required to keep up the natural heat of the body, and when warmly lodged, cows require a less amount of food; while regularity in feeding is a very important point in dairy management; as a greater quantity of milk is absolutely obtained by regular feeding upon a smaller quantity of food, than a larger one irregularly given. In the latter case, a marked diminution of the milk yielded takes place, which lasts for some time; even when regularity of feeding has been resumed after temporary discontinuance, it may be, from accidental causes.

The most essential points in the management of a dairy are:

First—To have a good breed of cows that are well adapted for the land and climate, and for the purpose

ESSENTIAL POINTS IN MANAGEMENT. 41

for which they are mainly intended—*i.e.* whether for the production of milk or butter.

Secondly—To have proper buildings and implements for the dairy, and for the best methods of feeding.

Thirdly—To have efficient servants, able to carry on the business of the farm in a thorough and proper manner.

Lastly—Gentle treatment, combined with good and regular feeding, and sufficient shelter for the stock.

Dairy produce has advanced steadily in price of late years, and there is every prospect of its being maintained in the future; and the mixed system of dairying and feeding is extending very much amongst practical farmers, as it enables them to be less dependent upon one variety of produce, while it affords a better division of labour; and greater profits can be secured under a system of good management by the combined methods.

It does not necessarily follow that a farmer must have plenty of meadow land to carry on a dairy business, for on the soiling system, of which I shall speak at length under the head of *Feeding*, a very small amount of grass land is necessary upon which to turn out the cows for air and exercise. There are, indeed, only two kinds of farms on which an union of the two systems cannot be adopted with advantage; those in the one case being stiff clays, on which only a small breadth of turnips can be raised, and dry turnip soils of inferior quality, which require the practice of sheep-farming to maintain the land in proper order.

The arable-farmer has an advantage over the dairy-farmer, who alone has grass land, in the ability he possesses of furnishing a greater variety of food to the cows, and by efficient house-feeding and warmth in well-arranged buildings, the cows can be maintained in good health and full profit, the house-feeding system being well adapted for milch cows, and quite compatible with the production of the finest quality of milk; the quantity, too, being much greater in proportion to the food consumed, than when cows are pastured in the open fields; while the large amount of manure made of the best quality by well-fed cows, adds materially to the fertility of the farm.

A mixed system of tillage and dairy-farming, where now only the former is carried on, would be found by many to be highly advantageous so far as profits are concerned.

Saving One's Hay.—I had acquired a little experience, and the time came round when, having read various accounts of the management of cows, I began to think for myself what would be the most profitable course to pursue; and I quite astonished my man, at a very early stage in our dairying business, when I had only two or three cows and an odd calf or two, by telling him that I intended to shut up all the fields for hay—the whole thirty acres that I first began with, reserving only a small enclosure near the house, of two or three acres, in which our few head of cattle could run.

He, however, loyally assisted me in my project, and a strong young fellow was engaged to assist him; and we mowed the grass, and carried it to the cows in their stalls as they wanted it, their provender being eked out with carrots and cabbages, some of which we had grown ourselves, and the remainder bought of neighbouring farmers.

We used first to mow all the long grass near to the hedges round all the fields—some of which grew rank and luxuriant, from being near the watercourses, and sprang up again quickly—and continued to cut grass wherever we thought it would best answer our purpose.

This was thought rather a bold stroke for a man to do who had plenty of grass, in shutting off his dairy cows from it, being quite opposed to the "custom of the country;" and the wisdom of my proceeding was of course challenged. I was told that I was keeping my cows away from the meadows when they were in their prime, and would most benefit the stock, and that I should lose in milk what I gained the other way. But I stuck to my plan, and found it answer uncommonly well. Towards hay-harvest, the cows stood well shaded from the heat of the sun, with no flies of consequence to torment them; and in the early morning and cool of the evening they took their exercise in the small field allotted to them—and being abundantly fed, they did exceedingly well, and looked in better condition than most of my neighbours' animals; the result being that I had a very large haystack, instead of a comparatively small one, and we experienced no falling off in dairy produce.

At first there seemed a good deal of trouble in cutting the grass, but it soon became a matter of *routine*; and the first thing in the morning sufficient was mown to last the cows through the day, and put in a cart, and taken to the cow-houses, and the same operation performed again at evening, when the cows relished that which was freshly served to them at milking time. Without trouble, nothing can be done successfully; but when even troublesome jobs become a matter of routine, and part of the daily work, they are soon got through easily enough. The first thing thought of was the cows' provender for the day, and the task was set about with a will; and it did not so very much interfere with the other business of the place, after it had become a matter of custom— custom, which makes everything easy, and causes difficulties to consist mainly in a change of everyday habit.

After we had secured our hay, we turned the cows into one field after another, to eat up the after-math; so that while they were consuming the grass off one, that of the others was growing.

My man, imbued with the prejudices of his class and the comments of our neighbours, was extremely doubtful at first of the success of the expedient; but after it was accomplished, and I pointed to the fine stack of hay we had secured in fine condition, he could not but acknowledge the plan was a good one, although opposed to the ordinary practice followed in our part of the world; and I need not say that I invariably pursue it. I never cut the after-math, contenting myself with a good crop of hay, which we are generally fortunate enough to get—though I did it the first year, in accordance with the advice given me—considering it exhaustive to the meadows. In the early stage of my operations, when I had more of this second crop of grass than my own cows could eat,

SYSTEMS OF DAIRY PRACTICE. 45

I used to take in the sheep of a neighbouring farmer at so much per score; making the bargain that they should be folded on the land at night, by which more manure was left than if they had been driven off to the farm.

Dairy Practice in various Counties.—The practice, or method of management pursued in dairy operations, differs very much in various parts of the kingdom, necessarily so on account of certain restrictions in the management of the land which are imposed upon tenants by the landlords, and which form "the custom of the country;" as, for instance, in Cheshire, the dairy-farmer is prohibited by his tenure from having more than a fourth, or at most one-third of his land in tillage. With few exceptions, cheese is the principal product of the dairy in Cheshire, but little butter being produced, except that made from whey, which is of good quality, as the cheese is made from whole milk. Bone manure has been largely used upon the Cheshire meadows, to which has been attributed much of their fertility; and the cows are tied up in stalls from the 1st of November till the 1st of May, being allowed a few hours each day for air and exercise, on the most convenient fields to the farm.

The calves are usually sold off in what is termed half-fed condition, when about a month old, except those which are reserved to make good deficiencies in stock. On the clay-land farms, the cows after calving are fed for some time on bran-mashes, then about half a bushel of oats is given per week, a small quantity every day; in exceptional instances, turnips and mangold-wurzel are also given, but the common practice is to feed with hay and cut grain. On the sandland farms, however, cows are commonly fed on turnips during the winter, the tops being given to them first with straw, and the bulbs with hay afterwards.

In Gloucestershire, except in those instances where the improved modern methods of feeding cattle have been adopted, the principal reliance is placed on the product of the meadows for the sustenance of the cows, both in summer and winter, in the shape of grass in the former and hay in the latter; very little extra food, such as oil-cake or bruised grain, being given to them, or even roots. The cows, too, are kept exposed very much in the meadows; and although the mildness of the climate, and the richness of the grass, will allow the Gloucestershire dairy-farmer to take, greater liberties with his animals than others can do in less favoured counties, there can be no question that in carrying hay twice a day to open fields in which to feed the cows, where it is thrown down, a good deal becomes wasted and spoiled in rainy weather.

As roots are but little grown, the discarded cows are seldom or never fattened, but sold to dealers; but the meadows are managed well, the cows being changed from one field to another, as regularly as possible; and the milking cows are kept as near the homestead as possible, to avoid the fatigue consequent upon driving them a long distance to be milked, which both lessens the quantity of the milk as well as deteriorates its quality.

In these and some other respects, the management of the cows is conducted upon a good system; the most faulty part of the method pursued in Gloucestershire being the deficiency of house and shed accommodation for stock, both in winter and summer—in the winter from the inclemency of the season, and in the latter from the annoyance caused by the buzzing and biting of insects, which are often very troublesome to cattle, and congregate alike under trees for shelter from the rays of the sun, in the hottest period of the day.

In Leicestershire, the pastures are naturally rich, while roots are grown extensively, it being the common plan to stall-feed in winter and to let the cows graze the fields in summer. Stilton cheese is celebrated, while the ordinary Leicester cheese bears a good reputation in the market; a large breed of cows being mostly kept, which the rich pastures are well able to carry, being either shorthorn, longhorn, or a cross betwixt the two. A good many years back, longhorns were the principal stock kept, but the facility with which the shorthorn breed lay on flesh and fatten has caused them to make their way in this county, for which they are admirably adapted.

The practice of winter feeding differs on various farms; straw, with a small quantity of hay, saturated with linseed, boiled in fifteen times its quantity of water, with bran, or oatmeal in addition, being given by many; and when in milk, the cows are fed with mangold-wurzel, and get a larger quantity of meal or bran. When straw only is given, eighty pounds of roots are allowed daily, or twenty-five pounds of hay, when no roots are served out, or forty pounds of roots with eighteen pounds of hay; or again, if the hay is mixed one-half with straw, sixty pounds of roots.

Early in spring, clover and Italian rye grass are given to the cows, and vetches and clover if they are plentiful in the summer, when they are pastured, as well as in the autumn ; the feeding, as a rule, adopted in Leicestershire being high.

In Dorsetshire, which has long been celebrated for its butter, the custom used largely to prevail of letting off the cows to dairymen at so much per annum, the dairyman having a portion of the farm allotted to him called the "cow-lease," to the extent of from one to one-and-a-half acre per cow, according to the quality of the land. After the cows cease to give milk for the season, they are kept in the straw yards, the sheep being turned into the pastures during the winter months, the mixed system of dairy, corn, and sheep-farming prevailing a good deal in Dorset. The cows used mostly to be of the Devon breed, which yield rich milk, and are hardy of constitution, though not of large size, but a great variety of breeds has lately been tried in the county, as Alderneys, Ayrshires, as well as Herefords and Durhams; the former being kept where there are numbers of others, to raise the average quality of the milk.

In some parts of Scotland, the dairy management is upon a very thorough and comprehensive system. In the western districts, dairy farming is carried on upon arable farms, combined with the breeding and rearing of stock. In Wigtonshire and adjoining counties, the Ayrshire breed of cows is mostly kept, yielding a large quantity of milk in proportion to their size, and fattening quickly, when it becomes no longer desirable to keep them as milch cows. In hot weather, in summer, they are housed for a few hours in the middle of the day to spare them from being tormented by flies, and are brought into the "byre" regularly at night and morning to be milked, and the cows are kept in good thriving condition up to the time they calve; an erroneous practice prevailing in many parts of England, of nearly half starving a cow when she is dry. When they calve early in the season, in addition to a full supply of turnips, they are supplied with bean meal, or artificial food of some kind or another, to keep them in high milking condition until they are turned out to grass.

In Fifeshire, the raising of dairy produce is looked upon as secondary to the breeding and rearing of cattle; but the practice gives a very fair illustration of the results to be obtained by the mixed system. The calves are hand-fed mostly, being seldom suckled by the cow except when dropped in May, in which case two calves are allotted to her to bring up. The calves are fed three times a day with warm milk from the cow, beginning with three pints daily, till the quantity is increased to six quarts up to the end of four weeks, as the calf grows and requires more, day by day, increasing the quantity to eight quarts for another four weeks. After six weeks, linseed and oatmeal well boiled together are given with one of the meals, generally either night or morning, beginning with a quarter of a pound, and increasing to one pound to the end of another six weeks, by which time they are ready to turn out to grass.

In this case, the object is to get the calves on early to arrive at maturity; and they get sweet milk in plenty, a little hay, or oats in sheaf. The mode is expensive, and does not pay, unless carried out in its entirety, by continued high feeding, so as to get an animal ready at two years old for the butcher.

The plan is no doubt good enough in its way, for many Fifeshire farmers make it answer; but it is quite a different course to the one I have pursued myself, bringing up my calves at a very trifling cost, upon an economical system of rearing which I shall hereafter describe in full. It is true they do not reach maturity early, but I deal with the matter as one of *profit*, and I give a brief notice of the plans and methods pursued elsewhere, because circumstances are so widely different in different districts.

Now in the solitary instance which I attempted, of which I have spoken before, of fattening a young steer for the butcher, I began with the wrong breed to start with—the specimen being an Alderney; whereas, had he been a shorthorn, the result would have been very different, inasmuch as I should both have had an animal of larger size and greater weight, which would have arrived at maturity in a much less time; and consequently, food is thrown away, as it were, upon the fattening of a wrong breed of animal, and there are certain conditions essential to success, which must be understood before that success can be ensured.

In making a comparison between the two systems of dairy-farming, where, in the one case, the food eaten by the animals is either in the shape of grass or hay, the product of the meadows, and in that of mixed arable and dairy farming; where old pasture grass and meadow-hay forms the sole food of the cows, the quality of the butter, and cheese, is doubtless superior; but in the latter, there are many opportunities of feeding, and management, which may be turned to profitable account, and when milk only is sought to be produced, the opportunities of feeding the stock are very considerable, in the varied items that are produced in the course of general cultivation.

CHAPTER III.

Situation of the Dairy—Dairy Utensils, etc.—Produce to be aimed at—Quality of Milk—Management of Milk—Butter-making—Clotted or Clouted Cream—Butter from Clotted Cream.

SITUATION OF THE DAIRY.—A north aspect is the best situation for the dairy, and the next best an east one, and it should be well protected from the rays of the sun, it being important in summer time that it be kept cool. It should be removed far away from the source of any impurities, as dunghills, or anything that emits unpleasant smells; not only extreme cleanliness being necessary in all the processes connected with the management of the dairy, but even distant sources of contagious influence should be guarded against, as nothing more easily receives and retains the odours of putrescent matters than milk, its chemical constituents causing it to turn acid, and inclining to decomposition, when near other substances undergoing the process of decay, whether animal or vegetable; even the presence of cheeses undergoing the process of drying on the shelves, which are sometimes allowed to remain for convenience' sake in the dairy, being highly objectionable, and a thorough draught near the ceiling, to be controlled at will, is

THE DAIRY.

very desirable to keep the atmosphere fresh and sweet.

For this purpose, cloths dipped in a solution of chloride of lime and hung up on cords fastened from one corner of the milk-house to the other, have been found of service; no pains being neglected by those who aim at doing things thoroughly to ensure this important end. The quality of the cheese and butter materially depends upon the construction and situation of the dairy-house; which, although it ought to be placed conveniently near the house, ought not to be near any pond, or stagnant water, the milk and cream soon acquiring an unpleasant taste.

As a uniform temperature is of importance, the sides of the building should be liable to be affected by the extremes of heat or cold as little as possible, so as to be cool during the summer and warm during the winter; shaded, if possible, by a wall or trees from the south and west. A span roof rising from the centre, and projecting downwards over the sides, to shade the body of the house, is the best for this purpose, and upon anything like a large and effective system of dairy management, there should be one room for milk, another for churning butter, or for scalding, pressing, and salting cheeses, and another for the implements used in the various processes. Windows, both latticed and glazed, supplied with shutters to regulate the temperature of the dairy, will be found of advantage; and the floor should so slope as to carry off immediately all water that may be spilled, together with milk accidentally dropped, though this declination may be advantageously made use of, during the summer months, for cold water to be thrown down occasionally to remove the traces of spilled milk, or to cool the atmosphere in very sultry weather.

Dairy Utensils, etc.—Instead of keeping the milk in dishes on shelves in the dairy, and in any nooks and corners of the milk-house, the best plan is to have a stone table, built of pavement upon a few bricks, which can be readily done at a small expense, to stand in the centre, for the milk dishes, or basins, to stand upon. By this means the fresh air surrounds them equally, which can never be the case when they are stowed away in out-of-the-way places, or on shelves against the walls.

This table should be made water-tight, easily done by using a little Portland cement, and all crevices stopped thoroughly, and a ledge should be formed round the outsides, also water-tight, so that cold water may be thrown upon it in summer time, to keep the basins cool; and warm water in winter to keep them from being chilled in very severe weather. A flat ladle and a few woollen house-cloths will always quickly dispose of the water when it is wanted to be got rid of.

I am assuming that there are already existing dairy conveniences; but if there are not, before proceeding any farther, perhaps it would be as well for me to mention, that suitable accommodation could be provided for a comparatively trifling outlay, as a sunk dairy—so that there is drainage, and it is high enough to admit the air—which need not be more than seven or eight feet at the sides, answers very well. In arranging a dairy in the first place, it should consist of three apartments, the principal one in the middle, in which the milk is kept. This centre portion is required to be kept at equal temperature as nearly as possible at all seasons of the year—about sixty degrees; and this is best done by excluding all direct communication with the outer air, except at will; and the outer walls of this portion should be made of sods of earth, rammed firm, to the breadth of four feet in thickness, while the other walls of the building need only be one brick in thickness, or even lath and plaster. A large tin funnel should run through the roof to act as a ventilator, the upper part projecting a couple of feet above it, a valve being fitted to it, which, by means of a pulley, will allow of its being shut or opened at pleasure. Through the thickness of the walls of this centre apartment, the windows must be formed upon the same principle as the embrasures for guns in fortifications. These windows are closed with lattices covered with gauze wire in summer to keep out the flies, and closed with glass in winter.

On either side of this centre apartment there should be two others; the one on the right hand, we will say, to be used as a churning-house, with a boiler in one corner, and on the sides frames for cheese-presses and vats, with slate vessels for holding the whey, and pipes for carrying it to a cistern outside for pigs' food. In old-fashioned dairies, the vessels for holding the whey are mostly of lead; but when any sour liquid is allowed to remain in them, bad effects follow at times; and with some metals that have been used, crystals have been known to be precipitated, on account of the action of the acid upon the metal. Whey keeps sweet in lead longer than in wooden vessels, and it is easier to clean them out; but slate is the best of all. The other apartment, at the opposite end, should be used as a wash-house for cleaning the utensils, and should have a furnace, with a cauldron, for scalding them, and a pump. The entrance should be through this first room, and at the doorway a bench should be placed, under the projecting roof, upon which to lay all the vessels to dry and sweeten in the air and sun, after having been washed.

When all the accommodation cannot be had under one roof, apartments must be organised, and arranged for, as near as possible to the above in those instances where persons are not desirous of going to any expense themselves, and who cannot get their landlords to make the required alterations, if any are necessary.

At the same time, it is surprising, where there is a handy man or two upon a farm, how readily necessary conveniences can be improvised. A cleverish bricklayer's labourer can make concrete, or concrete slabs, out of which the walls of a dairy-house could soon be constructed ; and a handy man, who is a bit of a rough carpenter, is always useful on a place.

Two of my best labourers can do something in this way. One was a London bricklayer's labourer who earned nineteen shillings a week, but having a delicate wife, he was glad to take service with me at fourteen shillings a week, all the year round, with the extra perquisites and privileges agricultural labourers obtain—as overtime, vegetables gratis, the skimmed milk for a trifle, and so on—so as to come and live in the country. He acknowledges himself that he is far better off with me, with constant employment, at fourteen shillings a week, than he was with nineteen shillings a week in London, and often out of employment, for a month or six weeks at a stretch, during the winter.

This man, I am sorry to say, still retains the habits of his class, though I do all I can to reform him, and he *must* go to the public-house, and drink a pint or two, as he calls it, on a Saturday night, after cleaning himself, when he has received his week's wages on Saturday afternoon. This is his drawback, for although he comes to his work regularly enough on the Monday, and continues at it all the week, yet he has taken more than has been good for him at times, and has come near the house, and quarrelled with the foreman, which he would not have done when sober.

He is a very fair bricklayer, and can do all the odd jobs we want executed; while another man is a rough carpenter, and can put up gates, fences, and perform any odd carpentry jobs that are needed to be done. And I refer to these particulars in this place, because the bare mention of constructing any buildings, or edifices of any kind, would frighten a good many people, as the cost is often made very formidable when regular tradesmen are set upon a job, which somehow grows under their hands in a most mysterious manner. Now, by having a handy man or two about the place, nearly all the tradesmen's bills can be saved. Our jobs may not be done so thoroughly, but they answer my purpose very well; and we are in the habit of "knocking up" quite extensive erections, and conveniences out of *hurdles*, which we thatch with straw or furze. Is a cow-shed wanted in a distant part—perhaps at the extreme end of my little farm, which is of a long straggling character? We fell a few straight young fir trees from out of the plantation, which we fix as uprights at the corners, and at convenient distances, to act as supports for others, placed across them at top; and fill up the spaces, and cover in the roof with thatched hurdles. A large roomy building is thus constructed by my men in a very short time. If a door is wanted, so that the whole may be closed entirely in, one hurdle placed upright, and working on stout "withy" hinges, gives us a door at once. In this way we build sheds for the cows, which gladly avail themselves of them in hot weather, to get away from the flies; and we have these handy erections all over the place, wherever they are wanted, and pull them down without ceremony, when they are not required to be permanent, and we can do without them.

Some time ago, being desirous of keeping my breed of black Spanish fowls distinct from the others, my foreman's wife, who lives in a cottage on the land, which stands by itself, but without any out-building save their oven, agreed to look after them, and we accordingly put up a fowl-house of the above-named materials. It is warm, roomy, and everything that can be desired for the purpose, and in one corner of it my foreman keeps things, for which he was sadly pinched for room before, having rigged up some shelves within it, the opposite end being used for the fowls' roosting-place.

To me, all these little improvements are a constant source of interest, and I make this digression, in order to show how comparatively easily things may be done where one has the right sort of men about, who can turn their hands to something a little different to ordinary farm work. It is not of course necessary that they *all* should be able to do this, but out of a number of men, two or three could easily be found who would prove useful upon these emergencies.

In some parts of the country, as in Devonshire, "stud and mud" houses are built, the walls being made up of straw mixed with earth wetted, sods, etc. These get firm and dry, and are "rough-cast" outside and whitewashed, and an erection of this sort on a small scale would answer as well for many purposes as a proper brick building. To the citizen, and dweller in towns, who has to pay for everything that is brought to him, the item of carriage in some of the bulkier articles forming the greater portion of the cost, this sort of thing cannot be so readily realised; but in the country, often, the stones, which sometimes can be used for these purposes, and always the earth, are beneath one's feet for use.

Tiles, as a roofing for a dairy-house, are objectionable. They are hot in summer and cold in winter, and a thatched roof is perhaps as good as any for the opposite seasons; but there is one drawback, that when a thatch gets old, it is apt to get musty, and therefore liable to harbour vermin. Good thick slates form the best roofing, being more impervious to the weather than any other material. Slate, indeed, should be used wherever it can in a dairy, even for the floors, for they imbibe less moisture than bricks. For, although water may be occasionally used in a dairy to advantage, as I have before instanced, yet, as a rule, it should be kept as dry as possible. When the floor is laid with brick, the spilled milk gets into the crannies, and also the water, and from these a certain amount of unpleasant odour will arise, however trifling, so that a slate flooring, raised a few inches above the outer ground, to make sure of a fall for water, is preferable to anything else ; and anyone making new arrangements in connection with their dairies should have recourse to slate as much as possible, and a floor with slanting gutters, to carry off the water used in washing, or "swilling" down, will be found advantageous.

In the same way a slate table will be liked by those who make use of them, but slate is not always so procurable as slabs of stone, or pavement, and one has to deal often with the materials which are readiest to hand. Marble is affected by many gentlemen who like to see their dairies handsomely fitted up, but slate is even preferable to marble, fishmongers finding that it preserves fish twenty-four hours longer than marble does.

Slates are easily laid upon a bed of mortar upon the ground, and where the earth is loose or soft, a bottom of concrete should be first spread. This is composed of seven parts of dry gravel, free from clay or loam, mixed with one part of pounded quick-lime, mixed with water at the time of using it, till it attains the consistency of thick mortar. A little Portland cement would be found very useful in stopping up chinks and crannies in the floors of dairies.

When it is necessary to build a new dairy altogether, a very economical method is to set up a framework of timber quartering, cased outside with half-inch slates, the cavities between the quarters inside being filled up solid with concrete, made as before described, or lime and hair mortar, with rubble of bricks, or stone, and made smooth inside with the trowel. When lime is used, it preserves the timber from decaying.

The requirements in the shape of dairy utensils will comprise milk-pails, shallow pans or dishes for holding the milk, sieves for straining it when taken from the cow, dishes for skimming the cream, churns for making butter, with scales, prints, and boards for weighing and making it up.

When cheese is made, there will be required ladders, vats, tubs, curd-breakers, and presses, with vessels large enough to hold the whey, or buttermilk, thermometer, weighing-machine, etc. The milk-pails are of various sizes, holding from two to seven gallons of milk, and are of wood mostly, with a handle fastened to the side, and rising above the edge of the pail, which, being a fixture, makes no noise when the cow is being milked, which is to be avoided as much as possible, all clatter and noise being highly objectionable at milking time.

The milk is carried to the dairy, and strained, in the case of butter-making, through an horse-hair sieve into shallow milk-pans, which are made of various materials, glazed earthenware, tinned iron, or glass, which hold one-and-a-half to three gallons, and from two to three inches in depth. Brass, and tin milk-dishes are also sometimes seen.

Where cheese is made, the milk is strained into tubs holding thirty gallons or more, according to the size of intended operations. For butter-making, the small-sized milk-dishes are preferable to the larger, the object being to give as much surface as possible, so as to remove all the cream, as it rises to the top after standing. Six quarts, perhaps, would be about the best quantity to place in each.

The cream is skimmed off the surface of the dishes by a shallow pierced tin ladle, and is stored in cream-pots, or stone jars, until enough has been accumulated to be put in the churn and made into butter. In cold weather especially, the milk-dishes will bear skimming twice.

The churn is of various forms and sizes, the old plunge-churn having given way to the barrel-churn, which is the easiest to work; the barrel being turned by a handle. The common box-churn is a rectangular box of wood, which contains a revolving frame of flat wooden beaters, and is made of various sizes. The American box-churns have been largely used in small dairies, and for the use of private families, but there are many modifications of the box-churn, of which it is not worth while to speak at length, as new churns are continually being brought before the notice of the public. There are also churns worked by power, designed for the production of a large quantity of butter, but in some of the largest dairies the barrel-churn is commonly used of various sizes, made to hold from twelve to twenty gallons and upwards. There is also a pneumatic churn, which gets the butter very quickly, but there is a knack in using it that all operators do not seem able to acquire, and I have seen several of these put by in despair, though others have spoken highly of their use; but never having tried them myself, I am not qualified to speak on the matter. One, belonging to our squire, who lent it to my wife at a time when I had not paid much attention to these matters, stood in our dairy for a considerable time, but they could do nothing with it, and it was sent back, our luck having been no better than the squire's people, who could not make anything of it.

In making cheese, the utensils used are the milk-pail at first, the cheese-tub, the cheese-vat and circular board, skimming-dish, and bowl. The cheese-tub is of sufficient size to hold the milk of which the cheese is made, the vats being mostly made of elm turned out solid of the size of the cheese. The cheese-tub will depend on the size of the dairy, there sometimes being two of them, one for use in the summer, and one for spring and autumn. These should not be too deep, as if so, it is inconvenient for the person leaning over them to turn the curd. The cheese-presses are also of various modes of construction, chiefly upon the lever principle, for the purpose of squeezing the cheese into shape in the vats. Of these I need not speak at greater length just here, as I will farther on give a brief notice of the different methods of cheese-making followed in various counties.

Produce to be aimed at.—Before proceeding to give an account of the different methods that are followed in various parts of the country, for making butter and cheese, or the management of a dairy for the sale of milk only; I cannot lay too much stress upon the point that the dairy-farmer, whether he be seeking to obtain a living from his undertaking, or whether he be simply a private person naturally desirous of turning matters to the best account, should, in either case, make up his mind clearly as to the course he intends to pursue with respect to developing produce. Nothing, perhaps, in a profitable point of view, can beat simple milk-selling; but then it is a somewhat lumbering business, and necessitates the employment of horses, carts, and drivers, to take the milk-cans to the station, bring home the empty cans, and perhaps have a long running account with the milk-sellers in London, or any large town to which the milk may be consigned, with whom he may, occasionally, make a bad debt perhaps.

Or, it may answer his purpose to make butter best, butter being a very profitable commodity, for which there is always a ready market, and cash ready too in payment from responsible dealers, who are always anxious to obtain a first-rate article in the shape of butter.

If he aim at cheese-making, there are different considerations to be entertained; and all these require first to be well deliberated upon, for the profit will hinge entirely upon a right choice being made to suit particular circumstances.

To the inland dairy-farmer, it is of primary importance that the cows he keeps be of such a breed, or breeds, as will yield rich milk; even though the quantity should not be so very great, for the reason that the refuse, either of butter or cheese making, can be turned to little account.

In my own case, situated three-and-a-half miles from a station, when I began to understand matters, and could see for myself, I perceived readily enough that butter-making would suit me best. I did not want to have the trouble of a milk business, involving long and troublesome accounts, and a certain risk about payments; while a trade in butter I could manage without the slightest difficulty. I was driven daily in a dog-cart to the station, and a hamper containing butter was put into the cart and went up to town with me, being properly labelled, and when I got to the terminus in London, one of the porters carried it to the Parcels' Delivery office, and it thus cost me nothing for carriage up to town.

Of course everyone is not situated in the same way, but the principle will hold good, that butter is very portable, and can be moved about at a very trifling cost in proportion to its value; and anyone, however far they may happen to be from a railway station, could easily send away a hamper of butter, or as many hampers as they chose, once or twice a week.

Cheese I never make, because it is not so profitable as butter-making, the produce of America entering into competition with it; and it does not fetch nearly so much money as butter, when the expenses of making are deducted, although, at the first glance, cheese-making would appear to be the more profitable of the two; a pound of cheese being made from a gallon of milk, the cost of a gallon of milk to produce being estimated at about sixpence; while the best cheese, as Cheshire or Gloucestershire, would fetch wholesale about sevenpence halfpenny or sevenpence three farthings per pound. Cows, however, fed in a certain manner, which I shall speak of again, for the production of milk only, could be made to produce milk at a cost of about fourpence per gallon, and the money value of the produce of the cow fluctuates very much according to the purpose for which she is kept, whether for milk, butter, or cheese. In Cheshire, and Gloucestershire, cheese-making is aimed at, and the produce commands a comparatively high price in the market.

Quality of Milk.—Fed alike in the same manner, and on the same food, the quality of the milk of different cows varies exceedingly. The component parts of milk are distinguished as the butyraceous, or oily substance, producing cream, of which butter is composed; the caseine, or caseous matter, out of which cheese is formed, and the serum, or whey; in round numbers, an average proportion of each being:

Cream-forming	4·5 parts
Cheese ,,	3·5 ,,
Whey ,,	92·0 ,,
	100·0

But these relative proportions will differ in degrees like the following, when the yield of separate cows are carefully compared:

Butter	4·318
Caseine	3·017
Whey	92·665
	100·000

Butter	2·900
Caseine	3·144
Whey	93·956
	100·000

In the two cases above instanced, the quantity of milk yielded per week by each cow respectively was seventeen gallons in the first, against twenty-four gallons per week in the second; the latter being a larger breed of cow, consuming more food than the first, and thus costing more to keep. The butter churned from the milk of the first cow weighed seven-and-a-half pounds, and that of the latter a little over seven pounds, so that the larger quantity of milk produced rather less butter, though the money value was greater altogether with that of the cow that gave the most milk. I have got eighteenpence per pound for my butter in most cases, and never less than sixteenpence, so that reckoning up the proceeds of the first cow at the rate of eighteenpence per pound for butter, and three farthings per quart, or threepence per gallon, for the buttermilk, the money result would stand thus:

	s.	d.
7½ lb. butter at 1s. 6d.	11	3
16 gallons buttermilk at 3d.	4	0
	15	3

The second as under:

	s.	d.
7 lb. butter at 1s. 6d.	10	6
21 gallons buttermilk at 3d.	5	3
	15	9

There was rather more than seven pounds of butter in the latter instance, so the gain in fact was a trifle more than the figures above stated. Had the milk of each cow been sold at eightpence per gallon, the larger profit would have been realised upon the produce of the second cow.

In a third instance, ten pounds of butter was churned from the milk of one cow—the money value of which was fifteen shillings—and there were twenty-one gallons of buttermilk, coming to five shillings and threepence; or a total of one pound and threepence altogether.

I do not dispose of my skimmed milk as an article of commerce, though I let any of the villagers have it as a matter of convenience and service to them, as well as my men; for it is very valuable to me in rearing calves—a line in which I have been very successful—and for feeding pigs, of which I keep a great number; for although the latter have but rough fare as store pigs, we "finish off" with barleymeal and skimmed milk.

It will be seen from the above instances quoted how various is the yield of milk from different cows, of which the ordinary average in individual instances, without any extra forcing, is generally assumed to be from 550 to 600 gallons in the year; out of which a cow is necessarily dry for a certain period.

The quality of milk differs too, as respects the time at which it is drawn from the cow. That which is milked first is always thinner than that which comes afterwards, increasing in richness till the last is obtained which can be drawn from the udder.

Management of Milk.—A great deal depends upon the management of milk, which, in the first place, when taken from the cow, should be carried as gently as possible to the dairy. Milk which is carried in a pail, or bucket, from any considerable distance, and is shaken about a good deal on the road, or gets cold before it is put into the milk-pans to settle for cream, never throws up so much, nor so rich cream, as if the same milk had been directly placed in the pans immediately after being milked. This is one advantage of milking the cows at home, instead of at the field. The advocates of the latter system say in defence of it that the cows are not made to take extra exertion, often in hot weather, and are not hunted and driven about so much when milked in the field in which they are grazing; but cows with proper treatment will stroll leisurely along towards home to be milked of their own accord, and will assemble at the gate of the enclosure in which they are confined, waiting to be released—especially if they are fed during the time the milking is going on, which I always make a practice of having done with mine, even if they are known not to be wanting anything in the shape of food, a handful of something different being given to them. I would not, indeed, keep a man who drove the cows about, or who was hasty and hot-tempered with them. I have seen men lose their tempers while milking, and even throw the milking-stool at a cow, but I would take care not to have such a man about my place, if I knew of any acting in such a manner.

Butter-making.—The milk, after being left in the shallow milk-pans which are used to collect the cream, will throw the latter up to the surface in the course of a few hours, according to the temperature of the air. If, as the Americans call it, a *fancy article* of superior quality is desired in the shape of butter, it is skimmed within twelve hours; but it is more generally left till twenty-four hours, and, in exceptional cases, even thirty-six hours, according to the time of year—sometimes more than one skimming being necessary.

A small quantity of water, cold in summer, or warm in winter, is sometimes put into the bottom of the pan, with the object of assisting the cream to rise, as it equalises the heat to that of the milk-house at times; but this course is not always to be recommended.

That portion of cream which rises first to the surface is richer in quality, and greater in quantity, than what rises in the same time during a second interval—the more in quantity, and richer than in a third interval—the milk declining in quality, as well as quantity, each time the pan is skimmed, and the cream will continue to rise to the surface.

The analysis of skimmed milk has been given as under:

Water	928·75
Cheese, with a trace of butter	28·00
Sugar of milk	35·00
Muriate of potash	1·70
Phosphate of potash	0·25
Lactic acid, with acetate of potash	6·00
Earthy phosphate	0·30
	1000·00

When milk is thick, it throws up to the surface a smaller proportion of the cream it actually contains, than milk which is thinner; but the cream is of richer quality. If the thick milk receives the addition of water, it will throw up a greater quantity of cream than it would have done had it been allowed to remain pure; but the quality of the cream at the same time becomes deteriorated.

Butter is usually churned from cream alone, but it can be made with the whole milk, unskimmed. And although this difference in practice would lead one to suppose the results would be something different, yet they have little perceptible difference, either upon the quantity or quality of the butter produced; though the produce of the dairy may be affected in its relation to the demand for skimmed milk, or buttermilk. Butter is made from whole milk mostly in Scotland, where the buttermilk enters largely, as an article of food, in the consumption by farm-servants and others; care being taken not to allow the coagulum, or curd of the milk, in the stand-vat to be broken till the milk is about to be churned. If it is not shaken till it is turned into the churn, it may stand from a day to a week without injury, and the buttermilk has a pleasant acid taste, very agreeable to those accustomed to partake of it; but is not usually given to servants, or consumed to any extent in England.

The churning from whole milk, on account of the larger quantity, is much more laborious; so that in large dairies where butter is made upon this system, churns moved by machinery are sometimes employed, and the method requires more time to complete the process of obtaining butter.

When butter is made from cream alone, the milk is usually skimmed two or three times in summer, and as often as four times in winter, till no more cream rises to the surface. This should be separated from the edges of the milk-pans to which it adheres, by running an ivory paper-knife closely round it, and the cream carefully drawn to one side, and lifted off with a skimming-dish—which requires a little knack in the doing, so as to avoid leaving any of the cream behind, and to prevent any portion of the milk being taken up with it; which, although the skimming-dish is pierced with small holes, will sometimes happen unless care is used.

The length of time milk may be allowed to stand before skimming must depend very much upon the temperature, and the ultimate design of the dairy-farmer; but in moderately warm weather, for ordinary good butter, it may safely be allowed to stand for twelve hours, and during cold weather much longer.

The cream, after being skimmed, is placed in a deep vessel called a cream-pot or jar. A good many of these are simply stone or earthenware vessels, for holding the cream until the desired quantity is accumulated to form enough for a churning; but one that has close to the bottom a tap, or cock and spigot, for drawing off from time to time any of the thin serous part of the milk that may be in it, is the best, as it acts upon the cream in an unfavourable manner, and diminishes the richness and quality of the butter.

Cream, when churned alone, should not be of a higher temperature than sixty degrees; some advocate even lower, as between fifty and sixty degrees, for if kept at a high temperature in the process of churning, it will be inferior in taste, appearance, and quality; but whole milk needs to be about seventy to seventy-five degrees Fahrenheit before the butter can be separated from the milk. A thermometer should, therefore, be hung up in every dairy; yet it is strange they are very seldom to be seen, experienced dairy-maids generally trusting to their sense of touch to guide them in this particular; depending upon their hands for trying the heat, which by long practice they are enabled to judge of pretty accurately.

Experiments made with milk churned of various

degrees of heat, from fifty-five to seventy degrees, demonstrate that the lower degrees bring butter firm, rich, and well tasted; while the higher produces it soft and spongy, and inferior in flavour.

In some parts of the country the cream is scalded by being placed in a tin, in a water-bath, and the water is boiled till the cream registers 165 degrees. In Devonshire the belief prevails, that more butter is got by this method. I have only, however, tried a few minor experiments myself in this way, and cannot speak positively as to results, it being a departure from the method laid down and arranged for, requiring somewhat different appliances and utensils to those we are already supplied with.

In winter time, the churn should be heated by pouring boiling water into it before the churning is begun, the practice being the reverse in summer time, cold water being placed in the churn; and the vessel which contains the cream should be put in cold water (hot water in winter), which is best done overnight, and the churning performed at early morning, before the heat of the day sets in. In summer time the handle of the churn should be turned slowly, for if too fast, the butter will be soft and of a bad quality; but in winter it must be turned briskly, or it will be difficult to convert the cream into butter.

When the butter comes, it will fall from side to side of the churn in large lumps, when the buttermilk should be drawn off, and the butter removed from the churn; a great many dairymen cause the butter to be well washed in cold water, with the object of extracting the whole of the buttermilk, any of which, left with the butter, being apt to cause it to turn rancid. In order to guard against this, it is often washed in repeated waters by anxious dairymaids, until the water comes out pure, which shows there is no trace of buttermilk in it; but when a dairy is conducted upon a system of superior management, there is no occasion for this being done; if, when it is taken out of the churn, it is well worked with the hand, and the milk squeezed out, and a cloth repeatedly pressed down upon it to absorb any milk that may remain. The less, however, that butter is beaten, or worked about, the better; for the more it is kneaded, the tougher it will become. Experience proves that butter retains its sweetness much longer when no water has been used in making it up.

If butter is to be salted, either for market or to be put aside for winter use, after the whole of the milk has been carefully pressed out, the salt should be well mixed, by working it in equally with the hand. If this is not done thoroughly, the butter will be of different colours, which will reduce its value as a merchantable commodity, as well as cause it to look unsightly—as it will be yellow where the salt has fallen, but white where it has not. It should be done at once, after it has been churned, for if deferred, the butter loses some of its firmness and flavour. If enough is not churned at one time to fill a firkin, it should not be put into the package in layers, but the surface left rough and broken, so as to unite better with each succeeding churning.

Fresh butter needs to be salted very lightly, so that the salt can be scarcely tasted; and when made up for market, is usually put up into the form of two-pound rolls, the hamper in which the rolls are packed being just deep enough to receive the rolls of butter standing up endways in it. This is the method in which it is usually prepared for the London market, but it is sometimes formed into a lump, and then stamped with a butter-print, in "pats" of the size most approved by those who want their butter made up in this form.

Clotted or Clouted Cream.—In the western counties of England, the dairymaids say that, by the method usually pursued there, about one-fourth more cream is produced than by the common way; and in making it into butter a churn is not used, the cream being stirred by the hand, the following being the method pursued:

The milk is carried warm from the cows, and strained into shallow brass pans, tinned inside, in which a small quantity of cold water has been placed, to cause the cream to separate itself more thoroughly from the milk and be thrown to the top; the morning milk standing till the middle of the day, and the evening milk remaining undisturbed till the next morning. They are then carried gently to a slow clear fire, or charcoal stove, the heat of either of which must not be allowed to get sufficiently great as to cause the milk to boil—or, as it is called, to "heave"—which would injure the cream. It is a very nice point to determine when it is scalded sufficiently, which an experienced operator, is enabled to form a tolerably accurate opinion of, by the texture of the surface of the cream, and the wrinkles upon it, its texture becoming somewhat leathery. In summer time, the process of scalding is quicker than in winter; for, in very hot weather, if the milk is kept too long over a slow fire, it is apt to curdle.

The milk having been duly scalded, is then carried back in the pans to the dairy, and in summer time is placed in the coolest situation—should the floor of the dairy be of stone, on that, or on slate benches. But in the winter season, it is desirable to retain some of the heat, by putting some kind of slight covering over the pans, as if cooled too suddenly it causes the cream to become thin, and consequently the yield of butter is diminished.

Butter from Clotted Cream.—In summer time, butter is made from clotted cream the next day, but in winter it is thought better to allow the cream to remain one day longer upon the milk. The cream, being collected from the pans, is put into wooden bowls, which are first rinsed in hot, and afterwards with cold water. It is now briskly stirred round one way, by the hand of the operator, which must also have been washed in hot water first, and afterwards in cold water, not alone so as to ensure perfect cleanliness, but as well to prevent the butter from sticking to either.

The cream, after having been briskly agitated for a short time, quickly assumes the form of butter, and separates from the milky part, which is poured off. The butter is washed, and pressed in several successive waters, quite cold, to get out any of the milky portion which may remain in it; after which it is well beaten on a wooden trencher, previous to which a little salt has been added to season it; and when the watery parts are thoroughly eliminated, it is finally formed into shape by the butter-prints, and is ready for market.

Butter, according to various writers, appears to

have been made in England from time immemorial, being a common food of the ancient Britons at the time of the conquest of Britain by the Romans, who were not a butter-making people themselves, and were unacquainted with the process, until they were taught by the Germans, which however cannot be a matter of surprise, as a warm climate is unfavourable to the production of butter; nor does the human system appear to demand the aid of oily substances for the furnishing of the animal economy in warm climates, as in cold ones; which causes the Russian moujik to relish tallow; an arctic traveller having related his experience that the most delicious meal he ever partook of was a piece of a raw fish and a lump of fat. Truly, indeed, may it be said that "a good appetite is the best sauce."

Nor do any of the Greek writers refer to butter when speaking of pastoral productions. Though made in England at the time I have spoken of, while the Romans might have learnt the art of making butter from the Britons, the former certainly taught the latter how to make cheese. The ancient history of buttermaking has been said to be very imperfectly known, for though mentioned in the Scriptures as "being brought forth by the churning of milk," it has been asserted by certain writers that the word "butter," as translated from the Hebrew, ought to have been rendered as "cream." The patriarch Abraham is described as entertaining his heavenly visitors with butter when on their way to warn Lot of the impending destruction of Sodom and Gomorrah; and while a dish of cool cream would be a welcome refreshment in an eastern country, butter would be scarcely so.

CHAPTER IV.

Cheese-making—Cheshire System—Gloucester Cheese—Egg Cheeses—Stilton Cheese—Cream Cheese—Skim-milk Cheese—New Cheese—Cheese made Abroad—Parmesan Cheese—Potato Cheese—Whole-milk Cheese—Rennet—Scotch method of preparing Rennet.

CHEESE-MAKING.—The best kinds of cheese made in England are produced in the counties of Cheshire, Gloucester, and Leicester; the latter, in the form of Stilton cheese, fetching the highest price in the market; and it is an indisputable fact that much of the peculiar flavour and excellence of cheese must be attributed to the quality of the pastures upon which the cows feed. Old Fuller wittily points this out in his "Worthies," when speaking of Cheshire: "It doth afforde the best cheese for quantitie and qualitie, and yet the cows are not, as in other shires, housed in the winter. Some essaied in vaine to make the like in other places, thoughe from whence they fetched their kine and dairie-maides, it seems they shoulde have fetched their grounde too, wherein is surelie some occult excellence in this kind, or else so good cheese will not be made." The numerous salt-springs which abound in Cheshire have probably a good deal to do with the special flavour of the cheese produced there, which is so highly appreciated by connoisseurs; but the rule may be taken as universal that the quality of the cheese produced is always best when the cows are turned out upon the pastures during the summer months. Good cheese may, however, be made all the year round, if the cows are fed upon good nutritious food, of which hay forms a large part throughout the winter; though in the best dairies, in nearly all counties, cheese-making does not commence until the cows are turned out to grass, and receive nothing but green food.

Cheshire System.—In Cheshire, cheese is always made in the morning, the evening's milk being poured into coolers till the succeeding morning. The cream is then taken off, and about half of it is warmed in a shallow pan with a flat bottom, till it attains about 100 degrees, and is poured into the cheese-tub together with the morning's milk, and the remaining portion of milk belonging to the last evening which has not been warmed. The cream, mixed with a little warm milk, is now added, which will cause the temperature to be somewhere about eighty to eighty-five degrees. The rennet and annatto (used for colouring) are now added, and the whole well stirred up together; about half an ounce of annatto being sufficient to colour seventy-five pounds of cheese; the annatto being dissolved overnight in a pint of warm milk. The tub is covered up closely for an hour, when, under ordinary conditions, coagulation will commence, and be completed in about a quarter of an hour. The curd is then broken, which takes about twenty minutes for the large cheeses turned out, which usually weigh about sixty pounds, and is allowed to rest for a quarter of an hour, to get separated from the whey, which is removed by gently pressing down a flat-bottomed pan on the curd, and allowing it to fill. The whey is poured into the set pan from the cheese-tub. The curd, to a certain extent freed from the whey, is broken up again, and again allowed to settle and separate; the whey being ladled out in about half an hour's time, and as the curd begins to get more solid, it is drawn to the side of the tub. When the free whey has been removed, a semicircular board, perforated with holes, which fits one-half of the tub, is placed upon the curd, and a thirty-pound weight put on the top of it, which gently squeezes out the whey, which is poured into the set-pan to catch the particles of curd that float into it. The weight is then removed, and the curd cut into pieces six or eight inches square. A weight, twice as heavy as the one previously used, is now placed on the board to press out more whey, and this operation is successively repeated with ever-increasing weights, according to the condition of the curd, which is then ready to be placed in the cheese-vat. The curd is sometimes broken up into smaller pieces by the hand, when, being placed in the first, or large cheese-vat, which it should not quite fill, a close-fitting board is then applied, and it is put under a light press. When the whey leaves off draining from the sides of the vat, the curd is again taken out and broken as before, and then put in the proper vat, in which a cheese-cloth has been previously placed. The ends of the cloth are neatly drawn over the curd, and covered with the circular board called a "sinker," and is then submitted to heavier pressure than it has received before. Iron skewers are thrust into the cheese through the vat-holes, to cause the whey to come from the interior of the cheese, which, after being withdrawn, will be the means of causing whey to drip from the punctures thus made. After the whey has ceased to drip, the vat is taken out from beneath the press, and the curd is cut into sections, as it lies in the vat, with a blunt knife, every two or three inches, and again pressed and skewered as before for twenty minutes. When this is done, the curd is taken entirely out of the vat, cut into large pieces, each of which is afterwards broken by the hand, and is then placed in a dry cloth in the vat, covered over, pressed, and skewered as before, until the whey is sufficiently extracted. From first to last, beginning at the time of coagulation, these operations will take up five or six hours, by which time the curd ought to be in readiness for being salted.

The process of salting lasts for three days, and sometimes even for four; the curd, now comparatively free from whey, being taken out of the vat, cut to pieces, and crumbled with the hands, or passed through the curd-mill. Salt is then added at the rate of one pound of salt to forty-five of curd, and thoroughly incorporated with it. The curd, now salted, is returned again to the vat, in which is a dry cloth of finer quality than that used before; and in order that the curd should be pressed properly, it should more than fill the vat, a tin hoop being used to retain that portion which projects above the vat, the lower edge being within the vat, and sinking with the curd when pressed.

The pressure is still further increased this time, and the cheese is again skewered. After being under the press for an hour, the cheese, completely formed, is taken out, and its edges pared; the parings being put into a hole scooped out of the top for that purpose, turned upside down, and put into the vat with a dry cloth round it, and pressed again. In the course of the evening, the cheese is again inverted, and is supplied with another dry cloth; which ends the first day's operations.

On the second day the cheese is turned three times, dry cloths being given, and the skewering continued. On the third day the turning is repeated twice, dry cloths being supplied upon each occasion; but the skewering is discontinued. This usually completes the process, but sometimes the pressure is continued for another day.

Gloucester Cheese.—There are two kinds of cheese made in Gloucestershire—single and double Gloucester —but the mode of making either is the same, except that the former is thinner, being called "toasting cheese," and originally intended for that once favourite dish "Welsh rare bit," is somewhat less salted, and pressed one day less in the course of its manufacture. It is occasionally, also, made somewhat less rich than the double Gloucester, by being partially mixed with skimmed milk.

As soon as the cows are milked in the morning, which is usually at five o'clock in the summer, the milk is carried to the dairy-house and strained into the cheese-tub, and the rennet and annatto mixed with it. But in autumn and winter, when the weather is cold, a small quantity of the milk is warmed in a tin pitcher, so as to raise the whole to the temperature of eighty-five degrees, which is considered the proper one, before adding the rennet.

The milk is then allowed to remain perfectly still

for an hour, being covered over with a woollen cloth to exclude the cold air. Under ordinary conditions, the curd will form in this interval, and be ready for breaking up, which is done by passing a three-bladed knife made for the purpose, or a coarse wire sieve with large meshes, gently downwards to the bottom of the tub. After the curd has been divided into as small pieces as its suspension in the whey will allow, it is left undisturbed for ten minutes, or a quarter of an hour, to give the curd time to sink enough to allow of the whey to be ladled off at the top. As soon as all the thin or clear whey is removed, the curd, which will be more condensed in consequence, is broken a second time, care being taken not to perform the operation too roughly or quickly, so that all the butter may be retained in it. When the curd has been broken up to a proper degree of fineness, it is left to settle for a short time, after which, more of the whey is removed, and poured through a sieve, so that not any small particles of curd are lost. When most of the whey has been removed, the curd is divided into lumps, and laid aside, one upon another on the bottom of the tub, which is then tilted up, so as to allow the whey to run on one side, in order to allow of its being conveniently removed. When this has been drained off, the curds are placed in the vat, over the top of which a fine cheese-cloth is spread, and the curd pressed down by the hands in an equal manner. When all has been carefully placed in the vat, the ends of the cloth are tucked up, and made as smooth as can be at top, with as few creases as possible, and covered with a circular board to fit the top of the vat exactly inside. It is then put in the cheese-press for half an hour, and lightly pressed, after which the curd is taken out, cut in slices, and passed through the curd-breaker, which separates it into small pieces without squeezing out the butter, which it is the great object to retain, so as to ensure a rich quality. A dry cheese-cloth is then spread over the top of the vat, which is turned upside down, so that the curd stands upon the cloth. The vat is now rinsed with whey, and dried, and the curd with the cloth on which it stands placed within it. The ends of the cloth are then neatly and evenly folded over the top as before, and covered with the cheese-board, or another cheese-vat, if more than one cheese is to be placed in the same press. The vat is allowed to remain under the press for two hours, by which time the cheese will have become consolidated, when the edges are pared off, and it is inverted, after being put in a dry cloth, and pressed again. Two or three presses are usually employed, beginning with the lightest, and ending with the heaviest, the process so far taking four or five days in its course of manipulation.

The salting, in the case of Gloucester cheese, is performed when the cheese has been made, and not in the course of its manufacture, as in that of Cheshire cheese; although the latter is sometimes done so as well, after the cheese has been made. After the cheese has been twenty-four hours in the press, it is ready for the salt to be applied—some do this as early as twelve hours—but it should not be applied until the skin is firm and free from openings, for these never close completely after salting, however heavily they may be pressed.

The salt is rubbed over the whole surface of the

cheese, as long as it will take it in, by hand, after which it is wrapped in a dry cloth and put beneath the press. In twenty-four hours afterwards it is salted as before, but upon this occasion it is put in the vat without a cloth, and pressed, so as to secure a smooth and even surface. A final rubbing with salt is given after the same interval of time, and the cheese, after having been pressed as before, is then ready to be taken away to the drying-room, where it is well wiped with dry cloths, and turned every twenty-four hours. In about a month after leaving the press, the cheeses are ready for scraping, and when intended for the London market, they are painted outside with Indian red or Spanish brown, or a mixture of both worked up with table beer, which is rubbed in with a woollen cloth.

If the salting was performed in the same way as first described, by applying the salt to the curd before it is put into the vat, it would be more crumbly, and not possess the waxy texture which is the distinguishing trait of Gloucestershire cheese; and therefore the salting is done outside, as described, with finely-powdered salt. The quantity of the latter used is about three-and-a-half pounds to the hundred-weight.

The double Gloucester cheese generally weighs about twenty-two pounds, while the single Gloucester seldom exceeds a dozen pounds in weight.

Egg Cheeses.—The single Gloucester, as before stated, was chiefly made up in its adopted thin shape for the sake of toasting, its waxy texture enabling it to be cut in thin slices without crumbling; but this result is attained in some parts of the north of

England, by adding the yolks of four or five eggs to every pound of the curd with which they are mixed. These "egg cheeses" are very much relished in those places where they are made, and toasted cheese is looked upon complacently as a leading feature in farmhouse fare.

Stilton Cheese.—Stilton cheese owes its name to having been first made at Stilton, near Melton Mowbray, in Leicestershire, but it is now manufactured in various parts of the country; and cheese is made upon the same plan in the counties of Cambridge and Huntingdon, its celebrity having begot many imitations.

Stilton cheese is very rich in cream, the night's milk being set aside and skimmed in the morning, the cream alone, without the skimmed milk, being added to the milk of the following morning; and those who desire to make a very rich cheese, add even a greater quantity of cream, its richness, of course, depending upon the quantity of cream of which it is composed, butter also being said to be mixed with it at times. The rennet is added, but no colouring is used, and the whole is made of the temperature of eighty-four degrees.

An hour and a half should be allowed for the curd to form. If formed in a shorter space of time than this, it becomes poor and tough; and if it takes longer, on the other hand, the extra time proves injurious to it, as it requires to be warmed, which deteriorates its quality. The curd is removed in slices by the skimming-dish—not being broken up in the ordinary manner of cheese-making—and is placed upon a canvas strainer or sieve. When the curd has all been placed on the strainer, it is either pressed by weights, until completely cleared of whey, or the ends of the cloth are tied up, and the whey squeezed out by gently twisting round the whole mass suspended on a stick across the cheese-tub. It is left to drain till next morning, when the curd is removed from the strainer and placed in a cool place, where it is cut into three slices and put into a shape, made of tin perforated with holes, rather larger than the intended cheese. A clean cheese-cloth is put between the tin and the curd, and as the slices of the latter are laid in a small quantity of salt is sprinkled upon every third layer. Next morning the curd is removed from the hoop, and clean strainers and cloths are applied; and it is then inverted and placed in the tin as before, and afterwards pricked with iron skewers in the sides, so as to drain off the whey and dry the curd. This is done for four or five mornings successively, until the curd is found to have become quite firm.

While this process is going on, the cheeses are kept in a warm place, and should the weather be cold, they are placed in tins before the fire, or in heated ovens, which some cheese-makers have constructed for the purpose of drying the cheeses, the temperature of which it is necessary to raise to one hundred degrees to thoroughly extract the whey. The latter should run freely from the curd, and each time the strainers are changed, those which have been used should be washed, and dried thoroughly in the open air.

When the cheese has become sufficiently firm to be handled, it is pared and smoothed, and any inequalities there may happen to be in the sides are filled up with the parings, and the top and bottom are also smoothed. A strip of canvas, large enough to go two or three times round the cheese, is then tightly bound round it and pinned together, a clean dry cloth being placed below and above the cheese—every morning the cloths and binders being removed, and the cracks filled up—which is continued till the outside, or coat, becomes hard and wrinkled. After this, the cheeses are removed to the drying-room, where they are regularly turned upside down, and brushed.

Nearly two years is required to bring Stilton cheeses to perfect maturity, which are not generally considered at their best until somewhat decayed. The blue mould may be communicated from an old cheese to a much younger one, by removing pieces of the former with the cheese scoop, or taster, and interchanging them. This operation, in fact, consists of the transposition of the mould plant from one to the other, which grows most in damp, warm cellars; but the cheeses selected for this inoculation should, however, of themselves be dry, and the blue mould of the older cheese be quite free from any portion bearing a more decayed aspect.

The modes I have indicated are those followed in three of the best cheese-making districts in England, which, as will be seen, differ very materially from one another in certain particulars. This is strikingly so in the application of rennet, the bag itself being used; while in Scotland, the liquid decoction extracted from it is so much stronger, that it occasions the curd to coagulate within fifteen minutes, whereas in England, the operation is allowed to extend to a considerably longer period—from an hour to two hours. The degree of heat at which the curd is set is one of the nicest points of cheese-making, and there certainly is a great risk in allowing the curd to stand a long time cooling in the cheese-tub. On the other hand, if too much rennet is used, or if it be unusually strong, it will make the cheese "heave," by causing fermentation. In order to avoid the risk of this happening, at some of the best dairies in Gloucestershire the "maws," or "vells," are not made use of till they are twelve months old; but of these I will speak more fully again. In cheese-making, it is necessary to obtain some little knowledge before commencing operations, as there are various nice points connected with it which can hardly be obtained from a written description; though the art of butter-making, as well as cream cheese, is easy enough to acquire—the latter a luxury often relished in private families.

Cream Cheese.—Cream cheese is simply thick, sweet cream, dried by being put into a cheese-vat, or shape, about an inch and a half in depth, perforated with small holes in the bottom, to allow any of the milk which may have been taken up with it to escape. It is covered with rushes, or a substitute, so as to admit of its being turned without being handled, and it is not put between a press, but gently pressed by hand between two cloths.

Being generally wanted for immediate use, it is kept in warm situations to sweat and ripen, for if only chilled, it becomes comparatively insipid, and much of its mellow richness is lost. If, however, it is kept in too hot a place it becomes rank, so that extremes of both heat and cold have to be guarded against.

DAIRY FARMING.

Skim-milk Cheese.—Skim-milk cheese, as its name implies, is made of milk from which the whole of the cream has been taken, except any minute quantity that may remain behind, and is more or less palatable according to the time the milk has been allowed to stand; for, if so long as to be entirely deprived of its butyraceous matter, it is not only very indigestible, but so hard that it is scarcely possible to bite it. In Suffolk, when large quantities were made in a former generation, it used to be called "bang;" "Suffolk bang" having the reputation of being so hard as to need cutting with a chopper, an ordinary table-knife being unfit for the purpose.

The best method of making it is, not to allow the milk to become sour, but the moment it has been skimmed, to warm it gently, until it attains the heat of ninety degrees. If it is made too hot its toughness will be aggravated, as the curd coagulates more readily than that of whole milk. This is the principal item of difference in the management, except that the curd is more difficult to break, and its natural adhesiveness causes it to require less pressing, but in all other respects the mode of making it is the same as that of other cheese. It will also be sooner ready for use than whole-milk cheese of the same weight.

New Cheese.—In some parts of the kingdom, in early summer, a description of cheese is made called new cheese, which also bears the provincial term of "slip-coat." It is made when the cows have been permanently turned out to grass, and is formed entirely of new milk, with about one-third of its volume of warm water added to it before the rennet is put in. The whey is then gently poured off, and the curd is carefully kept entire, until put into a vat of considerable diameter, but only about an inch in depth. It is very gently pressed for a few hours only, and when removed from the vat, it is covered with a cloth, which is frequently changed, and as soon as the skin is formed, it is considered fit for use.

Cheese made Abroad.—Large numbers of cheeses made abroad are annually imported into England, the largest quantity we receive coming to us from America. There, the system is followed of associating dairies, the milk being sent from several farms to be made up at one dairy-house, by which manufacturing expenses are minimised; the whole being conducted upon a very excellent system of routine, with every appliance and convenience for carrying on the business thoroughly; and both butter and cheese are made of the very best, as well as inferior, qualities; very high prices being sometimes obtained for dairy produce in the United States.

Cheese is turned out, too, in large quantities all over the Continent; Holland sending a good deal to England, made from both whole and skim milk. Of butter we get also a large quantity, as well as the imitation, which is often sold as genuine butter, and passes under the name of "butterine," being chiefly composed of mutton and beef fat. At one time, mutton suet was rather a "drug" with London butchers, but happily for them, they found a ready market for this, which has recently been put up into bags and shipped to Holland, returning to us in the shape of the compound referred to. It is not injurious to the health of those who partake of it, and perhaps answers the purpose of any other oily substance required by the human system, but the imposition is, of course, very reprehensible, and is now pretty well known and understood by the general public ; but, for a long time, a thriving trade was done in this line, before it was discovered—extensive factories having been started in Great Britain, even, for the conversion of this fat into imitation butter—and it now gives no little occupation to the officers appointed under the Adulteration of Food Acts, for the detection of this and similar frauds upon the public.

The cheeses sent from Holland, under the name of Gonda, Eidam, and Friesland, are made much in the same manner as the cheese in England; but another cheese, familiarly known, which comes to us from Italy—that of Parmesan—is made upon the same principle as the one carried out in the United States, of a number of dairymen clubbing together and sending their milk to be made up into cheese by one person. These are invariably of large size, weighing from sixty to one hundred and eighty pounds, being made in that part of Italy known as the Lodesan, which lies between Cremona and Lodi, comprising the richest portion of the Milanese, where the meadows have been irrigated from time immemorial, as described in another portion of this work ; the cows being kept in the house nearly the whole year round, being fed during the summer upon cut grass and during the winter upon hay. If I remember rightly, it was reading an account of the management of these celebrated Milanese meadows, and Sydney Smith's remark of cows grazing in pastures, "What would be thought if we were to walk over our bread and butter?" combined, that caused me, in the first place, to shut up my cows in the summer till the hay was got in. Who can tell what an effect a stray remark like this of Sydney Smith's is capable of producing, which I again am re-echoing?

As Parmesan cheese fetches a high price, perhaps some persons who keep a large number of cows may be induced to make an imitation of it. I therefore insert an account of the method followed in its manufacture, which has been given in the *Journal de Physique*, as follows:

Parmesan Cheese.—" The summer cheese, which is the best, is made of the evening milk, after having been skimmed in the morning, and at noon, mixed with the morning milk, which is also skimmed at noon. Both kinds of milk are poured together into a large copper cauldron, of the shape of an inverted bell, which is suspended on the arm of a lever, so as to be moved on and off the fire at pleasure. In this vessel the milk is gradually heated to the temperature of about 120 degrees; after which it is removed from the fire and kept quiet for a few minutes, until all internal motion has ceased. The rennet is then added, which is composed of the stomach of a calf, fermented together with wheaten meal and salt; the method of using it being to tie a piece of the size of a hazel-nut in a rag, and steep it in the milk while held in the hand, squeezing it from time to time. A sufficient quantity of the rennet thus soon passes through the rag into the milk, which is now to be well stirred, and afterwards left at rest to coagulate.

Within about an hour, the coagulation is complete; and then the milk is again put over the fire, and raised to a temperature of 145 degrees. During all the time it is heating, the mass is briskly stirred, till the curd separates in small lumps; part of the whey is then taken out, and a few pinches of saffron are added to the remainder, in order to colour it. When the curd is thus sufficiently broken, nearly the whole of the whey is taken out, and two pailfuls of cold water are poured in. The temperature is then lowered, so as to enable the dairyman to collect the curd, by passing a cloth beneath it and gathering up the corners. It is now pressed into a frame of wood, placed on a solid platform, and covered by a round piece of wood fitting into the mould, with a heavy weight at top. In the course of the night it cools, parts with the whey, and assumes a firm consistence. The next day one side is rubbed with salt, and the succeeding day the cheese is turned, and the other side rubbed in like manner; this alternate salting being continued for about forty days. After this period, the outer crust of the cheese is pared off, the fresh surface is varnished with linseed oil, the convex side is coloured red, and the cheese is fit for sale."

Considering that Parmesan cheese is made from skimmed milk, it must be confessed that it is of very superior quality to any skim-milk cheeses produced in this country; and in quoting the method of manufacture followed in Italy for possible imitation, I am rather fearful that old Fuller's quaint remark will apply here, as in the case of the Cheshire example—that to have an exact similitude, it would be necessary to import the pastures, as well as the method of making the cheese.

The pores of Parmesan cheese, showing by its texture its origin from skimmed milk, are yet filled with an oily substance, which proclaims the quality to be superior to the skim-milk cheese which is familiar to us in England.

Potato Cheese.—Potato cheese is made from a mixture of potatoes and sour milk, very little being made in England, but in some parts of Saxony it is to be met with of very fine quality. As the making of various articles appertaining to rural economy is very interesting to many people, I append the following account of its method of manufacture (*Bullet. de la Soc. d'Encour. Ag.*): "Potatoes of a large white kind are those to be preferred, and after being boiled they are peeled, when cool, and reduced to a pulp of equal consistence, either by being grated, or ground in a mortar. To five pounds of this pulp there is added one pound—or about a pint—of sour milk, with the usual quantity of salt, to impart a flavour. The whole is then kneaded together, and being covered up is allowed to remain for three or four days, according to the season. At the expiration of this time, the pulp is again kneaded and placed in one or more small wicker baskets, in order to get rid of the superfluous moisture; the pulp is then moulded into form by being placed in small pots, in which the cheeses are allowed to dry in the shade, during about fifteen days; after which they are put in store. The older they are the better they become; and if kept dry, they will keep for a great number of years. Three kinds of this cheese are made : the first, or most common, according to the above proportions ; the second, with four parts of potatoes and two parts of curdled milk ; and the third, with two parts of potatoes and four of milk. Ewe milk is as frequently employed as that of cows and imparts a pungent taste, which to many palates is found agreeable."

Formerly a good deal of cheese was made from the milk of sheep and goats in England, especially the former—either separately or together, or sometimes mixed with that of cows—which is still practised in many parts of the Continent. The greater importance that the breeding and rearing of sheep has attained of late years in England, owing to the extensive development of turnip-feeding husbandry, has caused this to be discontinued, except in some of the mountainous parts of Scotland and Wales. The flavour of the cheese is esteemed by some persons, and, to a certain extent, in request by those who are familiar with it—of which there may be said to be a decreasing number every year—at all events, in England, where the case is somewhat different to the warm climates of the East, or the mountainous countries of Asia and Europe, where certain breeds of sheep and goats browse in safety on the verge of precipices and in the clifts of rocks that are inaccessible to cattle, to the owners of which, milk or cheese is a necessary article of food.

Whole-milk Cheese.—Though seldom made in England, cheese is commonly made from whole milk in Scotland; that is to say, of milk which has not been skimmed.

The method usually followed in making cheese from unskimmed milk is, to place the ladder across the cheese-tub with a large canvas cloth covering the whole, in order to prevent any of the milk falling upon the floor, or any foreign substance into the tub. Above this cloth the sieve is placed, through which

WHOLE-MILK CHEESE.

the milk is to be strained, which should be of the temperature of ninety to ninety-five degrees. If it happen to be below eighty-five degrees, some of it should be put in a deep brass pan, and immersed in water kept hot in the wash-house. By this means the whole is warmed equally, which is a very important point to see to, for if the milk is not warm enough when the rennet is added to it, the curd will be tender, and the cheese will bulge out at the sides. If, on the other hand, it is too hot, it will swell—or "heave," as it is technically called—and become spongy; either of which defects is injurious to the appearance and quality of the cheese.

The rennet is at once added to the milk, which is thus coagulated at its natural heat; but as many dairy-farmers have not a sufficient number of cows to form a cheese at every milking, it must of necessity be then allowed to cool. In doing this, it of course throws up cream, which is sometimes taken off for butter, while the second meal of whole milk is used along with that which has been already skimmed; but if the cheese is needed to be of good quality, the cream must be also added. This, however, should be at the same time skimmed, for the milk, when cooled, must be afterwards heated to full ninety degrees Fahrenheit in the summer, and to a higher temperature still in cold weather; and were the cream to be warmed to that degree it would be melted, which would cause a considerable part of the butyraceous matter to be lost in the whey. It is therefore generally considered the better practice to gradually bring it to a liquid state by the admixture of moderately warm milk before it is poured into the cheese-tubs. The curd is then broken into small pieces, and the whey being thoroughly squeezed out, it is salted, wrapped in a cloth, and placed in a chessart, of such size as may be convenient, and is then pressed with weights proportionate to its size, and turned occasionally, until it becomes sufficiently firm to be taken out of the mould, and placed either on a cheese-rack, or on the floor of the cheese-room, where it is occasionally turned, and rubbed dry with salt, and remains until fit for market.

Rennet.—Rennet, being a very important factor in the manufacture of cheese, requires a special mention, for although it can be made from the curd, which has been formed by the coagulation of the milk when it turns sour, yet, when done in this way, it is hard and ill-flavoured. Recourse is therefore had to rennet to produce it, which is made from the gastric juice of animals, commonly that found in the maws or stomachs of sucking calves, that have been fed entirely upon milk. These are occasionally preserved by salting, along with the curd, but the most usual way is to employ the skins of the stomach bags alone, by putting a few handfuls of salt into and around the stomachs, which are then rolled up and hung near the chimney to dry, after which they are put by for a long time before being used.

If the skin be good, a piece no larger than a sixpence is put into a teacupful of water, with a little salt, and allowed to soak for about twelve hours before it is wanted. This will be sufficient for eighteen or twenty gallons of milk.

The manner of preparation and preservation of these " vells," as they are sometimes called, is, however, very various; and as the quality of the cheese depends a good deal more upon the application of the rennet than upon any other part of the manufacture, too much pains cannot be taken with them.

One method is to clean the maw of a newly-killed calf, salt the bag, and put it in an earthen jar for three or four days, until it forms a pickle, when it is taken from the jar and hung up to dry, after which it is replaced in the jar again, the covering of which should be pierced with a few small holes to admit the air, where it is allowed to remain for twelve months.

In many old-fashioned dairies it was customary to add leaves of sweet-brier, dog-rose, and bramble, a handful of each, with three or four handfuls of salt, and boil them together for a quarter of an hour in a gallon of water, when the liquor was strained off and allowed to cool. The maw was then put into the liquid, together with a lemon stuck round with cloves, and the longer it remained in it, the stronger and better the rennet was thought to become; half a pint, or less, of the liquor being sufficient to turn fifty gallons of milk, thus verifying the truth of the Scripture adage, "A little leaven leaveneth the whole lump."

The lemon, undoubtedly, would perform a useful office, but it is very questionable if the sweet leaves mentioned possessed any influence in furthering the business in hand.

According to the "Cheshire Report," in making the rennet, it is customary in Cheshire to take part of the dried maw skin in the evening previous to its being used, and put it into half a pint of lukewarm water, to which is added as much salt as will lie on a shilling. In the morning, the skin, being first taken out, is put into the tub of milk; but so great is the difference in the quality of these skins, that it is difficult to ascertain what quantity will be necessary for the intended purpose. A piece the size of half-a-crown, cut from the bottom of a good skin, will commonly be sufficient for a cheese of sixty pounds weight; though ten inches square of skin are often found too little. It is customary, however, to cut two pieces from each skin—one from the lower, the other from the upper part, but the bottom end is the strongest.

But, however, according to Aiton on "Dairy Husbandry," when speaking of the chief dairy district in Ayrshire, it is customary there, so far from washing away the chyle contained in the maw of the calf, to take steps to increase it as much as possible, by giving the animal as much milk as it can be made to swallow, a few hours before it is killed. The chyle being formed by the mixture of the gastric juice with the food, and that gastric juice being the coagulating power, both are carefully preserved, and are regarded necessarily as forming a stronger rennet than can be derived from the bag alone.

A tablespoonful of rennet made upon this method will, it is said by Mr. Aiton, coagulate thirty gallons of milk; but it has been pointed out that its great superiority over the English practice is, that it will curdle the milk in five or ten minutes, whereas the rennet used in South Britain requires from one hour to two, or even more, in order to form the curd—a defect chiefly to be attributed to the removal of the curdled milk.

The opponents of the system have asserted that

the chyle gives a harsh taste to the cheese occasionally, but in opposition to this is adduced the fact of the universal mild flavour of the cheese made in Scotland. It is admitted, however, that unless great care be employed in the immediate preparation of the rennet so made, there is a danger of the curd becoming rancid; and thus a certain degree of rankness may be imparted to the cheese. The following is its method of preparation:

Scotch Method of preparing Rennet.—"When the stomach, or bag, is taken from the calf's body, its contents are examined, and if any straw or other food be found among the curdled milk, such impurity is removed; but no part of the chyle is suffered to be lost. At least two handfuls of salt are put into the bag, and upon its outside, after which it is rolled up in salt and hung near a fire, where it is always allowed to hang until it is well dried—and it is understood to be improved by hanging a year, or longer, before being infused.

"When rennet is wanted, the 'yirning,' as it is called in Scotland, with its contents, is cut small, and put into a jar with a handful or two of salt; and a quantity either of soft water, that has been boiled and cooled, to about sixty-five degrees, or of new whey taken off the curd which is put upon the bag in the jar. The quantity of water, or whey, to infuse the bag is, more or less, according to the quality of the yirning. If it is that of a new-dropped calf, that has not been fed, three English pints will be enough; but if it has been fed for four or five weeks, a couple of quarts may at least be put on the bag to mash. It should, however, be observed, that the yirning of a calf four weeks old yields more rennet than that of one twice that age. After the infusion has remained in the jar from one to three days, the liquid is drawn off, and an English pint more water, or whey, put on the bag in the jar; and that, after standing in mash one or two days, is also drawn off, and, with that of the first infusion, strained, if any impurities appear in the liquor; the whole being put up in bottles for use as rennet, and the bag being thrown on the dunghill, without ever being put into the milk. Some put about a dram of good whisky into each quart bottle of the rennet, and it may be either used immediately, or kept for as many months as may be convenient."

Rennet is, however, made much more quickly than by any of the methods instanced, as the following: Place sufficient salt in a gallon and a half of boiling water to make it of a consistency that will float an egg. After it has got cool, it is strained, and six maws are placed in it, and after standing a few days the rennet so made will be fit for use.

CHAPTER V.

Milking—Quantity of Milk yielded by Cows—Feeding—Straw, chaffed, as Food for Cows.

THE subjects connected with dairy farming run somewhat into one another, yet I am anxious to keep them distinct, and not to put the cart before the horse. Before dairy operations can be commenced, the cows must be provided, and the dairy-house and implements must be ready to receive the milk; but before the milk can be obtained, the process of milking must be gone through, and this in proper order ought rightly to have been referred to before butter and cheese making were described. Yet, when in speaking of the implements of the dairy, it seemed only natural to describe the processes in connection with their use, which I have done in the preceding pages, and I will now speak of milking the cows, upon the proper method of doing which a very great deal depends—much more in fact than many people give credit for, who are somewhat careless over this necessary operation.

Milking.—Cows are sometimes milked oftener than twice a day; but this is unnecessary, the udder of the cow being of sufficient capacity to hold the milk.

The time of milking will have to depend upon

circumstances. Where a trade is done in selling milk, it will be necessary to fix a time in the morning which will suit the railway trains that carry it off; and this sometimes must needs be done as early as possible in the morning, four o'clock being a common time in the country during summer, and as soon as it is light generally all the year round, when no special circumstances have to be taken into account; whilst the evening milking is nearly the same throughout the year. But whatever the times of milking may be, the operation should always be performed with the greatest regularity.

A dozen cows are generally considered enough for one person to milk, as, if the cows are good ones, and yield plenty of milk, the arms of the milker get tired, and he or she cannot perform the task effectually. Some men will milk as many as fifteen or twenty, but this is too great a number for one person to undertake.

The time a cow takes to milk varies very much in individual cases. Some cows, which give their milk readily, can be milked within four minutes, while in that of others, it will take twenty minutes to milk them properly; and the operation needs to be thoroughly performed, and not hurried over; for if the cow has not given up all her milk, besides the loss to the owner of the milk, the cow herself receives an injury.

If the milking is not carefully and properly done, both the quantity as well as the quality will be seriously diminished. By the illiterate milker this is not understood very often, especially with regard to the quality of the milk being affected by incomplete milking; the fact being that, the first milk that is drawn from the cow is the poorest, it gradually becoming richer as the milking is proceeded with, until the last draining of the udder, which passes under the technical terms of "afterings," "strippings," and "stroakings," which must be thoroughly drawn from the cow, with the double object of securing this latter portion, as well as of ensuring a continuance of the usual supply; for if any is left in the udder of the cow, she yields a smaller quantity at the next milking.

This fact is accounted for by the supposition that the portion left behind is absorbed into the system, and nature generates no more than to supply the waste of what has been taken away. It will thus be readily seen that the greatest care should be used in milking the cows.

The following facts, which will throw a clear light upon this subject, related in the Bath papers as ascertained by Dr. Anderson, prove that the loss of half a pint of this milk occasions the loss of as much cream as would be afforded by a far greater quantity of the first milking, besides that portion of the cream which gives the greatest richness and flavour to the butter.

"Having taken several large tea-cups, exactly of the same size and shape, one of these was filled at the beginning of the milking, and the others at regular intervals till the last, which was filled with the dregs of the stroakings. These were each weighed, the weight of each cup being settled, so as to ascertain that the quantity of milk in each was precisely the same; and from a great number of trials frequently repeated, with many different cows, the result was thus:

"The quantity of cream obtained from the first drawn cup was, in every case, much smaller than from that which was last drawn; and those between afforded less, or more, as they were nearer the beginning or the end. The quantity of cream obtained from the last drawn cup from some cows exceeded that from the first in the proportion of sixteen to one. In other cows, however, and in particular circumstances, the disproportion was not so great; but in no case did it fall short of the ratio of eight to one.

"The difference in the quality of the cream, however, obtained from these two cups was much greater than the difference in the quantity. In the first cup the cream was a thin tough film, thinner, and perhaps whiter, than paper; in the last the cream was of a thick consistence, and of a richness of colour that no other kind of cream was ever found to possess.

"The difference in the quality of the milk that remained after the cream was separated, was perhaps still greater than either, in respect to the quantity or the quality of the cream. The milk in the first cup was a thin bluish liquid, like as if a very large proportion of water had been mixed with the ordinary milk; that in the last cup was of a thick consistence and yellow colour, more resembling cream than milk both in taste and appearance."

From this interesting experiment, it will be seen that thorough and effective milking would make a very sensible difference in the increased product of butter, as against milking inefficiently performed, and the necessity of its being done in the most skilful manner, so that the whole milk be drawn from the cow, will be readily seen. There are what are termed "hard," and "soft," or easy cows to milk; and much depends upon the milker. If he, or she, be rough and unkind, or noisy, the cow will often not give the whole of her milk, but retain a portion; and many of them have certain little fancies during the time they are being milked, which it is best to humour, if of a harmless nature; and the whole operation should be conducted in as quiet and orderly a manner as possible. Some cows will not stand very quietly—these should be humoured a little, and allowed to choose their own attitude, as they require careful treatment. The tempers of cows are often spoilt by bad management and rough usage at milking time, and therefore considerate persons should always be chosen to perform this office.

If a little of their favourite food be given to them while they are being milked, they will not only remain more quiet, but yield their milk with less reluctance; and in arranging the hour for milking, it is as well to leave as nearly as possible an interval of twelve hours, that is to say, about five o'clock in the morning, and four or five o'clock in the afternoon.

As I have before stated, I always make a practice of having my cows milked at home; but if the meadows wherein cows are placed are a very long way off from the farm, and it would be undesirable to drive them so great a distance, it will be found a good plan to form a milking enclosure with hurdles, after the fashion previously indicated in another place, in one corner of the field.

Quantity of Milk yielded by Cows.—Both the quantity and quality of milk yielded by cows are extremely various, that produced in autumn and winter being richer than that given in spring and summer, from which the greatest quantity of butter is to be obtained, but the least cheese; about 600 gallons in the course of a year being considered a fair average; but a much larger quantity than this has been given by individual cows.

An instance is on record of a cow belonging to a Mr. Cramp, which during five years yielded the extraordinary amount of 23,559 quarts of milk, producing 2,132 pounds of butter; and similar instances of productiveness have been cited. Mr. Aiton, whom I have quoted before, has estimated the yearly average return of the best Kyloes at 4,000 quarts within 300 days, or until they run dry, thus:

First fifty days,	24 quarts per day		. .	1,200
Second "	20 "		. .	1,000
Third "	14 "		. .	700
Fourth "	8 "		. .	400
Fifth "	8 "		. .	400
Sixth "	6 "		. .	300

But he adds that many cows will not produce half that quantity, and that probably 600 gallons in the course of the year may be about a fair average of the Ayrshire stock. Few herds of cows will exceed this average, but by a judicious course of selection and rejection, by turning out from the herd the inferior milkers and the old cows, and by continually adding productive young cows to it, a herd may be raised considerably above the average by painstaking dairymen.

The yield of milk, too, can be greatly stimulated by certain methods of feeding, which the London cowkeepers have carried out in a very marked degree, feeding their stock upon brewers' grains and other stimulating food, calculated to increase the flow of milk, without reference to its butyraceous properties.

Some of the county agricultural surveys give the average quantity of milk yielded by dairy cows to be:

In Devonshire	12 quarts per day
„ Cheshire	8 „
„ Lancashire	8 to 9 „

Though, unquestionably, some prime animals in full milk, in the height of the season, when grass is abundant, will show much larger quantities, as is evidenced by a trial on record, made at Bradley Hall, the seat of the Earl of Chesterfield, in Derbyshire, some years ago, of the milk and butter produced by four cows of different breeds; the result of which was as follows:

	Gals.	Qts.	Butter.	
From a Holderness cow	7	1	38½	ounces
„ Ayrshire „	5	0	34	„
„ Alderney „	4	3	25	„
„ Devon „	4	1	28	„

But such a large yield as this only lasts for a short time.

It is, however, well to know what cows are capable of producing, for in many private dairies, where gentlemen are at the mercy of careless and inattentive servants, the entire produce is frequently not obtained from the animals, which are thus rendered less profitable than they otherwise would be, under a good and thorough system of management, while the cows themselves become deteriorated through bad or careless milking.

In Dickson's "Survey of Lancashire," five short-horned cows, of the ordinary quality of that breed, are stated to have given in one year as follows:

One which did not go dry at all	.	4,857 wine quarts
„ dry eight weeks	. . .	3,985 „
„ „ six „	. . .	3,987 „
„ „ „ „	. . .	3,695 „
„ „ eighteen „	. . .	3,383 „

These cows were in summer out at grass, and in the winter were fed on hay and turnips, for two months on hay alone.

Others, chiefly of the shorthorned breed, produced on an average of the whole year, nine and three-quarter quarts per cow per day, and three small Scots, with an equal number of the long and shorthorned breeds, gave an average of eight quarts; that is, supposing the cows to have been dry about forty days in the year, which thus adds one-ninth to the real quantity produced when in milk.

To sum up, the milking of the cows ought only to be entrusted to persons of unremitting care and even temper, who take a pride in the herd, and are partial to the animals they tend—which will never let down their milk to a person they dread or dislike. The utmost cleanliness also needs to be practised all through the operation. The udders of cows that have been kept in stalls often need washing, and this should be done in tepid water; but care must be taken that they are wiped dry, for which purpose proper cloths should always be kept in readiness, and not left to the makeshift of a handful of hay as a substitute; as if any of the droppings get mixed with the milk the consequences will be worse than if the udder had been left untouched. Some advocate the invariable practice of washing the udder before milking, but cows frequently take cold when this is done too often, and should be only practised upon occasions of necessity. The quicker the job is got over the better, though no speck or taint of dirt should ever be allowed to come near the milk-pail.

Feeding.—As may be readily imagined, upon the methods adopted in feeding the cows will mainly depend both their productiveness and profit, and the quantity and quality of the milk will be found proportionate to the nourishment of the food that is given to them.

Linseed, pea, and oat meal will produce richness; and in Holland, where a great deal of attention is paid to milch-cows, when fed in the house, it is usual for them to have their water mixed with oil-cake, rye, or oatmeal. Brewers' grains will occasion a profuse yield of milk, but it will be of the poorest kind. But even the effect of these may be considerably modified by the addition of oil-cake and other rich foods of a concentrated nature.

The winter house-food is generally made up with roots of various kinds, and these should always be supplemented with a certain amount of good, sound hay—the most economical plan being to cut it up—while sweet oat straw tends very much to correct the watery nature of roots.

Straw, Chaffed, as Food for Cows.—Amongst those who have turned their attention to feeding with chaffed straw, every kind of straw is sometimes given; though that of barley and wheat are decidedly inferior.

Wheat straw is said to make cows run dry sooner than oat straw, while, according to "Holland's Survey of Cheshire," the former is said to occasion more than the usual time to be required when churning the cream of cows that have been fed with it. But the practice of using straw for fodder is a very diversified one, and the results, as stated by many who use it, very contradictory; but then the circumstances under which it is administered are often widely different. Mr. Joseph Darby, in a paper contributed to the *Journal of the Royal Agricultural Society of England*, has collected together a great number of instances where straw, chaffed, enters largely into the food of cattle. Straw has long been given as fodder to young stock, but its usefulness as a corrective to food given to milch-cows is also considerable, under various forms and modifications; and thus Mr. Darby says "the Aylesbury Vale furnishes the following as the experience of one of its farm occupiers: 'Straw is generally used as litter, this being more of a grazing and dairying district than a farming one; but I myself, having 160 or 170 acres of arable land, out of a 500-acre farm, generally cut up a good deal of straw. I use straw for horses in chaff consisting of about three-fourth straw, one-fourth hay; no long hay or straw being given. For beasts I vary according to circumstances. In a good year of hay, perhaps, I give one-fourth straw to dairy cows, and three-fourths straw to dry beasts, always mixed with pulped mangolds, or swedes—generally mangold. Cake is used, and varied, according to circumstances. I always use the food fresh mixed. In a plentiful hay season I do not always use it as chaff, but give the dairy beasts the hay whole, and the young beasts whole straw and roots, or three or four pounds of cake, which I prefer with the whole straw. No doubt more cattle can be kept by using chaff and pulped roots; as I myself, I should think, keep twenty or thirty more beasts through the year since I have adopted the system I now yearly pursue—mowing less and grazing more—but the increased price of labour makes it a question with me whether it now pays. But this year I shall be compelled, through the shortness of hay, to cut up everything I can.'"

In giving another example, Mr. Darby says that nothing can possibly show the variability of custom and opinion in the straw question more than the fact that, whereas the last statement gave as a reason for straw being chiefly used for litter in the Vale of Aylesbury, the circumstance of its being a dairy and grazing district; the following, posted to me from Shaftesbury, points to dairy-farms as the very places where straw ought to be used as food. The writer says:

"On well-managed dairy-farms as little straw as possible is used for litter, all the wheat and oat straw, except what is used for thatching, being fed, and even some bought for the purpose. But some farmers do not make the most of it by any means, and of course are obliged to do with less stock in consequence. I always put wheat or oat straw chaff with corn for horses, but never any whole; but I keep cows, before calving, on either wheat straw or oat straw, or barley, if it has clover in it, whole, giving a little cake—about four pounds—once a day. After calving, I give, generally, straw and hay chaff, with linseed and ricemeal, twice a day, and hay besides. I prefer cows, before calving, to eat straw whole, as it saves labour, but afterwards I advocate giving chaff, mixed with some kind of meal. A neighbouring farmer chaffed the whole of his hay and straw, giving the cows nothing but chaff mixed with meal during the last winter, and they did exceedingly well. If cattle are littered with cut straw, the manure will, of course, drill after getting rotten, but I do not approve of using much straw for litter, if it is fit for feeding. I prefer sparred floors to perforated bricks, which economise straw, but of course some straw is occasionally absolutely necessary. If straw was more extensively employed as food, I think cattle might be increased ten to the hundred acres, and in some cases certainly less hay might be made, were straw used for feeding as much as it ought to be."

Quoting still from Mr. Darby's paper, Professor Buckman considers there are no feeding properties in wheat or barley straw, and that it would be much more profitable for farmers living near a railway or large town, if they were allowed to sell a portion of their straw, and buy extra quantities of artificial manure in return. If straw were more generally used as food, stocks of cattle might be considerably increased, but with no profit to the farmer, as wheat and barley straw have no feeding properties. Straw is employed in this district about half-and-half; wheat straw for litter, and spring-corn straw for food, etc.

Mr. George Adams, of Pidwell Farm, Faringdon, not only supports the views of the desirability of using straw as a fodder, to lessen the extravagance of hay-making and hay consumption, but states decidedly that by giving it up, and feeding on straw and artificial foods as substitutes for hay, he has been enabled to double his stock of cattle and sheep. Mr. Adams says:

"In answer to yours, I keep 100 dairy cows, and 220 breeding Oxfordshire ewes, with the produce of the latter; the ewe lambs being kept for stock and the ram lambs fed for sale. I could not possibly winter so much stock if it were not for the cutting of fifty acres of my best straw into chaff for the young and store animals; particularly as my land lies low, and heads very much. I reckon on yarding 250 beasts from Christmas up to the 1st of May, and all the young and store stock live on wheat, oat, and barley straw cut into chaff by steam. I grow from thirty to thirty-five acres of golden tankard mangolds each year, and pulp on an average five cartloads each morning, to mix with the straw chaff; and I have 100 gallons of good linseed gruel thrown boiling hot over and mixed with the straw chaff and pulped mangold every morning, ready for the night and next morning; and on Saturday I have a double quantity done, to last till Monday. I find my young stock do far better than they did when living on hay, at double the cost. The dairy cows are fed the same till near calving. The boiling of the linseed, and putting it into the chaff boiling hot, causes the chaff to ferment; and the cattle eat it eagerly, and do well. My ewes live on the same food, with two or three bushels of malt-dust mixed with it each morning, when they can be got near the feeding-shed. All my barren cows are fatted out on the same food, with four or five pounds of cotton and linseed cake per day each; and I find that my dairy cows do not thrive so well after going to hay, with four pounds of cake each per day after calving, as they did before, at one-half the cost, upon the straw mixture. I assure you, if it were not for cutting up all my oat and barley straw and about fifty acres—which is one-half—of my wheat straw, I could not keep more than half my present stock of cattle and sheep."

These kinds of examples are extremely interesting to those who are seeking for general information, as well as for the correlative facts which they contain; although the estimation in which straw is held as food for stock varies very considerably. But there is one great fact which must of necessity strike those who have studied the subject, which is this:

The stomach and digestive organs of the ox being evidently formed with the view to his subsisting upon bulky, but moderately nutritious, food, such as grass or hay, it is necessary that his capacious stomach be constantly full, if the animal is to enjoy that placid contentment which, in the case of the cow, is favourable for the production of milk. And this capacious paunch must be filled before she goes to rest, and proceeds with her rumination and digestion.

Now if fed upon too great a bulk of rich food— and oxen can eat nearly as much of one as the other —the powers of assimilation are not correspondingly expansive, and often stomachic derangement ensues; the result being diarrhœa, produced from irritation of the stomach, if not more serious disease. Not only is there a considerable waste of food, but the constitution of the animal becomes injured.

When care is not taken in feeding them, excessive purging is produced when cattle are first put upon turnips in the autumn, or upon green food in the spring; but by judiciously using these, with a portion of straw chaffed and mixed with the other, these evil consequences can be avoided, and the hurtful purging be prevented.

So far as my own experience is concerned, having but little arable land, I get but a small amount of straw; but I wish I had more, as I grow a good many carrots, and also some heavy crops of mangold wurzel occasionally, while I always have a comparatively large quantity of hay to use—my grass land being four times the amount of acreage of my arable—and I have a very large number of mouths to feed altogether, when all are reckoned up, upon my small place; the finding food for them all being at times a matter for much consideration and arrangement. And a quantity of good straw chaff would often prove very useful to me; and when I see the vast quantities of straw that are often thrown down in open yards, upon which all the rain falls that comes down naturally, as well as that poured upon it in extra quantities, in certain places, from the unspouted sheds of many farmyards, I cannot help regretting the waste of what might often prove an additional source of food; but if not, even as manure, undergoing sad deterioration, by which farming profits are much reduced.

When roots and straw chaff are mixed together, for the purpose of being given to the cows, they should be mingled twenty-four hours before being required for use, as a slight fermentation will then have taken place, which is much relished by the animals. Inferior hay, or any that may have been somewhat spoiled in the getting, which by itself the cows would scarcely eat, can all be used up by chaffing it, and mixing with other items of food; and pulped roots are always better than when sliced, as the beasts are not so likely to get choked, and they are unable to separate them from the chaff, which they will sometimes endeavour to do.

In some districts in England that are considered first-class dairy ones, as in Gloucestershire, little or no extra food is given to the cows, as oil-cake, bruised grain, malt-dust, mangolds, or even turnips, carrots, bran, pollard, palm nuts, bean and pea meal, decorticated cotton cake, or brewers' grains; all of which are capital adjuncts and additions to the food of cows, when properly used under judicious management; pea or bean meal, especially, when mixed with other food, being extremely useful to milch-cows.

In that county it is generally estimated that a cow requires for her support the produce of three acres of pasture. One-and-a-half-acre from May 1st to December 1st; in the winter and spring, hay only being given, perhaps assisted by a little chaffed barley straw, which is given to the cows when they are not in milk, it being reckoned that a cow will consume two-and-a-half-tons of hay, which requires an acre and a half to grow it.

Good sound hay, it must be admitted, is good food for cows, but it is an expensive method of feeding, and not so great a supply of milk is to be obtained as when more generous food is given; the cost of which, by various economical contrivances, can be very much reduced.

In some parts of Fifeshire, where dairy farming is carried on in a very thorough and complete manner in the summer, cows are sometimes pastured for about ten hours daily, upon one or two year old clover and rye grass lea; and when the feed gets short, it is supplemented by a plentiful allowance of clover and vetches in the house at night, as well as a quantity of brewers' grains.

In the winter, the cows are tied up in pairs in the stalls, and boiled food is given to them, consisting of thirty pounds of swede turnips, one and a quarter pound of linseed, two pounds of pea or bean meal, and plenty of oat straw, which is given at eight A.M. Two hours afterwards, sixty pounds of yellow turnips are given, and straw again. At two o'clock P.M., one-sixth of a bushel of grains is given; and lastly, at five P.M., sixty pounds of yellow turnips, and oat straw again afterwards.

Regularity in the time of feeding is of the utmost consequence; and the cows should be disturbed as little as possible when fed upon the soiling, or house-feeding system; uninterrupted high feeding while they are in full milk is the surest way of making a profit.

Cooked linseed, bean, and pea meal, and distillers' or brewers' grains, are all valuable articles of food for milch-cows. The grains, as already stated, will produce the largest quantity of milk, but its quality will be thin and poor; while the artificial grasses, as clover, rye grass, etc., swede-turnips, and mangold, given in conjunction with bean-meal, oil-cake, etc., will produce a fair yield of rich milk.

When too great an amount of brewers' and distillers' grains have been given to cows, they often become what is termed "grain sick;" straw chaff mixed with the grains will prevent this, as will also boiled linseed, when mixed with them.

Cows resemble human beings in liking a change of food, and where they appear to surfeit upon any particular one, it is very easy to make a change for them. Potatoes are not often given to cows in England, but they have been employed with advantage in Scotland, steamed with hay and other mixtures, which has afforded them a variety of soft food, till green food again comes into season.

There cannot be the least doubt but that the system of house-feeding, or soiling, is considerably cheaper than allowing the cows to graze the meadows; so that even if there be but little pasture land attached to a farm, a good many cows may be profitably kept upon this system, which many farmers never attempt, appearing to consider it a branch of farming business which they are not qualified to undertake, or account of the nature and disposition of the land they occupy; experiment having amply demonstrated that cows can be fed upon roots, steamed chaff, and oat straw, and, including all other expenses, produce milk at a cost of fourpence per gallon, the general estimate of cost being about sixpence, when the acreage of grass necessary to support them has been calculated against its product in the shape of hay, at average market price.

When feeding cows in winter upon roots, many dairy-farmers have to put up with a considerable reduction in price obtained for their butter, on account of its tasting of turnips. To many people the taste of turnips in butter is very unpleasant and sickening; "turnip butter," as it is called, being indeed objectionable to most persons; and thus, many who can make a good article enough in the summer time, when the cows are fed chiefly on grass, have the mortification of being obliged to accept a lower price during the winter months, on account of the inferiority of their article; being, perhaps, obliged to grow turnips more or less upon their plan of rotation.

It is supposed by some that this unpleasant taste given to butter by common turnips may be corrected by the use of a small quantity of dissolved saltpetre being mixed with the milk, or of a proportion equal to one-eighth of boiling water being added to it, when left to stand for cream; but the use of these expedients has only a partial effect, as also the recipes of stirring the milk some time after it is drawn—to add to every gallon of milk a tablespoonful of the clear solution of half an ounce of the chloride of lime in a gallon of water—to feed the cows with turnips immediately after milking, by which means the cows' animal economy will dispose of the taint, etc.; but if a certain amount of concentrated food is used, no taint will be perceptible, either from using turnips or cabbages, the latter being, at times, equally as objectionable as the former, only causing a different taste. The use of mangold-wurzel, too, though seldom referred to as affecting butter by its taste, does, indeed, communicate to it a slightly bitter and peculiar flavour, which is quite as objectionable to some palates as the other.

Mangold-wurzel is now given very largely to milch-cows, but as food it is not so enriching as turnips, the milk being very thin and poor, the chief value of mangold being, that it is such an excellent keeping root, and is sound, and good, late on in the season, when the turnips are done for, being all the better for the extra time they have been kept on hand, and their amount of acrid juices diminished, the yellow globe being the best keepers, though with me, and I suppose with all others, the long red mangold is by far the heaviest cropper.

During the summer time, there is usually very little trouble to be apprehended from the butter tasting badly, where cows are chiefly fed upon grass; though sometimes, even then some noxious weed or other may abound in the pastures, which ought to be got rid of; but there is no doubt that the butter made by some careless people is inferior in quality because sufficient care is not taken to ensure perfect cleanliness in the vessels in use in the dairy; from deficient ventilation; from allowing the milk to stand too long in the pans, or not churning often enough. By skimming the milk quickly, a certain portion of the cream, though not lost, will go with the skimmed milk, and here comes into consideration what is to be done with the latter. There is always a ready sale for skimmed milk, at fourpence per gallon, in the neighbourhood of any large towns, and thus a better return could be got for this article than if it were only given to the pigs; yet the two plans hardly go together, the butter-making and milk-selling—for the same facility that would enable the skimmed milk to be disposed of profitably, at fourpence per gallon, would perhaps admit of the whole milk being sold at tenpence per gallon, it being retailed at fivepence per quart, which would give a profit of 100 per cent. to the retailer upon the first cost; and each cow would thus bring in a revenue of twenty-five pounds per annum to the dairy-farmer, upon the average yield of 600 gallons per cow—an average which may always be attained under a system of good management.

Turnip-tasting Butter.—As cows are mostly fed upon roots during the winter and spring months, as few people have a large quantity of hay, the proper course of feeding with these becomes highly important; and if the roots given are sound, and have not been heated in pits, excellent butter can be made from the milk of cows fed upon turnips, but little inferior to that made in summer, without having recourse to any preventive expedients, by giving a certain amount of concentrated food of various kinds; of which the best are, perhaps, crushed oats, bean, Indian, and palm-nut meals, pollard, bran, and oil-cake, when turnips are used extensively. Bran is cheap enough, and a most excellent food to give, a good deal of stamina being contained in it.

It is an excellent plan to give boiled food to the cows in the winter and spring months, when they are fed largely upon roots; and these concentrated foods are then the most appropriate additions, the animals getting the full advantage of all the food so given.

When boiled food is not used, or there is no convenience for cooking, the concentrated food can be thrown into a large tub, and hot water poured over it, the steam being confined within by a cover. By this means it undergoes a certain amount of cooking, and the cows relish it very much. And when this is not done, the meal, or mixtures of meal, or whatever is given, should be sprinkled over the pulped turnips; which, as stated before, are better given this way than sliced. Many painstaking dairymen, however, make excellent butter from turnip-fed cows during the winter months, with the addition of hay only, and a few hours' run each day upon the pastures, in conjunction with thorough cleanliness and good management; but it is far better to enrich the milk, and keep the animals in first-rate health and condition, by the addition of more nutritious food.

Quantity of Meal, etc.—By giving concentrated food to the cows, the yield of milk is increased, and its quality is also greatly improved, which is a very important point in butter-making. From four to eight pounds of meal in a day forms an ample allowance, according to the size and appetite of the animals; the large heavy breeds needing more than the smaller and hardier ones, who do well upon comparatively scanty fare. Nor do the advantageous effects of good feeding end here, for the manure of animals fed upon a somewhat higher system is considerably richer and more valuable, which is of great consequence to one who carries on a mixed system of husbandry; or even to the cow-keeper alone, when a richly-manured plot for mangold-wurzel is highly desirable. But, although cows may be fed during the winter and spring months upon hay and turnips alone, without there being any very perceptible falling off in either quantity or quality of the milk, it is not so with hay and mangold-wurzel alone; in the latter case it being indispensable that meal, or other nutritious food, be given, if the owner is desirous of keeping up the health and stamina of his cows and the produce of his dairy to the fullest extent.

Quality of Butter dependent upon Feeding.—It will be seen from the foregoing that the quality of the butter produced will depend very much upon the methods of feeding adopted—and *quality* is the chief result which should be aimed at, and not so much the *quantity*; for where a high price is realised for produce, it pays relatively much better, and the plan of management pursued may always be modified to suit differing circumstances. Hence, we will say, the butter-maker has no opportunity of selling skimmed milk profitably; and thus, the latter being given to the pigs, it would be desirable to take all the cream which can be made to rise to the surface. The late skimmings should be put aside, and churned as an inferior quality.

In all markets for butter there are various gradations of quality, as first, second, third, etc. This is strikingly exhibited at the butter-market at Cork, which is under the superintendence of a public inspector, and the price of the best quality for the day is stuck up on a board in a conspicuous situation in the market.

The Butter made in Ireland.—In Ireland, this system of classing the butter in accordance with quality is carried out in a very effective manner, all good judges of butter being able to pronounce at once, from its taste, its marketable value; and in Ireland the butter trade is regulated by Act of Parliament, the mode in which it is conducted being as follows: The farmers assemble in the morning, and have all their casks arranged in the market-place.

The coopers then take out the head of each, and the inspector follows, without knowing to whom the casks belong, and marks the quality of each with these distinguishing characters:

  I for the best quality.
  II for the second quality
  # for the third quality.
  ## for the fourth quality.

  The coopers then replace the heads, and cut the character indicated upon the side of the firkin, together with the weight and tare of the cask, which is weighed at the market beam; after which the farmers proceed to sell their produce. This is done in open market, so as to exclude any possibility of favouritism, and the price is only named for the first quality, a regular diminution in value being understood to attach to each of the other sorts.

  While speaking of cask butter, I may incidentally remark here, perhaps, that the casks usually contain as nearly as possible eighty-four pounds each, and are generally made of white oak or ash. The wood of the lime-tree has been recommended, on account of its having been ascertained by numerous experiments as being the only wood free of acid, acids being well known to act powerfully on salt, which they decompose and turn into brine; the quantity of salt used being about ten ounces to the stone of fourteen pounds, more or less, according to the length of time the butter is intended to be preserved; the butter made during the summer months being the fittest for salting; that which is made in the latter part of the season not taking it so well, and requiring rather more. As lime-wood, however, is not always to be had, fir is supposed to come next in order. It is said, however, that by boiling the staves during four hours, the whole of the pyroligneous acid of all kinds of timber may be extracted, the method of doing this having been published in the *Transactions of the Highland Society*, thus: "Have a boiler the same length as the wood, with a weight to keep it immersed in water, and have a wooden cover on the boiler, as it must be done by close evaporation. The wood is then dried for use; becoming closer, and more condensed, from the fibres being more contracted, and while it continues hot, it can be easily brought to any shape."

While referring to the quality of butter, etc., being dependent very much upon the system pursued in feeding, it should be also mentioned that much good butter is spoiled, and quality sacrificed, from oversalting, which is sometimes done with a foolish idea of increasing the weight, by illiterate men; who are blind to the fact that this defeats itself, the loss arising from inferior quality more than overbalancing, and exceeding any advantage gained by extra weight.

Summer Feeding.—Although it is advisable to give concentrated food as a counterpoise to poor provender, too great an abundance of rich food, such as beanmeal, etc., without a due proportion of turnips, mangold, straw, or hay, will inevitably cause the cows to lose their appetite.

In the beginning of summer, and towards the middle of it, when young grass and green barley are given in some districts of the North, at the first cutting especially, the provender is mixed with a large proportion of old hay, and a good quantity of salt, to prevent swelling, is given to the cows. Salt, indeed, ought always to be given in moderate quantity to cows at all times, as it increases the quantity and improves the quality of the milk. As the season advances, with the plan of feeding on green crops, less hay and straw require to be given, as the grass approaches ripeness, till it is altogether discontinued; but young, or wet, clover should never be given without a mixture of dry provender.

In the same line of procedure, by inverse ratio, when grass becomes scarce upon the approach of winter, young turnips, and turnip leaves, steamed along with hay, will be found a good substitute for grass; in proportion as the grass decreases, the turnips to be increased, until the latter can be made a complete substitute for the former. In some Scotch dairies, where the house-feeding system is carried on largely, as the spring approaches, Swedish turnips and potatoes, when cheap, are substituted for yellow turnips. These two roots, steamed with hay and other mixtures, will give soft food till grass—and by grass must be understood artificials, such as clover and other trifoliated plants—again comes into season.

When cows are soiled, or house-fed, during the winter, and turned out upon the pastures in summer, although they stand quietly enough in their stalls during the winter, they show a restless anxiety to be at liberty as the season advances; and when pasture land is abundant, and not saved for hay, they should be turned out during the day, and brought in again early in the afternoon, and fed at night upon sound meadow hay. When the weather becomes warm, and the grass affords a full bite, they can be allowed to lie out all night, from the end of May till the beginning of October, being brought under cover in the middle of the day, in very hot weather.

This is not my practice, but there may be those who, for special reasons, do not want to take the trouble of house-feeding, and would rather sacrifice the profit, than have to incur the necessary amount of work ; for, by turning cows out in this way, there is little or no trouble with them, for five months out of the year.

Coarse grass will produce abundance of milk, but it will reduce the quality of the butter, and as long overgrown grass, although naturally of a good quality, will impart a certain degree of rankness, it will be found the best plan to hurdle off the fields in different enclosures, and shift the stock from one to another every ten days, by which means they will have a constant supply of close, short, and fine herbage.

The plan I adopt is, to mow all the rank grass, and give it to the cows, mixed with some dry food or other of a corrective nature. The after-grass, or aftermath, is always favourable to a good supply of milk ; and this I never cut, as before stated, but turn the cows into the meadows as soon as it will afford a good bite after mowing; using the artificial grasses during the summer, till this time comes round, giving it to them as each kind gets into season ; as rye grass, young clover, spring tares, lucerne, or anything that I can grow, or think it worth while to purchase of neighbours for my stock. These are, each in their turn, of excellent service ; producing a supply of rich milk ; though it is said by some that tares are apt to produce "ropiness," while clover is said to cause "hoving." But any green food, partaken of too greedily, will do this in the form of the succulent grasses, and all that is required is proper care in administering the food, and these unfavourable results can be obviated by mixing it with dry food of the kind suggested.

Feeding Dry Cows.—Cows vary very much in the time they run dry. In a few cases they do not get dry at all ; but, as a rule, the cow should be well and regularly milked until eight weeks before calving, when she should not be milked again, unless she happen to be an unusually good cow, and yields a very large quantity of milk. In such a case, the distended udder should be milked once a day, or once every other day, as circumstances seem to indicate ; but there is seldom any difficulty in drying them.

It is common for many farmers to turn them into the straw-yard when dry, and feed them upon very inferior provender till shortly before calving ; but this is a very bad plan, for, although it is not necessary to keep them in full flesh, yet, if allowed to fall off until they become lean, not only will their milk become thin, when the time for calving has arrived, but will be deficient in quantity ; and the loss in dairy produce will be much greater than any saving effected in fodder. Milking cows should not only be maintained in good condition, but in what may be termed a milky habit of constitution ; and instead of, perhaps, allowing them to feed only in the straw-yard, and pick up what they can, some swedes, or esculent roots of some sort or other, should be given, or their equivalents, so as to keep them in proper condition as milch-cows. And there should always be a plentiful supply of water.

It is the best plan also to put the cows upon better food a fortnight before they calve, by which means a greater secretion of milk will take place. Chaff, with pulped roots, will do very well for dry cows, and let them make out with good straw, morning and evening, the better food being given at midday.

In old times there was more propriety in turning cows into straw-yards when they were dry, than at present; for under the old system, the whole of the corn used to be thrashed out by a man with a flail, and as he thrashed, he would toss the straw out into the yard, and the straw would then be fresher, and more eaten, than when it has been stacked, as is now almost invariably the case, after having been thrashed by machinery. When this was done by the flail, the cows certainly thrived better than they do now, as in those farms where the practice is still continued; but the conditions which formerly made this a good custom are now changed, and thus from old habit, many methods of dealing with stock are perpetuated when they ought to be altered, to suit the varying circumstances of the day, to which they are no longer appropriate.

At the beginning of November, when everything in the shape of green food will be getting very scarce, it will be found useful to give cows the leaves of the mangolds, after they are drawn. I am in the habit of giving them, plucked off the roots as they stand in the ground, not stripping them entirely off, but leaving the centre ones, for I find an early frost will sometimes half destroy them, and I never allow the animals to eat anything in a frozen state; a common belief prevailing amongst farmers that cows are apt to slip their calves if they eat frozen grass, and we generally have our mangolds up before there is any danger of the frost touching them.

Feeding with Hay in bare Pastures.—Those dairy-farmers, however, who rely a good deal upon their pastures, and keep their cows out late upon them, as in Somersetshire and other southern counties, where they consider they understand their work thoroughly, carry hay to them in the fields, dividing it into small heaps, about twelve yards apart, so as to prevent them from standing upon two heaps at once, and thus spoiling a good deal of it. Where there is a large number of cows, it is generally customary with good dairymen to send the hay into the field in a cart, or waggon, with a man standing up in it with a fork in his hands, who throws the hay on either side in little heaps, while the horse is led at the pace required, or made to stop when necessary, by a boy. It is considered by this means that very little hay is wasted, by those who do their work well, but despite of every care that may be used, some must inevitably be wasted, and when done by careless men, a good deal is lost; cutting up the hay with chaff, and mixing it with pulped roots, being a much more economical method, which is the one I always adopt; for however plentiful hay may be, it is somewhat expensive feeding, and I always keep my chaff-cutter going, so that there shall be no excuse of shortness of ready provender, for the shortest methods—those which involve the least trouble—it will be found, will generally be in favour with the men most people have about them.

When the time comes for turning the cows out, of course there is a great amount of work saved, for where a large number are kept, there must necessarily be plenty to do, in providing a great bulk of food for them; but it will be found that a daily systematic practice of doing certain things, at certain times, causes work to come easy, and as a matter of course; and I never found any much greater amount of the general business of the farm transacted, when my cows were turned into the meadows after hay-harvest, than when a large amount of prepared food had to be got into readiness. The secret of all this is, of course, *routine*; and it will be found by all who adopt the painstaking methods necessary to economise the food which their animals consume, that the work soon becomes a matter of course, and is got through very quickly, when once the men are used to it, and know how to go about it.

Cows enjoy the air and exercise, if the pasture wherein they are turned be nearly bare, and their produce will be greater than when entirely confined to sheds, even when there is abundance of food given, the little change causing them to thrive, and keeping them lively, and more contented upon the whole; and they appear to relish their food more, as would appear to be only natural.

Advantage should be taken of fine days, even in winter, therefore, to give them a little exercise, so that there is no danger of doing damage by poaching the ground. But when thus turned out for exercise, it will be found a good plan to divide the field or fields into enclosures, and separate the cows, where there are various kinds and conditions; because the barren cows, when in season, are generally ridden by the others, which is dangerous to those in calf, as the calf is liable to be turned in the cow, and a bad calving time may be the result.

Cows, when turned out, often get little pickings from the hedges for themselves, even in early winter, which, however trifling, makes a little agreeable change of diet for them, which they show unmistakably enough they relish exceedingly, in average seasons being pretty well able to get the principal part of their living from the field up to November.

With dairy cows, it should be ever remembered that it does not pay to feed them insufficiently, and with a view to obtaining full profit, every owner of dairy cows should exert himself in order to give them appropriate food, and enough of it, every day throughout the year. Without full feeding, however excellent the management may be in other respects, the want of it will manifest itself in a diminished flow of milk, and consequent loss of money in the return made.

CHAPTER VI.

Calving—Time for Cows to Calve—Fifeshire System—Gloucestershire System — Milk Farms—Castrating — Cow-list — Mr. Hayward's Calculations.

CALVING.—The length of time a cow goes with calf is generally put down at forty weeks; but in most cases it will be forty-one weeks, whilst forty-two is often exceeded; the fact being that the time a cow goes with calf is very uncertain. A French writer (M. Leissier) made some very interesting experiments, which he duly chronicled some years back at Paris, respecting the periods of gestation in different animals; in the case of cows the result being that, out of 575, of which an account of the date was taken when they were put to the bull, and when they calved, it was found that:

21 calved between the 240th and 270th days, the mean term being 259½ days.
544 calved between the 270th and 299th days, the mean term being 282 days.
10 calved between the 299th and 321st days, the mean term being 303 days.

It may, therefore, be fairly assumed that between nine and ten months may be reckoned upon as the most common period; but it has been remarked that a cow generally goes about forty-one weeks with a bull-calf, and a few days under that number with a female.

The cow seldom drops more than one calf at a time; though, in rare instances, sometimes two, and even three have been known to have been brought forth; an instance having been recorded in the *Bulletin des Sciences*, of a cow belonging to a farmer in France which produced nine calves at three successive births, viz. four at the first, three at the second, and two at the third; all of which, except two of the first that were born, were brought up by the mother; but the heifers afterwards produced only a single calf each. The exploits of this anti-Malthusian cow must be decidedly regarded as a *lusus naturæ*.

In those instances where two calves are brought forth, and they happen to be male and female, the latter is generally incapable of breeding, and in some districts they go by the name of a "free martin" (though these supposed barren cows have been known to bring calves), while the bull is always perfect.

About six weeks, or, at the outside, not more than two months, before the cow is expected to calve—and the date of this anticipated event should always be carefully calculated beforehand, and entered, not only in a herd-book, kept in the owner's possession, but on a stout piece of cardboard, with ruled lines for the names of the cows, and the date at which they were served, to hang up in the cow-house to serve as a reminder—she should no longer be milked, but dried; but this will very much depend upon the constitution of the cow, which ought not, on any account, be allowed to get into poor condition. If the udder is very large and evidently gives the cow pain, it may then be advisable to milk her; but if once done, it will be necessary to repeat it; or, if the weather be very hot, and the cow suffers great inconvenience, milking may be deemed necessary.

When the full period of gestation has nearly terminated—which may be seen about a fortnight before, when the cow's udder increases in size, and is said "to spring"—she should be separated from the others, and put in an enclosure, or paddock, near the homestead, in order that assistance may be handy in case of a difficult time at calving. When this is close at hand, a hollow space appears on either side of the apparent junction of the tail with the back—which is locally termed "dropping," or "pitching"—and the beast will exhibit a degree of restlessness, as if seeking a sheltered corner. And they will calve sooner, and better, if left alone, but should be carefully watched in an unobtrusive manner, in case any assistance may be necessary, and there is a bad, or unnatural presentation—which will be other than the calf's head resting on the forelegs—and it is a difficult birth; in which case efficient help should be obtained. Under all circumstances, unless the cow should happen to be very relaxed, it will be found a safe plan to cause her bowels to be opened with a gentle dose of medicine.

The end of her term of gestation will not only be indicated by the springing of her udder, and the dropping of her belly, but there will be a discharge from her bearing; and her uneasiness, and moaning, will proclaim the event to be not far off.

In severe weather she should be housed for a few days, but not stalled, and a good bed of straw should be provided for her; but the natural progress of the birth should not be interfered with, the animal being better left to the course of nature, which will accomplish its object safely in most instances.

Youatt, a most careful and humane as well as very efficient writer, recommends that, in instances which present nothing more than usual delay, without any supposed wrong position of the fœtus, "a pint of sound warmed ale be given in an equal quantity of gruel. Warm gruel should be frequently administered, or at least put within the animal's reach; and access to cold water should be carefully prevented. To the first pint of ale should be added a quarter of an ounce of the ergot of rye (spurred rye) finely powdered; and the same quantity of the ergot, with half a pint of ale, should be repeated every hour, until the pains are reproduced in their former and natural strength, or the labour is terminated."

If the cow be kept in a loose-box at night, and allowed to walk out into an adjoining paddock, or yard, in the morning, where she can be quiet and undisturbed, the animal will do better than when entirely confined, and derive advantage from the air and exercise.

Immediately after the birth, the cow should be milked, and although she may have a very full udder, in some cases she will not give much, but if the calf is placed on one side of her, and the milker takes his place at the other, the matter can be got over without difficulty. Some remove the calf immediately it is born, but this must be condemned as an unnatural course to pursue, for as Youatt humanely says: "It is a cruel thing to separate the mother from its young so soon; the cow will pine, and will be deprived of that medicine which nature designed for her, in that moisture which hangs about the calf, and even in the placenta itself; and the calf will lose that gentle friction, and motion, which helps to give it the immediate use of all its limbs, and which, in the language of Mr. Berry, increases the languid circulation of the blood, and produces a genial warmth in the half exhausted and chilled little animal. In whatever manner the calf is afterwards to be reared, it should remain with the mother for a few days after it is dropped, and until the milk can be used in the dairy. The little animal will thus derive the benefit of the first milk, that to which nature has given an aperient property, in order that the black and glutinous fæces which have been accumulating in the intestines during the latter months of the fœtal state, might be carried off."

For my part, I have always acted upon the advice here given by Youatt, though my aim is to bring my calves up upon skimmed milk; and I always allow them to suck for a few days, which there is an advantage in doing, for the cow's udder becomes more soft and pliant, and especially in the case of young heifers, whose udders are invariably hard. The cow should be milked first, and sufficient left in the udder for the calf, which will not only get the richest, and most nourishing milk, and that best adapted for its support, but in its attempts to get it, the pushings with its head will soften the udder of the cow, which will thus be benefited by the calf's efforts.

It sometimes happens, that when the cow's teats

are sore, she shows a disinclination to allow the calf to suck her, when they should be fomented three or four times a day with warm water, after which she should be very gently milked by hand ; an operation best performed by women, whom I much prefer to see milking cows than a man employing his rough fist upon the animals, which, to me, seems scarcely a natural task for him to perform. After milking, the teats should be dressed with the ointment prescribed for sore teats, which will be found under that heading in the chapter devoted to " Diseases of Cows."

Immediately the calf is dropped, in most instances, the cow will commence to cleanse its skin, by licking off the slimy matter with which it is covered, but should she show any disinclination to perform this office, usually suggested by nature, the difficulty may be got over by sprinkling a handful of salt over the calf ; after which she will generally set about the job without further delay.

Some dairy-farmers make a practice of giving the calf about half a pint of warm gruel about an hour after its birth, and throw the first milk, or " beestings " from the cow away. This, however, is decidedly a wrong practice, for nature has intended the "beestings " of the cow, which are unfit for dairy purposes, to be at once the first strengthening food for the calf, as well as being an aperient medicine ; as it is a strong and viscid fluid, possessing that quality which powerfully assists in discharging the glutinous fæces before alluded to, while it contains a peculiarly nourishing quality, highly adapted for the early invigoration of the young animal.

On this subject Youatt, whom I am always glad

to quote, remarks: "Parturition having been accomplished, the cow should be left quietly with her calf; the licking and cleaning of which, and the eating of the placenta—that is, the afterbirth, or cleansing—if it be soon discharged, will employ and amuse her. A warm mash should be put before her, and warm gruel, or water, from which the chill has been taken off; two or three hours after which it will be prudent to give an aperient drink, consisting of a pound of Epsom salts and two drachms of ginger. Attention should likewise be paid to the state of the udder, for it is very subject to inflammation after calving. The natural and effectual preventive of this is, to let the calf run with her, and take the teat when it pleases, as the tendency to inflammation is much diminished by the calf frequently sucking; and should the cow be feverish, nothing soothes or quiets her so much as the presence of the little one."

The placenta, or afterbirth, is generally taken away altogether, which the cow, left to itself, will eat, which is commonly thought disgusting, and a great many people prevent them from doing so; but in the opinion of some, as the cow eats it with avidity, it is thought to possess medicinal qualities which her instinct teaches her to appropriate. If the placenta be not soon discharged from the body, the aperient drink recommended should be given, together with the ergot and ale, as serious inconvenience will be sustained by the cow if it be retained too long.

After the calf has been cleaned by the cow, and it has begun to suck, the navel-string requires to be inspected, in case it continues to bleed. Should this prove to be the case, a ligature should be passed closely around it, but if it can be avoided, not quite close up to the belly, and if at the place where the division of the cord occurred, which may be very sore, a pledget of tow well wetted with friar's-balsam is recommended by Youatt to be placed over it, confined with a bandage, and changed every morning and night; but caustic applications, which are resorted to by many, should be avoided.

Although to all appearance matters may appear to be going on very well at first, sometimes, between the third and tenth day, inflammation will suddenly show itself about the navel; hence the necessity of continued inspection, and examination, until all danger of this happening is well over. Should any swelling of the part exhibit itself, accompanied by redness and tenderness, it should be well fomented with warm water until it is thoroughly dispersed; but if it will not yield to this treatment, the assistance of a veterinary surgeon should be obtained, without further loss of time, or fatal consequences may ensue.

In the case of a heifer having a bad time with her first calf, it will be, perhaps, the wisest course not to attempt to breed from her again, but either dispose of her, or fatten her for the butcher; as, in all probability, her subsequent calvings will be equally unfortunate with the first; and it is by taking these kind of anticipatory precautions that a herd of cows may be got together that are perfectly healthy and above suspicion, and future trouble, annoyance, and loss will be avoided.

Time for Cows to Calve.—As to the time that cows should be made to calve will depend a great deal upon the course of management pursued. The cow is always ready to take the bull soon after calving, but this should not be allowed until a month or five weeks afterwards; but, as it occurs at various other times during the spring and summer, it gives an opportunity of regulating the calving-time as may be desired, at such period as would appear most convenient, and fall in with the course of management that is generally pursued. The inclination of the cow lasts for three or four days, and recurs again in about three weeks' time, if she has not conceived; otherwise she will not show any inclination. This state of affairs is, however, sometimes deceptive, as the period of her being in season sometimes passes over without conception, and it is not until between the third and fourth month after copulation that the fact of pregnancy can be ascertained, which is discovered by the dropping of the belly, and the motion of the foetus, so that sometimes these calculations may be thrown out, and the most experienced breeders are occasionally deceived.

Some writers have recommended March as being the best time for calves to be dropped, while all are unanimous that affairs should be so managed that the cows should be made to calve down by the middle of May at the latest; as late calves will not be sufficiently grown and strong enough to bear the cold of winter; and on this account some do not care for rearing calves that have been dropped after the 1st of March, avoiding, however, calves falling in the winter months, the aim of the dairy-farmer being, to have his cows calve before they are turned out upon the pastures, about the 1st of May.

The principle of this is correct enough, and is as it should be, although it is not the course I adopt; for I carry the same principle out much farther still, and like as many calves as possible to come in January—which is generally considered an unfavourable month, being in the middle of dreary winter; but my object in this is, as I bring up my calves on skimmed milk, and they are fed from the pail by hand, while the necessary feeding is going on for two or three months they are growing into strength, and they get the benefit of so much extra time, and get stout and strong, and have all the summer to run through; which builds them up by the time the winter comes round, and they are then hardy animals fit to stand almost anything. I have been very fortunate in rearing calves, my system not being very commonly adopted, and is mostly the result of my own observation and experiment; an account of which I shall reserve for a separate chapter.

Pursuing the method I do, I am more independent of the condition of the cow from prolonged milking, so far as the after-condition of the calf is concerned, when it is suckled by its mother; which is a principal point borne in mind by those who bring up their calves differently, a late-milked lean cow often having an easier time of parturition than those which have been dried earlier, but which affects the after-condition of the calf. For the matter of that, her aftermilking also bears witness of the too great strain that has been put upon her, and it is never desirable to tax the cow's producing powers too greatly; but I merely record the fact that, as far as my system is concerned, I have not to take into account, on the calf's behalf, the after-condition of the cow so much, which is a main point to be considered by many who bring their calves up upon a different system. The scraggy, poor condition of many calves, is often to be attributed to too late milking, and it is especially unwise to milk heifers with their first calves too close up to their time of calving. Five or six months after calving perhaps is long enough in this case. By this means her strength will not be so much impaired, and she will grow, and increase in size by the time she has her second calf; but from four years to eight years of age, cows in good condition can be milked up to within six weeks or two months of calving, as before stated; and, in exceptional cases, the flow of milk is so strong, that it continues almost up to the time when the new lacteal secretion commences.

Fifeshire System.—The ordinary aim is to have the calves well forward for early grass, by which means they become strong, and require less care and attention during the following winter; which is, without doubt, a very important consideration to entertain, upon whatever system their rearing may be conducted. Upon the Fifeshire dairy system, the cows are made to calve as much as possible during the three spring months—March being reckoned the best time for calves to be dropped—where they are mostly hand-fed, and seldom suckled by the cows, unless dropped in May, when two are assigned to each cow. The calves are hand-fed with milk warm from the cow, three times a day, beginning with one-and-a-half quart daily, the quantity being gradually increased to six quarts at the end of five weeks, and to eight quarts at the end of other four weeks. At the expiration of six weeks, in addition to the milk, linseed and oatmeal, well boiled together, are given with the milk, beginning with four ounces per diem, and served at one of the meals, either night or morning, till the quantity is increased by degrees, to one pound per day at end of another six weeks; at which time the calves are ready to be turned out to grass.

After this, the meal in the middle of the day is discontinued, and in the course of another week the morning meal also; and should there happen to be an abundant feed of grass, the night's meal is soon after discontinued as well, the calves being entirely left without milk, at ages varying from twelve to fourteen weeks.

The quantity of food consumed by the calf upon this (Fifeshire) system is considered on the average to amount to about 120 gallons of milk, twenty-eight pounds of linseed, oatmeal, or barleymeal (whichever is given), and as much hay as they choose to eat; those dairy-farmers who are desirous of bringing their stock early to maturity not grudging their food, but giving them plenty of whole milk, hay, or sometimes oats with the straw, the plan being an expensive one. By the use of linseed, or meal, a much larger number of calves can be reared than when they have to depend upon milk alone.

Gloucestershire System.—I have found, in the course of my experience, that there is often a good point to be gathered from a system—with the whole of which perhaps I may not agree—that may be applied with advantage; and in the Gloucestershire system, which is a very defective one, so far as the housing of animals is concerned, where the calves are fed on the best hay during the first winter, but are never sheltered with any degree of care, an economical system is pursued —the calf being taken from the cow at a week old, at which time two quarts of new milk are given morning and evening for the first month. After this, contrary to the Fifeshire system, the milk is *reduced* to one quart at each time, and half-a-pound of meal substituted. This feed is continued for a month or six weeks longer, after which the calves are turned out upon the best grass there is on the farm; the calves being taught to eat a little hay as soon as possible, while being fed on meal and milk, which is an excellent preparation for teaching them to get their own living when the time comes round for grass-feeding; their stomachs by that means being got into a certain preparedness, or condition of readiness, for receiving the grass, which otherwise might bring on scouring, which pulls down calves very much, and checks their progress very materially at a critical period of their existence.

Milk Farms.—This kind of arrangement of making the cows to calve as nearly as possible at definite times, suits very well the circumstances of both farmers who pursue a mixed system of dairy and arable farming, as well as those of Cheshire and Gloucestershire, and those counties where cheese is largely made, and the summer operations of the dairy have chiefly to be considered; but upon a milk farm, where a supply of milk is as indispensable in winter as at any other time, or in the case of a large private family, where the consumption of milk and butter is great, the time of calving will have to be arranged so as to suit requirements, and in the case of the milk farm, the cows must calve nearly all the year round; and the same with gentlemen's establishments, where the cows must follow each other in calving at appropriate intervals, and not only calve down in the spring season, but a sort of duplicate calving-season must be instituted, extending from October to June. If the calves are not considered worth rearing, or it be awkward to do so, they had better be got rid of at once. I always sell off those that come late in the autumn, or early winter, because they give a good deal of trouble to wait upon all through the winter months; my practice always being to get rid of the bull-calves, at whatever time they come, and rear the females, discarding any of the latter whose size, form, or colour I may not approve of, or that do not bear the appearance of being handsome, vigorous animals, though we seldom have to reject any on that score.

Castrating.—It will, however, well answer the purpose of those who have a good deal of rough pasture, to rear their calves of both sexes upon the plan I have adopted, and in this case the males should be castrated as soon as possible after a month has expired from their birth. The longer the operation is delayed, the greater will be the danger attending it; and an exact register can be kept of the various ages and breeds of the calves, by adding on to the list, hanging up in the cow-house, the date of the birth of each, which will save a good deal of trouble and guessing about ages, etc., where a large number of cows and calves are kept. It will be better, perhaps, if I give a *fac simile* of the form I use, which shows at a glance the necessary particulars relating to both cows and calves, without which, or some similar arrangement, there will often be a degree of uncertainty:

COW LIST.

No. in Herd Book.	Name.	Breed.	Served by.	Age.	Expected to Calve.	Calved.
12	Lady	Alderney	Duke	5	Jan. 12	Jan. 15
14	Violet	,,	,,	3	,, 30	,, 29
15	Polly	Ayrshire	,,	7	Feb. 6	
16	Rose	Shorthorn	Monarch	4	,, 20	
17	Spot	Devon	,,	6	Mar. 1	
18	Fanny	Cross	,,	5	,, 18	
19	Bell	,,	Duke	4	Nov. 20	
20	Frisk	,,	,,	3	Dec. 10	

Situated as I am, with only a small portion of arable land, I have never aimed at bringing up more calves than my own cows bring; but upon the inexpensive system I carry out, I can readily see that it would answer the purpose of many farmers, who have a large breadth of indifferent pasture, or the run of common land, to bring up a good many, not to fatten them for the butcher, but to sell them as store stock, at the end of the summer season, or autumn rather, when there is no longer a sufficient living to be picked up, or nearly enough, without incurring a heavy expense in the shape of purchased food for them.

The only experiment I ever made in fattening a young ox was such a decided failure, as before mentioned, that I never cared to repeat the experiment, although it was certainly by no means a fair trial, for the beast I essayed upon was an Alderney, the very worst breed that I could have selected for such a trial; and he ate an immense amount of food, and was a long time making himself fat; but the case would have been far different had I tried my "prentice hand" upon a shorthorn, as the latter would have clothed his frame with flesh in a much shorter period, and I should have got a considerably larger, and correspondingly more valuable, animal. But I saw enough of the transaction to be aware that I could make a great deal more money by giving the food to cows, and getting a return in milk, than by fattening beasts.

In some country districts, if the farmer has not grazing land of his own, there are often opportunities where stock is taken to grass for a small charge per head; and where this privilege is to be obtained, it would be found very profitable to bring up a number of calves upon the method I have adopted, the particulars of which I am about to give; but so much depends upon individual cases, and opportunities, that each person ought to carefully find out for himself what will be the best course to pursue in his own individual case, and then carry out a definite system which has been resolved upon after mature consideration.

The arable farmer who grows a large quantity of roots, might possibly find it to his advantage to feed young stock, and deal in cattle; giving them plenty of straw chaff and pulped roots, with the addition of oil-cake and cheap feeding stuffs, which are to be purchased so cheaply, that free-trade in this respect does not become an unmitigated evil, when the present high prices that are realised for stock are taken into account.

BUTTER, CHEESE, AND VEAL. 151

English farmers cannot compete in the production of corn with American produce and the grain of northern Europe; but if they were to add stock-keeping to their usual routine—I am now speaking of arable farmers exclusively—they would often command much more satisfactory results than they are at present able to obtain, and greatly increase their profits. Unfortunately, it is the case with a great many tenant farmers so situated, with only the produce of their arable land to rely upon, that they still stick to the old-fashioned methods in vogue many years ago, and do not adapt themselves to the altered circumstances which now prevail.

Various calculations have been made, at different times, as to the rate of profit to be obtained from diverse methods of dealing with production under what may be termed dairy produce, including the rearing of calves for veal, associated in an account, as against butter and cheese, in celebrated dairy counties, amongst which may be instanced that of Mr. Hayward, of Frocester Court, in Gloucestershire, a very intelligent and experienced farmer, who kept as many as a hundred cows in his dairy, and inclined in favour of cheese-making. But in the annexed account, which was drawn up a good many years ago, the difference between the price realised for cheese and butter was not so great, and the calculation of profit would, at the present day, be entirely different, and instead of fixing butter at tenpence per pound, fifteenpence per pound, or fifty per cent. upon the lower quotation, would be much nearer the mark; and the tendency of the present day is for cheese to drop in value, on account of American and other competition;

while that of superior fresh butter is to increase in price.

Mr. Hayward's Calculations.—Mr. Hayward viewed the production of fine cheese to be the most profitable application of milk—exceeding that of butter or veal; but the calculation must now be taken subject to the altered relations of value which prevail, although the figures are as much as ever instructive, his estimate being as follows:

	£	s.	d.
100 gallons of milk produce 112 lb. of cheese of the best quality, which at 6*d.* per lb. is	2	16	0
And 5 lb. of whey butter, which at 8*d.* per lb. is	0	3	4
Value of 100 gallons of milk when converted into cheese	2	19	4
100 gallons' produce of milk, butter 34 lb., which at 10*d.* per lb. is	1	8	4
And of cheese of the worst quality 74 lb., which at 3*d.* per lb. is	0	18	6
Value of 100 gallons of milk when made into butter	2	6	10
160 gallons produce 112 lb. of veal, which at 7½*d.* per lb. is	3	10	0
But calves, when dropped, generally sell at 10*s.* each, which, being deducted	0	10	0
Leaves, as the value of 160 gallons	3	0	0
And therefore, the value of 100 gallons in feeding veal is	1	17	6

In the above calculation, no expenses are reckoned in connection with the making of butter and cheese, nor of the value of the pigs that can be reared upon the whey and the skimmed milk ; and no reference is made to the time that cheese must be kept on hand before it is sold, or fit for consumption, by which so much capital is locked up, while butter can be sold at once ; and there is not much trouble in rearing calves ; but taking the figures as they stand, and substituting fifteenpence per pound for butter instead of tenpence, the difference will amount to one pound three shillings and fivepence, or a total of three pounds ten shillings and threepence, allowing the other items to stand as set down, which will show a very great difference in favour of butter above the others.

There can, however, be no question in the present day about the matter, that milk-selling ranks first in the order of profit, unless there are drawbacks in the shape of long distance from a station, or the wear and tear of a bulky trade, which may be disliked, and the consequent trouble attending it.

Next comes butter, which, no matter how far removed from a market, can always be disposed of profitably, on account of its portability and its relative high value in proportion to its bulk ; and, lastly, cheese.

I do not think a comparison can well be made as to calves, for circumstances are so widely different, and success or non-success in rearing them profitably, against the other products of the dairy, will depend so much upon contingent circumstances, that a fair comparison cannot well be drawn between them in ordinary cases ; for it is very apparent, that the dairy-farmer with plenty of good pasture-land would find it much, more profitable to keep cows upon it, which would give him a handsome daily return in milk, that he can at once turn into cash, than feeding calves upon it, which he would have to keep by him a long time, and the cost of whose keep would amount to something very considerable while they were "growing into money," as it is termed, though the case would be altered in that upon land where the pasturage was not good enough for milch-cows, but upon which growing calves might be able to glean a tolerable living.

CHAPTER VII.

Rearing the Calf—Scouring in Calves—Whole Milk for Calves—
Feeding Calves in Massachusetts—Various Methods of rearing
Calves—American and Canadian Cattle and Meat.

REARING THE CALF.—I have always regarded the rearing of calves oneself as the most important branch of dairy-farming. By paying attention to this department, one has the power of making his herd of cows just what he pleases, so as to suit his requirements in the shape of dairy produce, and rear cows that will best produce either butter or milk, as well as having a breed of animals suited to the land that is to carry them, besides knowing the quality and nature of his stock, and what he may expect from them; which is more than he can reckon upon when he buys his cows haphazard from dealers or neighbouring farmers.

If the dairy-farmer takes proper care of his animals when he rears them himself, he will seldom find them ailing; but in buying strange cows, heifers, or calves, the new importations may have some ailment or other, which, not perceptible at first, will be made manifest afterwards—some latent complaint or other, which may at a future time give him trouble—whereas, from his own healthy young stock, nothing is ever to be feared.

In all well-regulated herds, there will be constant changes going on, and cows leaving it, either for the fatting-stall, on account of approaching age, or from judicious culling, when an animal turns out not to be a paying one, and yields less milk than the average; or if not fattened for the butcher, should be sold, and got rid of, and the young heifers growing up will take their places.

My first aim is the product of butter, using the skimmed milk to bring up calves, the rest going to the pigs, keeping a large number of the latter; and as I want quality more than a large quantity of milk, there is a very large element of the Alderney in my breed, which prevails above all others. The purebred Alderney cows I cross with a shorthorn bull, which brings me a breed of animals very well suited to my pastures; which, though by no means rich, cannot be called very poor, being perhaps a shade under the average of English meadows, and not suited for the heaviest and largest breeds of cattle. When the shorthorn element begins to get too much developed in a heifer, I cross her with an Alderney bull, and where the Alderney decidedly predominates I adhere to the shorthorn cross; which I find suits my purpose uncommonly well.

I have several stray cows of different breeds amongst the older ones, and their progeny is always modified upon the system I have named, and the cows are moderate-sized animals, which suit my purpose; though upon one occasion I departed from this rule, and regretted it afterwards—the occasion being that, a neighbouring gentleman having died, his widow sold off the stock he had, and amongst it was a pet

Brittany cow of very small size, which my wife fell in love with, and which I became the purchaser of.

Although a small cow will often bring a large calf, particularly those of the Ayrshire breed, this one was *too* small—not being much larger than a good-sized donkey; its diminutive dimensions of course constituting its chief excellence in the eye of those who value them as pet animals—and after keeping the first calf, which proved to be a heifer, I saw that I should have to get rid of the others, or I should reduce the standard of my herd.

The natural food of the calf when first born is, of course, the cow's milk, but my aim being to rear my calf, and yet use the cream to make butter with, so that in keeping one I do not lose the other, I set about the task in this wise.

I allow the calf to suck its mother generally for five days or a week, except the rule requires modifying—either that the cow is a young one, and ought to be sucked longer, or for any other cause, if the calf for some reason or other cannot get along without the cow, or the cow without the calf; but in the average number of cases, I am generally able to rear them after they have received this assistance, or start, from the mother.

While the cow is suckling the calf, I never allow her to have any roots, but cause her to be fed upon good sound hay and a little bean-meal, or oil-cake, or other good food, if she appears to need it. Many persons feed their cows upon mangold and chaff whilst suckling their calves, and there is no doubt in my mind that this food is often the fruitful occasion of the calves scouring, by which many people lose a great number, and are surprised that this should be the case, as the calf is allowed to suck its mother to an unlimited extent. But this method is not so good as putting them at first upon shorter commons, and calves should not be allowed to fill themselves with milk till they are at least a week old. Many farmers are at a loss to understand why they should lose calves by scouring, sometimes when they are only twenty-four hours old; taking, as they say, the food provided by nature, while I, by "tinkering them, and messing them about," as they describe it, manage to rear calves, and hardly ever lose one!

The real reason doubtless is, in many of the cases where calves are lost in this way, that the little animal, suffering from diarrhœa, and weak, is often disinclined to move about and help itself, by sucking its mother when only a day, or a couple of days, old, and so sinks from want of support; and although it might help itself if it chose, it does not do so. Under these circumstances, a little milk should be *given* to it. If the scouring continues, three table-spoonfuls of linseed oil should be administered.

Scouring in Calves is sometimes caused when they are sucking the mother, by derangement of the stomach, owing to coagulation of the milk there, which at times occasions a large mass to form, the whey of the milk proceeding on its course and producing diarrhœa, the fæces when evacuated being of a white colour, these cases being attended with a good deal of danger, when alkaline medicines should be given with a view to dissolve the mass, and neutralise the acid which has accumulated to excess in the stomach; and for this purpose carbonate of magnesia and carbonate of soda will be found good medicines, in doses of one or two drachms each, according to the age of the calf.

Under ordinary circumstances of common scouring, the medicine recommended under the head of "scouring" in the chapter devoted to the diseases of cows, will be found a useful remedy to be used in a reduced quantity. Another very good recipe consists of two ounces of castor-oil, and mix half a tea-spoonful of ground ginger with a whisked egg. The castor-oil will carry off offending matter, while the ginger warms the little animal's stomach, and the egg performs a useful office in another direction. This will be found efficacious if there are feverish symptoms, accompanied with refusal of food. To keep up the animal heat, a woollen rug tied round its body will be found of advantage.

There are, also, often external reasons for diarrhœa, as, for example, when calves are kept in dirty, ill-ventilated, or damp calf-houses. Calves require to be kept both dry and clean, with not only plenty of straw under them, but the floor to be made to slope downwards, at a gradient of one inch in thirty-six, so that the urine may be carried off freely—calves voiding a good deal in proportion to their size.

They should be well littered up twice a day, and the straw well shaken up, and all dirty and wet patches thrown aside.

My calves are kept in an outhouse, without any fittings in it whatever, beyond what we "rig up" ourselves. It is simply the earth floor, with stout stakes driven down at suitable distances, to which we tie hurdles, so as to allow each calf to have sufficient space to walk about and frisk in while they are quite young; a little hay being twisted into the hurdles for them to nibble at, and learn to feed themselves, which they will do in a very short space of time. Bean straw makes capital bedding for calves, and wheat straw is better than barley straw for this purpose.

When we take the calf away from the cow at the end of five or seven days, which is the most usual time, it is fed with skimmed milk and boiled linseed mixed—the milk freshly skimmed, and perfectly sweet, warmed to the heat of cows' milk. A good deal of management is necessary to make them first take to the pail, and this is done by the man putting the calf's head in the pail, while he inserts his fingers, which he has wetted with milk, in the calf's mouth, and gently passes a little down its throat; care being taken not to push the little animal's nostrils into the milk, which will occasion it to withdraw its head so as to enable it to breathe. After a short time, the calf will learn to drink without the aid of the fingers, and come readily enough to the pail. Some, indeed, will be inclined to be greedy over it, and will gulp it down too fast, if they are allowed to have their own way; but this should not be permitted, sufficient time being given for its admixture with the animal's saliva. A good deal depends upon careful feeding, calves which are allowed to drink too fast being generally recognisable by their "paunchy" condition.

Some who bring up the calves from the pail allow two to drink at the same time, but this should never be allowed, as one will often get a great deal more than the other; and they should always be fed separately. The milk, too, must always be of the proper heat; and not sour milk, which has stood too long in the dairy. A mistake made by giving calves the milk out of the wrong dishes, where some is allowed to stand, would bring on diarrhœa; or cold milk, in winter time, is highly objectionable.

There are many other contrivances for bringing up calves, instead of allowing them to suck the cows, but I have never tried them, having plenty of skimmed milk as a rule; though I once made the experiment with hay-tea, which many have successfully brought up calves upon. Hay-tea is made by piling an earthen vessel with as much fine, sweet hay as can be pressed into it lightly with the hand, and then pouring boiling water upon it. The vessel is then covered closely up, and in a couple of hours a strong liquid is produced, which will last good for a couple of days, and should be used about the same heat as cows' milk. Hay-tea is good food mixed with linseed jelly, which is made with one quart of seed to six quarts of water, and allowing it to boil for ten minutes.

A good mixture is also made of seven pounds of bruised linseed cake, stirred into two gallons of hot water, with two gallons of hay-tea, and the addition of seven pounds of mixed meal, consisting of equal portions of bean, oat, wheat, and barley meals, stirred together with two gallons of water, and the whole commingled. Two quarts of this, with the same allowance of water, are given to each calf twice a day. While this is being done, the little animal should be invited to eat a little sliced carrot or turnip, which it can be quickly got to nibble at, together with the hay before recommended. They will soon learn to eat a few beans, or peas, which they prefer whole to ground; and after their stomachs have been accustomed to a little food of this varied nature, by the time the grass begins to spring they may be turned out for an hour or two, during a sunny day, in an orchard or warm enclosure, and they will begin to nibble a little grass. Carrots, either grated and mixed with chaff, or given alone, cut into thin slices with a knife, they will readily eat ; and as soon as they take to these kinds of food the supply of milk can be gradually decreased.

Whole Milk for Calves.—In those cases where it may be considered desirable to feed calves upon whole milk—which is never my plan after the period I have stated, except upon rare occasions—the quantity of milk given to a good large breed of calf, say a moderately-bred shorthorn, or a cross approximating in size, should not exceed the following :

4 quarts per day at 2 meals during the 1st week with the cow
5 to 6   „   „   2nd to 4th   „
6 to 7   „   „   4th to 6th   „

and for six weeks afterwards a couple of gallons a day, if fed for so long upon milk. In addition to the above, the calf will eat a little green hay as it nears the fourth week, and a week or two afterwards, sliced roots, meal, or crushed linseed cake, mixed with hay chaff. This kind of feeding is adopted by breeders who want to turn out fine large beasts at two-and-a-half years old, and who, perhaps, do not make dairy produce the first consideration.

In addition to hay twisted into the hurdles for the calves to nibble at, which they will soon acquire the knack of doing, I have some common semicircular hay-racks fixed against the wall, at a height of three-and-a-half feet from the ground, one of which serves two calves, being placed between two of the rough stalls formed by hurdles, and lower down, some small troughs, holding about a gallon and a half each, in which to place any other description of food, with which the calves may be fed. Too many beans should not be given to calves, as they are somewhat heating; but in cold weather, which is the time I rear most of my calves in this way, a little food of a warm nature is not by any means objectionable.

A convenient calf-house can thus be made out of any shed that is dry and warm, care being taken that the floor slopes in such a way that all the moisture drains off. At first, I was somewhat helpless in such matters, and thought any change, such as that of taking up a brick floor, involved a good deal of expense, and a long bill from the bricklayer; but we do all these kind of jobs ourselves, and would take up the bricks or stones forming the flooring of a barn or outhouse, shovel up the earth, so as to form any desired declivity, sink a small cesspool, and lay bricks inside and mortar them, lay down the bricks or stones again, and make any necessary changes we may require in a few hours' time, all the men lending a hand and doing certain parts, the man who formerly was a bricklayer's labourer laying the bricks and making the mortar, while the others are adepts at using the spade; and it is astonishing what convenient alterations we can make at the cost of a few hours' labour only.

Upon one occasion, having a large underground cellar with a brick flooring, which I used as a wine and beer cellar, and for storing away anything that

we could not find room for anywhere else conveniently
—experiencing much inconvenience when a sudden or
violent heavy rain fell, which penetrated through the
gravel and swamped the cellar at times—I took up
all the bricks, and dug the floor out for about a couple
of feet, taking care not to go too near the walls, and
wheeled the earth out and filled up the space with
broken brick-bats and coarse gravel-stones, upon which
we relaid the bricks again. We were never troubled
with any more standing water in the cellar, for the
natural drainage of the land on which the house
stands carried all water away where it used to stand
upon the bricks, but it was very troublesome whilst
the water was there, as we had to make use of a stout
plank to walk on, to get to the beer barrels, that had
been in use for many years by the previous tenant;
and by having a handy man or two about one,
any little difficulty of this nature may be soon got
over, so that there is really no occasion for having
damp, unhealthy buildings for stock, in which they
can never thrive.

Upon sand, and gravel, the natural drainage is
always good, and upon clay a capital dry floor may
be made by excavating it and burning the clay taken
out in a heap, with a few bushels of small coal, and
then filling the space up again with it after it has
been burnt.

Lime we buy at sixpence per bushel, at a lime-kiln
a mile or two off, and we have plenty of sand with
which to make mortar, and also whitewash, which we
use freely upon all the walls of our outbuildings, pigsties, etc., as well as the kitchen ceilings, or any other
that may require doing; and I have very little to pay

in the form of tradesmen's bills, for broken panes of glass, or any little jobs that always need doing about the house, as my man buys the glass and puts it in at a cost of from fourpence to eighteenpence for a large square, the glass being sold at twopence halfpenny per square foot.

In "The Sussex Report," a method is described of rearing calves in that county upon treacle and linseed oil-cake, in the proportion of half an ounce of treacle and one ounce of powdered oil-cake, mixed with a pint of skimmed milk, properly incorporated, and given together with lukewarm whey, or hay tea.

In some parts of the north of England, calves for the first four or five weeks are fed upon equal quantities of new and skimmed milk, after which they are gradually brought to drink gruel, made of bean or oat meal, mixed with one-half of buttermilk.

Feeding Calves in Massachusetts.—A plan of rearing calves in an inexpensive manner is pursued in Massachusetts, after the following method: The calves, when three days old, are taken from the cows, and fed with barley and oats ground together, which is made into gruel, one quart of the flour being boiled during half an hour in twelve quarts of water; of which one quart is to be given, lukewarm, to each calf, morning and evening. In ten days a bundle of soft hay is placed in the stable, which they will soon begin to eat, and a little of the flour is put into a small trough, for them to lick occasionally. They are thus fed during about two months, gradually increasing the quantity; and it is said that half a bushel of the corn is sufficient until the calf is entirely placed on grass, to which he is occasionally turned out during the day.

The greatest scourge to which calves are subject is scouring, and it is generally thought sufficient to feed calves twice a day, night and morning, allowing them as much as they can eat at the time. Some calves, having this opportunity, fill their stomachs so full, that the large quantity they take impedes digestion. As trouble should never be considered, when it is desired to perform anything in the best possible manner, it will be found the most advisable plan to feed calves three times a day, giving them less each time to make amends for the third feeding, and give food as well in the middle of the day. By this more frequent method of feeding, the growth of the calf will be found to proceed much more satisfactorily, and its general health and condition will be better. Many advocate tying calves up, but I think the little exercise they take, even when confined to a loose-box—if it can be so called, in which I place mine, between hurdles—is of great advantage to them, and I often laugh to see the little animals frisking about, throwing up their hind-legs, and merrily running round their small enclosure, which they would be unable to do if tied up by the head.

Care should always be taken not to change the food of calves too suddenly, but accustom them to what is coming by slow gradations, giving them a small quantity at first, and increasing it afterwards. They relish a little change of food, and administered in this way, their stomachs and digestive organs are not upset, or thrown out of order, which will often take place upon a sudden and entire alteration of diet.

The *quality* of the food, too, ought to be a point for consideration and examination. I have spoken of linseed-tea, or gruel, as being a capital article of food to give as a substitute for whole milk, when mixed with skimmed milk; but there is a great difference in the quality of linseed, Indian linseed not being sufficiently gelatinous, and boiling hard. A common idea of quantity to employ in making linseed gruel is, five pounds for about seven gallons, sufficient for five good-sized calves.

Nice green, soft hay should be given to the calves, which they will learn to eat when three weeks old. About six weeks old, the calf will begin to nibble grass, and in two or three weeks more it can be turned out, if the season is sufficiently advanced, and left to graze. But if the spring is wet, and cold, they should not be exposed to the weather, but merely turned out for air and exercise a few hours in the brightest part of the day, and then brought into a yard where there are sheds to shelter them, and they should neither be allowed to lie upon wet land or wet bedding, but be kept dry.

I have capital convenience for my calves so far as their *run* is concerned, for, having several patches of plantation, round the borders of which grass grows, and also in those places not entirely shaded by trees, they pick up the best part of their living in the early spring, and after our hay-making is done, which I always try to finish as early as possible, they graze the meadows with the cows, and we rear a number of good animals that cost me but a very trifling sum each, and those calves born in January or February, having been well set up, and their stamina established during the early part of their lives under cover, having run all through the summer, and autumn, upon the pastures, at the commencement of winter are fine strong animals, as hardy as one could wish to see them.

Most of these turn out well as heifers, and if, when they have brought their first calf, I am not quite satisfied with them, or think there is not a prospect of their turning out good milkers, I sell them. Upon these occasions a common question is put, and indeed is an invariable one: "Why do you part with her?" To which I always make a point of telling the truth, by saying, "I have enough young stock of her description, and have better amongst my herd;" and I give a true statement of what she does, which saves a good deal of after trouble and annoyance, which might occur from a charge being made of misrepresentation, and the would-be purchaser can either take her or leave her, as he likes. I always depute this part of the business to my working foreman, and fix a reasonable price, which we will not depart from. Sometimes a buyer wishes to see me upon the subject, so as to persuade me to take a pound or two less maybe; but my man is always ready with his answer, which is to the effect that "Master" would not do anything in the bargain-making line, and the price having been fixed, there was no departing from it.

Various Methods of rearing Calves.—Calves can thus be reared in a great number of ways. First, by sucking the cow, which is one designed by nature, but which is an expensive method to the dairy-farmer, and does not suit the purpose of an *economist*, who wants to make as much *profit* as he can, by giving it whole new milk from the pail; by feeding it with partly whole milk and partly skimmed milk, by part milk and other foods; by skimmed milk in conjunction with other foods, which is the one I adopt, and that which I consider the best, taking into consideration the objects I have in view, and which I have before explained; by bringing up two calves sucking one cow at the same time, following with two others, and finishing off with one, making five calves altogether, when a cow has a good flow of milk, and calves in spring, and is afterwards turned out to graze upon the pastures.

The latter always appeared to me a very good plan for anyone to follow who has plenty of pasture land desirous of raising stock quickly; but in my case, although the chief part of the land I occupy consists of meadows, yet I want to save my grass for hay, or at all events that part of it which is left uncut, and unused by my cows, which are fed upon the soiling or house-feeding system, while the grass is getting into readiness for hay. More grass is trampled down and spoiled than the cows eat when they are turned out, and the greater part of the grass I am thus enabled to save for hay; making it early in the season, as soon as ever it is ready for the scythe. I do not wait till the grass gets thoroughly ripe, and the seeds all developed, which makes weighty hay; for although giving me a less valuable hay-crop than I might otherwise obtain, I am enabled to get the cows on to the pastures early in the season; while the grass is stronger, and grows better, from the grass plants not being exhausted by the perfection and completion of their seed-formation; and the meadows are consequently richer and more succulent than they otherwise would be, for the after-feeding of my cows and stock.

The breeders of pedigree cattle allow the calf to suck the cow as a matter of course, their object being to rear as fine and large a calf as possible, which is best attained by this means; but all the methods enumerated will, at times, require to be modified by circumstances—as, for example, if a calf is not quite so strong as it should be, it may be desirable to feed it upon whole or unskimmed milk from the pail, for a longer time than I have indicated in the method I follow; or, if the presence of the calf is necessary to the comfort and well-being of the cow. But the system I have adopted has been found to be far the most profitable, as I rear my calves, make my butter, and save the best portion of my hay, which comes in for winter use, when otherwise, did I not save it, I should have to lay out a great deal of money every winter.

I shall speak of the management of grass land hereafter, but I may as well remark here that a change of pasture is highly desirable for milch-cows. Two of my meadows are very large ones, but I hurdle them off and make them of suitable size, and so let the animals have a constant change. While they are eating down one portion, the other is thus growing; and if the grass whereon they are is not quite sufficient, a little extra food is carried to them in the fields and placed in troughs; or a cut of fresh clover, or other artificial grass, placing those animals that want it most upon the richest pastures, where there is the best feed; and thus the milch-cows are put first into the fresh fields, and when they have taken off the best, the calves and dry cows follow, to eat it down close; the milking-cows being moved on to another fresh portion, and so on.

All this is so well understood, and is so entirely a matter of routine, that my plans are carried out day after day upon the principle laid down, and I have very little trouble with things beyond a daily consultation with my working bailiff, or foreman, who tells me how matters are going on—that a cow has calved, and is doing well, or ill; that he thinks of mowing that little "bit" of clover, or taking up the mangold; or that he considers it would be desirable to cut down the chestnut, or ash coppice, and get the man we employ to come and make some hurdles for us, as we shall be wanting a good many—and so on.

It may thus be readily seen that my calves give me but little trouble after they have done with the pail, and are reared at a very small expense till winter is reached, when their horns are branded with an inch brand, and the number entered in the herd-book. By keeping these particulars minutely, one may see how each cow's calves have turned out, and which answer the best to keep; while the exact particulars as to age, sire, dame, etc., are always there for reference and verification.

By breeding and rearing one's own stock great advantages are secured, which I have enumerated before; not the least of which is freedom from contagion. The importation of live cattle from abroad will, doubtless, in course of time, increase considerably, and notwithstanding the watchfulness of Government officials, contagion may be brought from supposed unsuspected districts.

American and Canadian Cattle and Meat.—In January, 1879, the Dominion of Canada steamer

Ontario brought to Liverpool 247 head of cattle from Portland, Maine; and when the vessel was brought into dock, it was found that several animals were affected with pleuro-pneumonia. The *Ontario's* cargo was bought in the markets of Buffalo and Chicago, and the animals were transported over the Grand Trunk Railway of Canada to Portland for shipment. During their transit through Canada they were under strict quarantine, and had no opportunity of acquiring the disease during the journey, or of communicating it to other cattle. The Canadian Government have always adopted the most stringent measures against the importation of disease into their territory, and have interdicted the landing of cattle from countries under the slightest taint of suspicion. But such has not been the practice in the United States, which has allowed free importation, especially from Schleswig-Holstein and Brittany; and it is said that it is more than probable the disease which has presented itself in the Western markets may have originated from these European imports.

If it should become necessary to prohibit the landing of United States cattle in England, it will have a very perceptible effect upon the English meat trade, in which all stock-rearers are much interested, and the importance of this trade may be inferred from the fact that, while these lines are being written, seventy additional steamers are being got ready for the trade at Liverpool, Glasgow, and Barrow. It is not expected that the interdict will be applied to Canada, as that country has always been exempt from the plague; and in view of possible danger, the Dominion Government are taking precautions by preventing United

States cattle passing over Canadian roads or railways.

The import trade from Canada has increased with great rapidity, the number of head imported in 1877 being 6,412; but in 1878 this increased to 32,115, or five times as many as the year before. With regard to the ultimate disposition of this live cargo of the *Ontario*, information was at once communicated to the veterinary department of the Privy Council, and the chief inspector visited Liverpool, and after making a careful examination of the beasts, an order was issued that none of the cattle should be allowed to enter the country, and the whole consignment on board was slaughtered on the quay. It appeared that, in crossing the Atlantic, owing to stress of weather, fifty beasts were thrown overboard from the *Ontario*, so that it was not so much a matter of surprise amongst experienced men that the disease became developed.

In the year 1878, England received from the United States 480,000 cwt. of fresh beef, being an increase of 230 per cent. in a couple of years over previous importations, the import of fresh meat of other kinds being of commensurate dimensions, while Canada has sent us a comparatively small supply of dead meat, because the relatively short sea route has made it more profitable to convey the animal across the Atlantic alive.

But, whatever may be the ultimate shaping of either the live or dead meat trade of Canada and the States with England, in which all breeders must be deeply interested in this country, fresh dairy produce will always find a ready and remunerative market here; especially milk, which now, on account of the provisions of the Adulteration of Food Acts, is obliged to be sold pure by the milk-vendors, who are not allowed to call in the assistance of the "cow with the iron tail" to increase their volume of what used often to be merely nominal lacteal fluid, which, in its genuine unadulterated state as an article of food, is more highly appreciated by consumers in consequence, of late, than it used to be formerly.

Sometimes arrangements can be made for the summer grazing of calves and dry stock in a gentleman's park, or other enclosure, where there will be shelter afforded by trees, a good bite of grass, and liberty and comfort for the animals. These advantages should always be made use of where they are to be obtained. But there are places where stock is taken in, which are so filled and overdone that the beasts cannot get enough to eat, besides running the risk of contagion from other cattle; and where there are any doubts on this head, it will be found the best plan to keep them at home, and make the best possible shift by economical contrivances in feeding, for which many suggestions will be found in the foregoing, but none that recommend under-feeding, which is the dearest and most extravagant method that can be pursued in the long run, in connection with the management of any species of stock, but more especially milch-cows, or young heifers that are destined to make cows in the future.

CHAPTER VIII.

Abortion (Slinking, Slipping-Calf, Warping)—The Drop—Inversion of the Uterus—Meteorisation (Hoove, Hoven, or Blasting)—Distension of the Rumen—Choking—Loss of Cud—Inflammation of the Rumen—Milk Fever—Garget (Diseases of the Udder)—The Cow-pox—Retention or Stoppage of the Urine—Sore Teats—Moor-ill, or Wood-evil—Pleuro-pneumonia—Foot and Mouth Disease (Epidemic)—Paralysis—Palsy or Tail-slip—Redwater—Hepatitis—Rheumatism (Joint-felon, Chine-felon)—Quarter-ill—Blood-striking—Black-quarter—Fardel-bound—Blain, or Gloss Anthrax—Foul in the Foot—Loo, or Low—The Thrush, or Aphthæ—Mange—Lice—Diarrhœa—Catarrh—Bronchitis.

ABORTION (SLINKING, SLIPPING-CALF, WARPING).— Cows are subject to abortion from various causes, which is known under the above names, according to the district, and it is usually regarded from a scientific point of view as being a disease, for which no remedy can well be prescribed, or preventive treatment suggested ; and a cow that has once been subject to this disease or accident, whatever it may be termed, is likely to be so again ; and it is the best course to get rid of her, though abortion is often brought about from bad treatment, over-exertion, and not unfrequently by being kept in too high condition. For these, there is an assignable reason, and also a preventive remedy ; but in proof of the justness of the view taken that it must be ranked as a disease, is the fact that it sometimes becomes infectious among a herd, and even occasionally throughout entire districts.

It appears sometimes to take the form of a contagion, as it were, for when a cow slips her calf, it is often putrid before it is brought forth, and the offensive smell which it emits, if only allowed to remain a short time in the field where other in-calf cows are, exerts some sympathetic influence, and perhaps will occasion several of them in the course of a few days to cast their calves prematurely.

Abortion is sometimes produced by fright, blows, or strains, or by jumping other cows, or by their being hunted about. I once had a young horse, which I kept for riding, that had been turned out into a field with some cows, and seeing from a distance the cows running wildly about the meadow, I found, when I got there, the rascal amusing himself by chasing the cows, who were doing their best to get out of his way, some of them with their heavy udders swaying to and fro, and slipping occasionally. I fortunately stopped his game shortly after he had commenced it, or Master Saucy might have done me a considerable deal of mischief, and I gave orders that the horses were never to be turned into a field where cows were grazing again.

A disturbance of the digestive organs will cause a cow to warp, and there are constitutional reasons in the case of many highly-fed and highly-bred animals which cause them to be more likely to abort than others. After prolonged wet weather, and in some particular seasons, the disease is much more frequent than at other periods, the time it mostly takes place

SYMPTOMS OF DISORDER.

being between the ninth and fifteenth week; but it may occur at any time during pregnancy.

The cows should be carefully watched, and if one of them show by her appearance the least danger of this happening, the animal should be removed from the rest. This is always a safe plan, even if the suspicion should turn out to be ill-grounded and without foundation; and men should be encouraged to err even on the safe side in this respect, which may occasion a misfortune to be averted.

Youatt describes the symptoms as these: "The cow is somewhat off her feed, rumination ceases, she is listless and dull, the milk diminishes or dries up, the motions of the fœtus become more feeble, and at length cease altogether; there is a slight degree of enlargement of the belly, there is a little staggering in her walk; when she is down she lies longer than usual, and when she gets up she stands for a longer time motionless. As the abortion approaches, a yellow, or red glairy fluid runs from the vagina—a symptom which rarely or never deceives—her breathing becomes laborious and slightly convulsive. The belly has for several days lost its natural rotundity, and has been evidently falling; she begins to moan, the pulse becomes small, wiry, and intermittent. At length labour comes on, and is often attended with difficulty and danger.

"When symptoms of abortion appear, the cow should be removed from the pasture to a comfortable shed. If the discharge is glairy, but not offensive, it may be presumed that the calf is not dead; this may be assured by the motion of the fœtus, and thus it is possible that the abortion may be yet avoided:

she should then be copiously bled, and a dose of physic should be given immediately after bleeding. The physic beginning to operate, half a drachm of opium and half an ounce of sweet spirit of nitre should be administered. The animal should be kept quiet, gruel may be allowed; but nothing like those comfortable drinks recommended by the cow-leech.

"The treatment thus differs little from that of parturition; but, should the discharge be fœtid, the natural conclusion will be that the fœtus is dead, and it must be got rid of as speedily as possible; if fever exists, bleeding may be requisite; or, perchance, the aforesaid comfortable drink may not be out of place."

If a cow aborts at a very early period of pregnancy, medical treatment is not necessary, and perhaps no disturbance to health will ensue; but at a late period, a dose of salts is often given to cause a copious action of the bowels, followed by a sedative, consisting of an ounce each of laudanum and spirit of nitrous ether; and when there is inflammation of the womb, hot fomentations are applied externally to the loins, for a long time together, and blood is sometimes abstracted.

Prompt treatment will sometimes stave off abortion. The cow should be bled, and afterwards kept very quiet, and one-and-a-half ounce of tincture of opium, and the same of spirit of nitrous ether, given; but in this course of treatment no purgative.

It most frequently happens that the after-birth is not got rid of after abortion has taken place, and as this ought to come away it should be removed gently by the hand, which, for the purpose, must be introduced into the uterus, and the placenta separated from it, by breaking down the points of attachment as carefully as possible.

The Drop.—Dropping after calving is supposed to be an affection of the nervous system, which is struck in the region of the brain, or the spinal marrow; but chiefly of the latter, at the region of the loins; but the disease is somewhat mysterious in its character, and very often comes on suddenly, just after the cow has given birth to a fine calf, and is in apparently good health and condition, and to all appearance in the way of doing well; and the disease has been attributed by competent judges to arise from the contractions of the womb after calving, in addition to the muscular efforts that have been put forth in expelling the fœtus, which produce an exhaustion of the nervous energy of the animal, particularly at the region of the loins—the drop seldom taking place till after the cow has had several calves, and with each succeeding one the uterus becomes more dilated, which causes the contractions to be greater, which brings on a great exhaustion of the nervous system.

Some breeds of cows are much more subject to this complaint than others, the mortality being greatest amongst highly-fed cows; and although cows should not be kept in too low a condition before calving, if they are allowed to become too fleshy, a dangerous condition of plethora may be induced.

Those cows which are naturally high feeders, as the shorthorn and other breeds, which put on flesh in great quantities when liberally fed, are not so subject to this complaint as the better milking varieties, whose secretions rather tend to milk than flesh. These are able to assimilate a greater quantity of nutriment without injury than those breeds whose excellence consists in their milking qualifications.

There are two phases of the disease—acute and subacute; and while the more serious form is very often incurable, the other can be got over, as some degree of appetite and animation is left to the animal, although it may possibly be neither able to rise nor stand. In acute cases, there is often entire torpor, the animal's sufferings being evinced by dismal moanings, and there appears to be an entire loss of all power, with no ability either to eat or discharge dung or urine—there being apparently an entire cessation of the natural functions of the bodily organs, the pulse being often imperceptible, and, when felt, weak and quick; till death, which generally takes place very quickly—from one to three days—terminates the poor animal's sufferings.

The curative system generally adopted is to bring on action of the stomach and bowels by purgatives and stimulants; and for this purpose large doses are given, as:

Sulphate of magnesia	1 pound
Flowers of sulphur	4 ounces
Croton oil	10 drops
Carbonate of ammonia	4 drachms
Powdered ginger	4 ,,
Spirit of nitrous ether	1 ounce

These are mixed in warm oatmeal gruel and given to the cow, slowly and carefully; the quantity of croton oil being increased when constipation is very obstinate. A blistering liniment is rubbed on the loins and spine, the cow being kept as warm as possible, a fresh sheepskin being recommended to be afterwards placed on the loins, with the wool outwards.

A fourth of the above mixture should be given every six hours, leaving out the croton oil until purging is produced, and if the animal cannot pass her urine, it should be removed from her by the catheter. Plenty of warm gruel should be given, and bran mashes, if the cow will eat them. When the disease assumes a milder form, the medicine recommended should be given in greater moderation.

The best methods of preventing the disease, is to allow the cows, some little time before calving, to have moderate exercise; to keep them well sheltered from the weather, and while allowing them to have enough, not to overfeed them. Before the cows are about to calve, I have always made it a point to give mine a strong dose of Epsom salts; the plan was never recommended to me, but it struck me that it must be a good one to get the bowels well emptied of food that might perhaps be difficult of digestion; and I attribute the invariable "good time" my cows have at the period of calving to this practice, and to not giving them the opportunity of leaping the fences, or being worried by dogs; in short, by having a watchful eye kept on them.

If the cow does not clean properly after calving, the best practitioners recommend that no haste be used in removing the after-birth, it being considered better treatment to wait a few days, giving it mild purgatives, when, if it is then not got rid of, the hand should be used, and the after-birth removed as gently as possible. There is no doubt, however, but that many of these misfortunes are brought about by want of care and due consideration for the condition of the cows, which demand the attention of a humane and thoughtful attendant to see after them upon these occasions.

Inversion of the Uterus.—Inversion of the uterus, when it does take place, is usually after parturition; but inversion of the vagina sometimes occurs before. In the case of either happening, the parts should be carefully cleansed, and returned as quickly as possible, the hinder parts of the animal being kept higher than the fore ones. Calving is sometimes delayed, or prevented by unnatural presentation; in which case it is necessary, if possible, to restore the calf to its proper position, which should be with its head resting on the forelegs, which protrude first, in some cases it being necessary to turn the calf. When the hind parts are presented first, care should be taken that both feet are freed before the buttocks. In difficult cases it is necessary to remove the fœtus piecemeal, so as to save the cow.

Meteorisation (Hoove, Hoven, or Blasting).—This is invariably brought about by the cow eating green food too ravenously, when driven first to the pastures, or when the first artificial grasses are brought to her in too great quantity; and consists of distension of the rumen by gas, given off by the food in consequence of its fermentation. Carburetted hydrogen is engendered principally in the early stage, and afterwards sulphuretted hydrogen: which so distends the stomach that, unless relief be given, suffocation will ensue. The symptoms are very apparent, as the animal's stomach gets an enormous size, and rumination ceases.

The usual course is, to pass the hollow, flexible probang down into the stomach of the animal, so that the gas may escape through it, before, or after which application, the following draught will be found efficacious:

Powdered ginger	3 drachms
Hartshorn	1 ounce
Water	1 pint

Should medicine not be ready at hand, of which a small supply should always be kept in case of emergencies, some lime-water may be given, or two drachms of chloride of lime dissolved in a quart of water. A purgative should afterwards be administered to remove any of the lingering causes, and to restore the cow's digestive organs to their natural state. Of course an accident of this sort may take place, despite all usual precautions, from a cow breaking her bounds, and eating greedily in a growing clover field, or of other succulent grasses, against her owner's wish, or knowledge.

In very obstinate cases, in order to save the cow's life, it may become necessary to make an incision in her flank on the left side, between the last rib and the hip-bone. For this purpose an instrument is used called a trochar, which is put into a tube termed a cannula, the former being withdrawn, while the latter is allowed to remain until all the gas has escaped. But if these professional instruments are not at hand, substitutes may be found in a common penknife and a quill, or stick of elder. The wound should afterwards be sewn up, or a little plaster applied.

Distension of the Rumen.—Distension of the rumen

is not nearly so common as the above, and though not attended with such acute symptoms in the early stage of its appearance, it is yet more difficult to apply relief; one of the chief objects being the necessity of distinguishing between the cause arising from distension of the rumen with gas, or by food, which is somewhat hard to do, as the appearances are similar. When distension is produced by accumulated hard and dry food, the swelling of the abdomen is not so great, and the signs of distress exhibited by the animal are not so urgent, though its real danger may perhaps be greater. Upon pressing the abdomen in the region of the rumen, it feels firm and hard; and if the probang is inserted no gas is liberated, and relief obtained thereby. In tympanitis, from a stomach which has been overloaded, meteorisation is often the first symptom, to which must be added the fulness and hardness of the paunch—that organ being in an after manner the origin or source of the inflammation of the organs of digestion. This form resists the power of drinks of the ordinary kinds, or of ammonia or ether, while puncturing does not give relief, the accumulated food being formed into hard lumps which can no longer be returned to the mouth for a second mastication. When ordinary means have failed, recourse is sometimes had to the trochar, in order to find out the nature of the contents of the rumen, and the degree to which the distension exists; which is ascertained by moving it about, and forming an opinion from the amount of resistance offered to it.

The method of treatment in mild cases is to administer a drench, composed of purgative and carminative medicines, as well as injections; sometimes blood-letting being resorted to. In obstinate cases, the stomach-pump is used, to inject a large quantity of liquid into the stomach, so as to excite vomiting; and in extreme cases, where the life of the animal appears in immediate danger, an opening is made through the flank into the rumen, large enough for the hand to be introduced, and the contents taken away; great care being taken in the meanwhile that the food does not escape into the abdomen; in the event of which great irritation would be produced. To prevent this occurring, the edges of the wound in the rumen should have a stitch, or two, to fasten them to the sides of the opening of the flank, and after the mass has been taken away, the internal wound should be closed by sutures, the ends of which hang out of the external opening, which is also closed by its own sutures. A soft diet has to be given after this operation, oily laxatives being administered, till the animal shows there is no occasion for their further use; and careful treatment must be pursued till the wounds are quite well.

Choking.—Choking is an accident of frequent occurrence; a piece of turnip or other root, being hastily swallowed, becomes fixed in the œsophagus, and, pressing upon the softest parts of the windpipe, impedes respiration, which, if not removed, will cause suffocation. When the obstructing object has been taken away, the œsophagus is sometimes so lacerated and injured that the animal is unable to recover from the wounds it has received; a smooth object being more dangerous than a rough or unequal one. Sometimes when cows have been turned into orchards, they have picked up apples that have fallen, and these are more to be feared than pieces of turnip, or other roots of unequal dimensions.

The symptoms of such an accident are exhibited in signs of distress—an attempt to vomit—and a discharge of frothy saliva from the mouth, accompanied by an enlarged stomach, from meteorisation of the rumen. The probang has to be used, which is best oiled first, or a little oil given to the animal by the horn. A rather large instrument should be used with a knob at the end, cut obliquely, and this should be passed gently along the roof of the mouth, till it enters the œsophagus. When the obstructing body is felt, the head of the animal should be alternately raised and depressed, and firm but moderate pressure used. If it cannot be pushed away at once, injudicious haste should not be used, for after waiting a little while it will, perhaps, readily yield to the next attempt, while it is getting softer in the meanwhile, and will often readily move upon the second trial.

The process requires to be done carefully and deliberately; as haste, and want of care, will perhaps produce laceration of the lining membrane of the œsophagus and its muscles, which is to be dreaded; a swelling of a hard, tense nature, commencing when in the neck part, which quickly increases, generally more above the place of injury than below it. Respiration becomes painful and difficult, the animal refuses to eat, the breath becomes fœtid, and death takes place from the third to the fifth day. When the obstructing object has been successfully removed, it is best to feed the animal upon soft food for a little time afterwards.

When the offending body, as is sometimes the case, gets impacted in the roof of the mouth, instead of pushing it downwards, it requires to be removed by drawing it upwards, which must be done by the hand, considerable force having sometimes to be used. Where it is possible to remove an obstacle by drawing it upwards, this course is always to be preferred, as the danger of lacerating the œsophagus is done away with.

Veterinary surgeons use an instrument for drawing an obstructing body upwards, with a spring forceps at one end, and a handle at the other end of a hollow probang, which is the better practice of the two, being attended with less risk.

Loss of Cud.—This is more frequently a symptom of disease, rather than a disease of itself, showing that there is a considerable derangement of the functions of the body, which is shown by a staring coat—the animal wearing a dull look, and belching wind, which indicates loss of power of the stomach. When this is manifested without any other appearance of decided disease, mild purgatives, and stomachics, will generally bring round a more favourable condition, the restoration of rumination being justly looked upon as a favourable symptom in cases of indisposition of this nature. Either excess of food, insufficient food, or bad food, will cause loss of cud, and sometimes bad teeth will assist in promoting it, and unsound or doubtful cows should never be retained in the herd.

Inflammation of the Rumen.—Inflammation of the rumen is somewhat uncommon, but is sometimes occasioned by the presence of poisonous plants in a pasture, such as hemlock, water-dropwort, wild parsley, henbane, and yew (the yew-tree being poisonous to cattle), and sometimes even the common crowfoot, and wild poppy.

The ergot of rye, and other grain and grasses, when moderately consumed bring on abortion, and when largely eaten causes death; but in the case of the preceding, the effects are usually seen to be of a narcotic character, when purgatives should be given, and the cows removed from the pastures.

Milk Fever.—When cows are fed too highly before, or after calving, with a view of stimulating the supply of milk, and it has been overdone, the result is sometimes milk fever; the udder becoming hard, and the flow of milk checked. The cow appears to totter, and wears a somewhat wild look. Aperient medicine should be given, and the cow fed upon soft relaxing food, if in high condition; and if the udder is large, it should be emptied, by milking twice a day for some days before calving, and by this means the consequences apprehended will be averted.

Garget, Diseases of the Udder.—The udders of cows, after calving, are sometimes subject to attacks of inflammation, swelling, feeling hot to the touch, the secretion of milk being interrupted, and a species of milk fever produced, sometimes occasioned by exposure to cold and wet. In bad cases, the loss of one or two quarters of the udder ensues, and sometimes it ends fatally. The treatment to be pursued, in the first place, is to apply hot fomentations, and if the inflammation is considerable, bleeding from the milk veins in the affected side is recommended. Opening medicine should also be given, and if the cow shivers, a stimulant should be added, consisting

THE COW-POX.

of an ounce of powdered ginger in warm gruel or ale, with two ounces of spirits of nitrous ether, which will occasionally stop any further progress of the disease.

After fomenting the udder, it will be found efficacious to rub an ointment, composed of the following ingredients, into the part: Powdered camphor, one ounce; mercurial ointment, two drachms; lard, eight ounces.

The Cow-Pox.—The cow-pox, although familiar enough to us by hearsay, in connection with vaccination and vaccine lymph, is by no means a common disease with cows. It consists of the formation of numerous pustules on the udder and teats, which, being very infectious, is communicated from one cow to another, by means of the hands of the milker.

Aperient medicine should be given, and a weak astringent applied to the sores on the teats. The astringent is easily made with a little powdered chalk, with the addition of one-fourth part of alum, which will be found a very effective application.

Retention or Stoppage of the Urine.—Pregnant cows are sometimes subject to a stoppage of the urine, owing to a pressure of the womb on the stomach. When this is found to be the case, the urine should be removed by means of the catheter, which is a hollow tube; and if accompanied with any other symptoms, the treatment must be in accordance with them.

Sore Teats.—Cows are sometimes troubled with sore teats, which causes the operation of milking to be a disagreeable one, both to the cow and the operator. A healing salve can be made of one ounce of yellow wax, which, when beginning to cool, should receive the addition of a drachm of alum, finely powdered, and a quarter of an ounce of sugar of lead, rubbed equally into it. Before milking, the teats should be well washed with warm water; and when the milking is finished, the teats should be dressed with a little of the salve.

Moor-ill, or Wood-evil.—These are the names given to a disorder which sometimes afflicts cows that are fed in the neighbourhood of woods and commons, and is somewhat singular in its effects. At its first commencement, the coat of the animal presents a staring appearance, and the external integument appears to adhere to the ribs below, so that there is quite a difficulty in raising it. The animal daily loses flesh, and goes about with her belly tucked up, being constipated from the beginning of the disease till its end, the constipation often being of a very obstinate nature. The appetite appears to be altogether depraved, and the animal will devour all sorts of rubbish, quite opposed to the cravings of a healthy condition, and will pick up bones, stones, bits of iron, oyster-shells, or anything that may be lying about, as well as any stray linen. She will swallow the filthiest urine, in preference to clear water, the appetite at best being very capricious. These are generally the first symptoms, which are succeeded by stiffness in some parts of the body, oftenest in the fore-shoulders and extremities, or the chest; and she may be seen uneasily shifting from limb to limb, and sometimes falling lame. When she moves, which the poor creature is often disinclined to do, her joints emit a cracking noise, as if they rattled in their sockets, while she will utter dismal groans, and altogether wear such an utterly forlorn and unusual aspect, as to cause illiterate country people, in some districts, to consider the cow's ailments the result of witchcraft.

The secretion of milk becomes lessened, and it is difficult to get her to take food, and if the disorder be not quickly arrested, it enters upon a new phase, and the cow begins to heave at the flanks, at times very violently, and the pulse is greatly accelerated.

The proper treatment to adopt is, at the first signs of the disease, to regulate the bowels, by giving a strong dose of aloes, in solution, to be followed up with Epsom salts ; the doses to be repeated every six hours till they operate. Bleeding is sometimes resorted to, but this is not considered good practice, unless there are signs of inflammation of the lungs, in which case the animal will experience relief from it, but bleeding requires to be done with great caution. The purgatives should be followed by febrifuge and alterative medicines, until the organs of digestion are brought back into their proper condition.

Some insert a seton in the dewlap, and take away ten pounds of blood in very severe cases. A recipe has been given, to administer, in very obstinate ones, six drachms of aloes, twelve ounces of sulphur, and sixteen drops of croton oil, the first day, in addition to a blood-letting of ten ounces ; repeat the bleeding to the extent of eight ounces the second day, and a smaller dose of the same purgative, and, in addition, blister the sides.

Pleuro-pneumonia. — Pleuro-pneumonia is the scientific name given to a disease which is supposed to have made its first appearance in this country in the year 1840, when it was said to be introduced into the north-west counties by some Irish cattle. It is a highly contagious disease, and consists not only of inflammation of the lungs, but also of the membrane which covers them, as well as that which lines the cavity of the chest; and perhaps the best breeds of cattle, as the Shorthorn, have suffered more from its ravages than the inferior ones.

Its highly infectious character is said by some to be due to poisonous atoms floating in the air, proceeding from the respiratory surfaces of diseased animals. It often makes great ravages amongst a herd of cattle before its presence is suspected, the earlier symptoms of the disease being very faint and obscure. A slight, but short cough, and a little staring of the coat, are the first indications to be dreaded; and these may continue for some time. The beast first struck with this disorder lags behind the rest of the herd, and does not feed so readily as usual, showing greater indifference to food. After a while, the breathing becomes accelerated, and the animal begins to lose flesh. At a later stage, the animal shows its distress much more plainly, the appetite falling off almost entirely, and rumination ceases; while the breathing becomes greatly accelerated, and is short and catching; till at last the animal pants for breath, and eventually dies of suffocation.

Where pleuro-pneumonia is known to exist, it is compulsory for the owners to have the infected animals slaughtered, but the question of treatment resolves into a suspicion of infection, and in a large herd, where there seems a probability that one or two may be infected, it is the most prudent course to have them slaughtered at once. It must be borne in mind, that the first stage is merely a short husky cough and a staring coat, and the curative measures which are best to be adopted at this very early stage, is moderate bleeding, which ought neither to be repeated nor to be of large amount; this course being resorted to merely as an immediate stay to the progress of the disease, while counter irritation in the shape of blistering is being instituted. This is best effected by removing the hair from the sides, and rubbing into them a combination of ointment of iodide of mercury, of tartarised antimony, and of cantharides. Croton oil as well, mixed with the preceding, will cause the blistering to be yet more effective, the thick hide making it difficult to raise a blister. A large seton may also be inserted in the dewlap, with the view of continuing the counter inflammatory action after that from the blister has spent itself. The bowels require regulating, and a good medicine for this purpose consists of one pound of Epsom salts, one ounce of powdered saltpetre, and half a drachm of tartar emetic, in two pints of gruel. This to be repeated about every eight hours.

Another recipe consists of first giving Epsom salts and linseed oil, and then administer afterwards a sedative, consisting of:

White hellebore, powdered . . .	1 drachm
Tartarised antimony	1 „
Nitrate of potash	2 drachms

The latter powder to be mixed up with gruel, and given morning and evening upon the first day, and once a day afterwards, for about five days. When recovering, bran and linseed mashes are good to administer, linseed in any form being an excellent food to give to animals that are either suffering or recovering from this disorder.

Foot and Mouth Disease (*Epidemic*).—When this disease attacks a herd of cows, a heavy loss is sometimes experienced, but its severity has greatly varied at different times, and in different places, the cause of the disease being altogether obscure ; but there is no doubt of its being communicated by contagion. A cow, when first attacked, strays away from her companions, eats but little, and is dull of habit. Sometimes the first presence of the disease is manifested by cold extremities, with a staring coat, followed by a reaction, when the extremities become hot, and a discharge of saliva takes place from the mouth ; the tongue being found swollen, while she appears to be tender in the feet, the muzzle feeling dry and hot, with evident feverish symptoms. In the course of the first day, vesicles are found on the tip and upper part of the tongue, as well as other parts of the mouth, the lips, and between the hoofs and the heels, the teats and udder being sometimes covered with vesicles like the tongue. After a while, the cow feeds slowly and with difficulty, and evidently experiences pain in mastication. The vesicles burst and discharge a thin serum, with increased soreness of the mouth, and greater discharge of saliva. Sometimes there are swellings, like small bladders, along the back and loins, which seem as if filled with air upon pressure. This goes on for about five days, when in favourable cases the animal gets better, and shows a disposition to eat, and although she may be pulled down a great deal, gets rapidly well afterwards.

These are the ordinary symptoms and presentment of the complaint; but sometimes a low typhoid form is assumed, and a putrid state produced. At other times, when there is a predisposition inherent in the animal to become so affected, it appears to be complicated with inflammation of the lungs, spasmodic affection of the bowels, or inflammation of the liver. Under a mild form of the disease, the animals affected will get well without any medical assistance; but when bleeding to excess, which has a very weakening tendency, has sometimes been done, or other improper treatment resorted to, it takes the form of typhus fever, which will carry off the animal.

The treatment to be adopted is, to apply astringents to the mouth and feet, relaxing the bowels, and moderating the fever which prevails, and afterwards encourage the appetite by giving tonics. Epsom salts is a good aperient medicine, and sulphur mixed with it has a cooling tendency, while a good tonic is made of gentian root, ginger, and sulphate of iron, in the proportion of two drachms of each. A solution of alum, with which a little treacle is mixed, will be found useful for the mouth, and the feet should be treated with an astringent.

A Mr. Bruce upon one occasion published an account of the method he followed upon his farm in Aberdeenshire, which was very successful. As soon as he discovered the disease amongst his herd of cattle he had all his healthy animals dressed with a solution of carbolic acid and water, in the proportion of one ounce of acid to one quart of water. He also applied to their feet a mixture of the acid and common gas tar—one-third of the former to two of the latter. The result of this treatment was that not a single animal was affected that had previously been dressed, although, in many instances, they had frequently come in contact with diseased ones, which were suffering acutely from it. I ought also to add that if the udder is affected, local bleeding and fomentations will be of advantage; and if the liver and lungs should prove to be out of order, appropriate treatment must be resorted to.

Paralysis, Palsy, or Tail-slip.—Most of the diseases to which cows are subject are brought on by bad management or neglect; and tail-slip, as it is vulgarly called, is a very prominent instance, mostly occurring with animals that are much exposed, or have been kept in damp places, or indifferently fed; young stock, for which almost anything is thought good enough by some people, being very subject to it. The seat of disease does not, however, arise in the tail, in which region of the animal cow-doctors say a worm has taken up its habitation, and who commonly make an incision in that part which is weakest, or where the joint appears to be loosest; the inability to raise the tail in making excretions of dung and urine, by which the hind parts become very filthy, arising from weakness or paralysis. It is true the sore in the tail will induce the animal to make efforts to move it about when it becomes painful, and the warm stimulating drinks which are generally given, coupled with improvement in keep, will sometimes strengthen the muscles which move the tail, and moderate or stop the scouring. But as to the removal of a worm by slitting the tail, there is never a worm there to move—though in some country districts it would be considered rank heresy to doubt of its existence—rheumatism being the first active cause, ending in palsy; so that making an incision in the tail, at best, will be merely a temporary remedy, caused by the bloodletting, which would be of advantage.

The proper treatment to be pursued is, to bleed in the first place, administer a purgative, combined with a carminative; stimulate, or blister, the loins, as well as any other affected parts; and insert a seton in the dewlap. Above all things, however, the animal must be comfortably and warmly housed, exposure to the weather being the most common occasion of the disease, particularly affecting cows in exposed situations, open to a cutting east or north-east wind. Plenty of good nutritious food should be given afterwards, coupled with warm stimulating medicine; linseed meal, or oil-cake perhaps, being about the best food to give. The disease sometimes comes on gradually, but is more often sudden in its appearance, resembling in its effects an attack of lumbago in the human patient; the first symptoms being that the animal is unable to rise, caused by want of power, and there will be tenderness upon the loins and about the rump, the skin being tight near those parts.

Redwater.—Redwater is a disease of the digestive organs, especially of the liver; the urine being surcharged with biliary matter which ought to have passed away by other channels. By many, it is attributed to disease of the kidneys, but this is not so, evidenced by an absence of any flakes of blood in the urine, the affected animal not suffering either from great tenderness of the loins, which is always associated with inflammation of the kidneys. The disease usually makes its appearance in hot weather, or after it, and is sometimes brought on by a change from poor pastures to rich ones, or from marshy and cold to dry and stimulating pasturage, or richer food. Cows are sometimes subject to it several weeks after having calved.

In most cases, diarrhœa first sets in, which is followed by constipation, when the pulse and the breathing become accelerated, and the appetite is impaired. The flow of milk is diminished, and rumination ceases; while the urine is brown, and perhaps afterwards becomes black. The main part of adequate treatment consists in regulating the bowels, and bringing back the system to a healthy condition from its temporary derangement; and a draught composed of the following should be given:

Sulphate of magnesia	12 ounces
Sulphur	4 ,,
Carbonate of ammonia	4 drachms
Powdered ginger	3 ,,
Calomel	1 scruple

The best form to administer it, is in warm gruel. After this, a fourth of the above, with the calomel, may be repeated every six hours, until the bowels are well moved, after which it will be found expedient to administer mild stimulants with diuretics, as:

Spirit of nitrous ether	1 ounce
Sulphate of potash	2 drachms
Ginger	1 drachm
Gentian root	1 ,,

The above should be given in gruel twice a day.

HEPATITIS.

Hepatitis.—An abundant supply of nutritious food being often given to cows, with the view of increasing the flow of milk, in some cases, owing to the predisposition of the animal, a too plethoric condition of the system is induced, which will bring on hepatitis, or active inflammation of the liver, which is a somewhat rare disease with cows; but is also sometimes brought on by exposure to heat, from their being overdriven, or by a sudden change in the temperature, or by a thorough alteration in their food, or from any cause which has the effect of deranging the digestive organs.

The first sign is a decrease in the quantity of milk yielded, and the cream presents a somewhat ropy appearance, the appetite falling off, and the cow showing signs of impaired activity; with a stiffened, staggering, or halting gait; the nose becoming alternately dry and moist. As the disorder progresses, rumination is only partially performed, or altogether ceases; and when the disease has lasted for a long time, and recovery is about to set in, a yellow scurf rises from the skin. Inflammation begins in one or more quarters of the udder, and tumours make their appearance in different parts of the body, which at length burst and discharge matter; and in some cases these indications are accompanied with a short, sore cough. Constipation is the usual accompaniment, the excretions being covered with mucous and vitiated bile of a dark-coloured appearance; which is succeeded by diarrhœa, after the lapse of several days. In some cases, the cow suffers from violent purging, the excretions being of a very dark colour, and extremely offensive, the pulse being intermittent and feeble—the result of the liver having lost its power, and the bile unfit for performing its usual office, being either inactive, or of a vitiated quality, and thus unable to carry on its wonted office. Like as in the human body, upon the occasions of derangement of the system, when calomel has to be resorted to, mercurial preparations need to be administered, so as "to touch the liver," and calomel, in doses of a scruple, should be given twice a day, with one or two scruples of opium. The treatment of the disorder must, however, be modified in accordance with the symptoms exhibited, but the bowels should always be cleared out by a dose of Epsom salts. A blister may also be applied with advantage.

In cases of chronic hepatitis, the same treatment should be pursued with this difference, that the doses should be smaller, but continued longer, and mercurial ointment rubbed into the right side.

I should never think of keeping an animal, myself, afflicted with any chronic disorder, for, however interesting prolonged treatment may be to the veterinary surgeon from a scientific or professional point of view, it is no joke to have to look after an ailing animal for a continued length of time; but in the case of a prized or valued beast, it may be sometimes deemed necessary to spare no pains or trouble to effect a cure; and under such circumstances it is, at all events, desirable to know how to set about it.

Rheumatism, Joint-felon, Chine-felon.—Rheumatism is often referred to under the designations of joint-felon and chine-felon; generally being produced by exposure to the weather, and is sometimes partial, and at others very severe; the fibrous tissues becoming affected, which is sometimes extended to the serous membrane lining the chest, and investing the heart. The disorder is manifested much in the same manner as in the human subject, being characterised by great stiffness of the joints and pain in moving.

Bleeding is generally recommended in the first instance, and purgative medicine given, together with an ounce of spirit of nitrous ether. The latter, being a very useful remedy, may be given twice a day, with a drachm of tartarised antimony and one of colchicum. It is also found advisable to foment the parts principally affected, and afterwards to rub them well with a stimulating liniment.

Quarter-ill, Blood-striking, or Black-quarter.— There are two distinct diseases described under the above names, or if they are not distinct, the same disease, or diseases, closely resembling each other are brought about by totally opposite causes, most frequently happening to yearling heifers and two-year-old heifers. The young animals mostly get it from lying on cold, damp soil, particularly when there have been hoar-frosts. In the one case, it usually makes its appearance in the early part of winter, and its course is so swift, that an animal, quite well to all appearance on the preceding evening, may be found dead the next morning. When the cases are not thus suddenly fatal, the animal is found with one quarter very much swollen, hence the term "quarter-ill," accompanied with a good deal of lameness, and if the swelling continues to increase, the case soon proves hopeless. After death, upon examination, the affected parts will be found nearly black, from distension of the capillaries with black blood; lymph being deposited amongst the muscles, and air infiltrated into the cellular membrane, which accounts for the crackling noise which is heard, when the hand is drawn over the beast while living; and unless these swellings can be dispersed, death soon ensues.

In consequence of the rapidity of the disorder, little can be done in checking its progress, the best course to pursue being to bleed, unless the pulse be very feeble; before doing which, a diffusible stimulant should be administered—as, two ounces of spirits of nitrous ether, together with a drachm of camphor, given with warm gruel.

The other phase of the disease is exhibited at a different time of the year, and may often be attributed to an injudicious change from poor winter food, when the animals are fed with difficulty perhaps, to rich and luxuriant pasture, or succulent grasses, which tend greatly to increase the supply of blood, which takes this form of disorder, instead of the more common one of diarrhœa, by which nature exerts a modifying influence, and endeavours to relieve the system. Bleeding freely should be resorted to as quickly as possible, and the bowels should be well opened. By gradually changing the pastures and the food, so as not to run from one extreme to another, the disorder, when it arises from this cause, may be prevented. The same also under the first-named aspect, which can be guarded against by housing the young animals at night, and putting them into sheltered yards, before the winter comes on, and not leaving it to the last minute.

I once lost, from this disorder, the handsomest one-year-old heifer I ever had, which was of a beautiful dun colour, a cross between an Alderney cow and a first-rate shorthorn young bull a neighbour of mine possessed. It was about the second or third calf that I had reared, and gave promise of turning out a splendid cow; and as I had only just then turned my attention to these matters, when it was found dead one morning, having been apparently in sound health the night previous, we none of us were able to assign any reasonable cause for such a sudden death. I knew very little about such matters then, but it was towards the close of autumn, or beginning of winter, and we used to allow the calves to stay out all night after they had had the run of the meadows for the whole summer, thinking the accessible part of the plantations sufficient shelter for them, and my subsequent experience, which I have derived from reading and observation, and hearing of similar cases, causes me to identify the mysterious loss, as it appeared to us at the time, with quarter-ill. I had the skin tanned, and it has been used as a hearthrug in an odd room that is set aside as a receptacle for odds and ends.

Fardel-bound.—A disease known under this name appears to consist in the retention of food in the reticulum, or second stomach of the cow, which is seldom diseased, unless in connection with some other disorder, such as derangement of the rumen. The stomachs of the ox are four in number, the digestive organs being of a somewhat complicated character, a much more elaborate course of digestion having to be gone through than in the case of the horse. The food seems to get impacted firmly between the plaits of this stomach, and this may probably be due to the presence of narcotic plants in the pastures, or to too large a quantity of dry food, unaccompanied with sufficient moisture, or by some other cause, which has resulted in derangement of the digestive organs.

The most appropriate treatment consists in giving opening medicines together with stomachics, such as Epsom salts, combined with ginger. The fine sense of smell possessed by herbivorous animals generally causes them to reject unsuitable food, when poisonous plants abound in a pasture, but they are accidentally partaken of at times, and the main object should be to empty the stomach of its contents as speedily as possible.

Blain, or Gloss Anthrax.—Blain is an inflammation of the membrane lining the mouth and tongue, which is sometimes confounded with the epidemic, as it is called, or foot and mouth disease. The tongue swells very much, accompanied with much soreness, upon which vesicles form, ending at times in mortification, the disorder being of a very virulent character, as the animal, under its worst forms, becomes either suffocated or starved.

The main thing is to lose no time, but lance any vesicle that has formed, and abstract some blood from the roof of the mouth. The bowels should be opened, but the animal not violently purged, and small doses of nitre and tartarised antimony given daily, either with linseed gruel, or in the water supplied. The mouth should be washed twice a day with a lotion formed of the following ingredients:

Powdered alum	2 drachms
Sulphate of zinc	1 scruple
Treacle	1 ounce
Warm water	16 ounces

Foul in the Foot, Loo, or Low.—Inflammation, and lameness, are generally the first indications of this disease, which resembles somewhat the foot-rot in sheep. This is followed by soreness between the claws, offensive matter being discharged from the foot. Sometimes abscesses repeatedly form, and prove extremely troublesome. Cows which are turned out on wet or marshy land are the most liable to it, which may be traced to moisture and the friction of mud between the claws. The affected part should be kept free from moisture, and a slough produced by means of an escharotic. A large pledget of tow covered with tar, on which sulphate of copper may be spread, should be placed between the claws, and renewed as often as necessary, which may probably be in the course of every forty-eight hours.

The Thrush, or Aphthæ.—This ailment takes the form of small pustules, which cover both the tongue and the membrane lining the mouth. These break, and become sores, and heal in the course of about ten days, and are produced by the heat of the system. Cooling medicine, as Epsom salts, should be given, and a weak solution of alum applied to the mouth. This treatment will hasten on the cure.

Mange.—Mange in cows is the result of either poor living or contagion, and proceeds from the presence of *acarus*, an insect that burrows beneath the skin, where it will breed to a great extent if not checked. The presence of these parasites causes an intolerable itching, and the animal rubbing itself, wherever it has the chance, the affected part soon becomes sore and denuded of hair, and the skin after a while becomes thickened and drawn up.

The mange may be cured by using an ointment composed of the following ingredients:

Sulphur vivum	4 ounces
Linseed oil	8 "
Oil of turpentine	2 "

This should be well rubbed in, plenty of friction being used in the operation.

In warm or showery weather, cows are subjected to the attacks of various insects, as breeze flies, clegs, and stouts, the irritation from which, at times, drives them almost frantic; while little flies (*simulium*), especially, congregate about cattle on heaths and marshes by thousands, getting into their ears; and there are others which alight on the lips, nostrils, and eyes. The discomfort and annoyance produced by these have a very unfavourable effect upon the general condition of the cows, while they are exposed to their onslaughts, and it is a good plan to get them under cover in hot weather, when they are likely to be thus tormented.

Lice.—When cows have been reduced by poor living, lice are apt to infest them, and prove the source of a good deal of irritation, though not so much so as mange. These may be got rid of by applying the ointment recommended for mange, or by a decoction of strong tobacco-water.

Scouring, the Scant, Diarrhœa.—Diarrhœa is mostly brought on by unwholesome or improper food, and a change of diet will generally remove the ailment; but if it does not stop, an astringent and tonic should be given, for which there are many well-known recipes in use, the following being a very efficacious one:

Prepared chalk	2 ounces
Gentian root, powdered	2 drachms
Opium ,,	½ drachm

This is best given in gruel, once or twice a day, the gruel being somewhat thick.

Diarrhœa may, however, proceed from other causes, the most simple form being the relaxed state of the mucous coat of the small intestines. In the worst cases there will be found to be either disease of the liver or the stomach, and particularly the maniplus. If the liver is affected, which may be seen from the offensive condition of the dung, calomel, combined with opium, in the proportion of half a drachm of each, should be given twice a day.

Catarrh.—Young animals suffer more than old cows from diseases affecting the air-passages, particularly in the spring, when east winds mostly prevail in England, as well as in wet weather in autumn. As the cows grow older, they get more seasoned, and accustomed to the weather, but when the disorder makes its appearance, the beast, at whatever age, should be comfortably housed, and supplied with a good warm bed to lie on, and warm bran mashes given to it, in which there is a little nitre. This treatment will generally be found sufficient to effect a cure; but should the ailment prove severe, and display signs of inflammation, moderate bleeding is recommended, together with a dose of Epsom salts.

A stimulating liniment can be rubbed into the

throat, or a seton inserted. The following will form an effectual liniment :

Powdered cantharides	1 ounce
Olive oil	6 ounces
Oil of turpentine	2 ,,

well mixed up together.

Sometimes catarrh is epidemic, the animals suffering from great debility, and in severe cases turning even to gangrene.

Bronchitis.—Neglected catarrh often turns to bronchitis, which consists of a more extensive inflammation over the same membrane, extending to a more dangerous degree to the internal surface of the lungs, the symptoms being similar to the former, but greater pain evidently accompanying the act of coughing.

It is best to bleed at an early stage of the disease, and insert a seton in the brisket, and give mild, aperient, febrifuge medicine.

By proper attention, and careful management, nearly all the disorders to which cows are subject may be avoided, as they mostly arise from causes which may be prevented; and, according to the well-worn adage, "prevention is better than cure."

I have, I believe, enumerated most of the disorders to which cows are principally subject, excepting a few —which I shall name under another heading—common to all cattle alike; and while in all serious cases it will be the best, and safest, course to call in an experienced veterinary surgeon—one who thoroughly understands his business—yet prompt treatment, taking things in good time, and applying a proper remedy will often be the means of keeping off an illness which may, at a later stage, be very difficult to cure. A general theoretical knowledge of the various forms of the most common ailments, with a description of their general appearance, will, at all events, guide the inexperienced dairy-farmer as to the nature of the primary treatment to be resorted to. Of course he can hardly be expected to perform surgical operations; and, in my own case, I take care to make myself "conspicuous by my absence" whenever some of the rather disgusting operations are obliged to be performed on the cattle, in the ordinary way, such as those connected with parturition, which my working bailiff has the sole and undisputed charge of; while I act the rôle of consulting physician only, and am quite content to leave all surgical operations to others better qualified to witness them; although I make a point of walking amongst my cattle, and inspecting them narrowly; and frequently on a winter's night, when the ground has been covered with snow, I have gone through the cattle-sheds in company with my foreman, carrying a lantern, to see that the animals were all comfortable for the night.

To me, this has never been a hardship; though, as I have said, I always shirk the grosser matters, which, on account of my squeamishness, I am rather helpless with—upon one occasion to my cost. For upon a bitter cold Christmas-eve, expecting a fine sow to litter that had been watched all day, my foreman came to me and said, "I have made the old sow comfortable for the night, sir, and don't think she will 'pig' before morning, and I should like to go away if you will allow me."

I did not like to refuse him upon such an occasion, when he wished to go away and enjoy himself—all our men having little presents given to them by my wife at Christmas-time. But, sure enough, he had not been gone an hour before somebody found out the sow wanted looking to, and before anyone could be found—for I would not have anything to do with the matter—two or three of the little pigs had crawled outside and were half frozen before matters were properly adjusted; and we had a smaller litter of pigs in consequence, as some of them died from the exposure to cold.

FEBRUARY, 1895.

A

CLASSIFIED

CATALOGUE OF BOOKS

PUBLISHED BY

CHAPMAN & HALL, Ld.

11, HENRIETTA STREET, COVENT GARDEN, W.C.

Contents.

	PAGE		PAGE
INDEX OF AUTHORS	2	MILITARY	17
NEW AND FORTHCOMING BOOKS	3	MISCELLANEOUS	18
AGRICULTURE, FARMING, HORTICULTURE, Etc.	5	MUSIC, DRAMA, Etc.	19
		NATURAL HISTORY	19
ART	6	SCIENCE AND TECHNOLOGY	20
BIOGRAPHY AND REMINISCENCES	9	SPORT	21
COOKERY, Etc.	11	THEOLOGY, PHILOSOPHY, SOCIOLOGY, Etc.	22
FICTION	12		
HISTORY AND POLITICS	14	TRAVEL	23
LITERATURE, BELLES LETTRES, AND POETRY	16	THOMAS CARLYLE'S WORKS	25-36
		CHARLES DICKENS'S WORKS	27-31

A Separate ILLUSTRATED CATALOGUE is issued,

CONTAINING

Drawing Examples, Diagrams, Models, Instruments, etc.,

ISSUED UNDER THE AUTHORITY OF

THE SCIENCE AND ART DEPARTMENT.

INDEX OF AUTHORS.

Name	Page	Name	Page	Name	Page	Name	Page
Ablett (Wm.)	5	Dickens (Charles)	12, 14, 18, 24, 27-32	Kelly (J. F.)	10	Rankin (T. T.)	21
—— (T. R.)	8	Dickens (Mary A.)	13	Kempt (R.)	10	Reade (Mrs. R. H.)	13
About (F.)	22	Diets (E.)	21	Kennard (E.)	22	Redgrave (E.)	8
Adams (H.), M.I.C.E.	20	Dilke (Lady)	6	Kennard (H. M.)	22	—— (R.)	8
Afalo (F. G.)	21	Dinarte (Sylvio)	12	Kent (Chas.)	18	—— (S.)	8
Aitchison (G.), A.R.A.	5	Dixon (Charles)	19	L—— (Major)	11	Reid (Sir T. Wemyss)	11
Alexander (Mrs.)	11	Douglas (J.)	20	Lacordaire (Père)	22	Renan (E.)	11, 16, 22
Allen (Grant)	13	Drayson (Major-Gen. A. W.)	10, 17, 20	Lainé (J. M.)	18	Riano (Juan E.)	8
Anderson (A. A.)	11			Laing (S.)	22	Ribton-Turner (C. J.)	16
Anderson (Capt. L.)	12	Duckill (H. J.)	11	Lamennais (F.)	23	Roberts (Morley)	13, 14
Angel (H.)	6	Ducoudray (G.)	14, 19	Landor (W. S.)	17	Robinson (J. F.)	5
Armstrong (W.)	6, 7, 9	Dyce (Wm.)	6	Lanin (E. B.)	15	—— (J. C.)	8
Aveling (E.)	20			Laveleye (E. de)	23	Robson (Geo.)	21
Avon	21	Earl (Mrs.)	23	Le Conte (J.)	19	R. O. C.	11
Bailey (Capt. H.)	21	Edwards (Mrs. S.)	12, 13, 14	Lee (F.)	10, 17	Rochfort (Louisa)	11
Bailey (J. B.)	9	Eliot (Mrs. F. M.)	15	Lefevre (A.)	23	Rock (Very Rev. Canon)	11
Baker (W. L.) A.M.I.C.E.	20	Ellis (Col. A. B.)	12, 15, 17, 22	Le Roux (H.)	19	Roland (A.)	5
Barfield (T. C.)	6	Engel (Carl)	6, 19	Leroy-Beaulieu (A.)	23	Roosevelt (R.)	11
Barrie (J. M.)	11	Escott (T. H. S.)	11	Leslie (R. C.)	10, 20, 24	Ross (Mrs. J.)	11
Beatty-Kingston (W.)	9, 19	Fane (Violet)	13, 17	Letourneau (Dr. C.)	23	Russan (A.)	12
Bell (Jas., Ph.D.)	6	Farr (Wm.)	18	Lilly (W. S.)	23	Russell (W. Clark)	13
Benson (W.)	6	Field (Henry M.)	24	Lineham (Mrs. R. S.)	7	Russell (Col. F.)	11, 18
Bentley (H. C.)	16, 21	Fiske (J.)	10	—— (W. J.)	21	Ryan (C.)	8
Bianci (G. H.)	8	Fitzgerald (Percy)	10, 15, 19	Linton (Mrs. Lynn)	13	Schadow (Dr. F.)	5
Billington (M. F.)	23	Fleming (Geo., F.R.C.S.)	5, 18	Little (Rev. H. W.)	10	Schauermann (F. L.)	8
Birdwood (Sir G. C. M., C.S.I.)	6	Forster (John)	10	—— (Rev. Canon Knox)	14	Scott (John)	16
Bloomfield, Lady	5	Forsyth (Captain)	27, 24	Lloyd (W. W.)	17	Seeman (O.)	8
Bonvalot (G.)	23	Fortnum (C. D. E.)	9	Long (J.)	5	Seton-Karr (H. W.)	22
Bos (Dr. J. R.)	5, 19	Foster (A. J.)	24	Low (Wm.)	11	Sexton (A. H.)	16, 21
Boulger (D. C.)	12	Fouqué (De la M.)	12	M'Dermott (P. L.)	15	Shepherd (Major)	5
Boyle (F.)	5, 12	Francatelli (C. E.)	11	Macdonald (A. F.)	15	Shirreff (E.)	11, 18
Bowne (E. S.)	9	Franks (A. W.)	6	McCoan (J. C.)	15	Shore (A.)	17
Brackenbury (Col. C. B.)	9, 14, 17	Gallenger (A.)	15	Malleson (Col. G. B.)	10, 11	Simkin (R.)	18
Bradley (Thos.)	7	Gardner (J. S.)	6	Mallet (J.)	11	Simmonds (T. L.)	21
Bridgman (F. A.)	23	Garnier (E.)	9	Mallock (W. H.)	12	Simpson (A. C. M.)	10
Brock (Dr. J. H. E.)	20	Gasnault (P.)	6	Marceau (Sergent)	10	Sinnett (A. P.)	13, 23
Bromley-Davenport (W.)	21	Gillmore (P.)	22	Marmery	23	Smith (Major R. M.)	8
Buckland (F.)	19, 21	Gingell (J. R.)	23	Maskell (A.)	9	"Snaffle"	22
Buffen (F. F.)	9, 19	Gleichen (Count)	17, 24	—— (W.)	7	Spalding (Lt.-Col.)	11, 18
Burchell (R.)	6	Gordon (General)	10, 17	Masp:ro (G.)	7	Spencer (Herbert)	23
Burgess (E.)	21	Gorst (Sir J. E.)	15	Meredith (Geo.)	13	Statham (H. H.)	8, 19
Burton (Lady I.)	14	Gower (A. R.)	20	Mills (John)	21	Steele (Anna C.)	13
Butler (A. J.)	14	Greater Britain (Author of)	14, 15, 17	Mitre (General Don B.)	15	Stoddard (C. A.)	24
Carlyle (Thomas)	9, 14, 16, 17, 18, 23, 26	Gresswell (Wm.)	15	Molesworth (W. N.)	15	Stokes (M.)	6
Carstensen (A. R.)	23	Greville-Nugent (Hon. Mrs.)	24	Moltke (Count von)	15	Story (W. W.)	16
Chamberlain (The Rt. Hon. J.)	16	Griffin (Sir Lepel)	13	Moorhead (W. K.)	9	Sutcliffe (J.)	8
Charlotte Elizabeth (Princess)	9	Griffiths (Major A.)	10, 17	Morley (Rt. Hon. John)	15	Sweetland (H. S.)	14
		Grimble (A.)	22	Muddock (J. F.)	13	Symonds (J. A.)	17
Charnay (D.)	23	Gundry (R. S.)	15	Muntz (E.)	7, 21	Tanner (Prof.)	5
Chaucer (Geoffrey)	12	Hall (Sidney)	18	Murray (Andrew)	20	Taylor (E. R.)	5
Chiplea (Charles)	7	Hardy (Thos.)	13	—— (H.)	13, 14	Temple (Sir R.)	17
Church (Prof. A. H.)	5, 6	Harper (C. G.)	6, 24	Necker (Madame)	7	Thomson (D. C.)	8
Collier (Hon. M.)	12	Harrison (John)	7	Nelson (W.)	21	Thrupp (G. A.)	8
Collins (Wilkie)	12	Hartington (E.)	7	Nesbitt (A.)	7	Topinard (Dr. P.)	23
Cook (Clarence)	7	Hatton (R. G.)	7	Newey (H. F.)	7	Tovey (Lt.-Col.)	18
Cooper-King (Lt.-Col.)	9, 17	Hawkins (F.)	19	Newton (E. T., F.G.S.)	20	Traherne (Major)	20, 22
Couperus (Louis)	13	Hawthorn (Julian)	13	Norman (C. B.)	15	Trollope (A.)	13
Courtney (W. L.)	17, 22	Hay (Rev. J.)	10	North (Barker)	21	Troup (J. R.)	24
Craik (G. L.)	16, 17, 29	Henry (Re)		Norris (W. E.)	13	Underhill (G. F.)	14
Crawford (O.)	19, 21, 23	Henslow (Prof.)	5	O'Byrne (R.)	16, 18	Vandam (A. D.)	13
Cripps (W. J.)	6	Hildebrand (Hans)	7	O'Grady (Standish)	16	Veron (E.)	23
Curzon (Louis H.)	21	Hill (Miss G.)	5	Oliver (D.)		Verschoyle (Rev. J.)	14
Daly (J. B.)	14	Holbein	7	—— (E. E.)	24	Walford (Major)	11, 18
Das (D. N.)	5	Holmes (G. C. V.)	20	Oxenham (Rev. H. N.)	11	—— (Mrs. L. B.)	13
Daubourg (E.)	5	Hope (Andrée)	12, 15	Papus	18	Walker (Mrs.)	24
Davidson (T. A.)		Houssaye (A.)	19, 19	Paske (Sur.-Gen. C. T.)	21	Walker (General Sir C. P. B.)	11, 18
Dawson (W. H.)	14	Hovelacque (A.)	22	Paterson (A.)	13	Wall (A.)	18
Doy (Wm.)	21	Hozier (H. M.)	10, 17	Payn (James)	13	Wallis (G.)	13
De Ainslie (General)	17	Hudson (W. H.)	17	Payton (E. W.)	24	Ward (James)	9
De Bovet (Mdme.)	24	Hueffer (F.)	19	Pelagius	22	Ward (R.)	9
De Champeaux (A.)	9	Hughes (W. R.)	15	Perrot (Georges)	7, 8	Watson (A. E. T.)	22
De Falloux (Count)	10	Hunt (Mrs. Alfred)	13	Philips (F. C.)	13	Watson (John)	21
De Koninck (L. L.)	9	Huntly (Marquis of)	22	Pilling (Wm.)	15	Wegg-Prosser (F. R.)	16
De Lesseps (Ferdinand)	10	Hutchinson (Rev. H. N.)	20	Pitt-Taylor (F.)	16	Westall (Wm.)	13
Delille (E.)	17	Jackson (F. G.)	7	Pollen (J. H.)	9	White (Walter)	13
De Mandat-Grancey (Baron E.)	24	James (H. A.)	7	Pollok (Col.)	22, 24	Wicken (H. F.)	11
De Windt (H.)	14, 24	Jeaffreson (J. C.)	15	Poole (Stanley Lane)	8	Wiel (Hon. Mrs.)	13
D'Haussonville (Vicomte)	20	Jeans (W. T.)	9	Poynter (E. J.)	8	Wolverton (Lord)	22
D'Orleans (Prince H.)	24	Jokai (Maurus)	12, 13	Pratt (Robert)	13	Woodgate (W. B.)	23
		Jopling (Louise)	7	Purcell (T. A.)	22	Wornum (R. N.)	9
		Junker (Wm.)	24	Pusbsin (A. S.)	13, 14	Worsae (J. J. A.)	9
				Rae (W. Fraser)	18	Wrightson (Prof. John)	5
				Ramsden (Lady G.)	18	Younge (C. D.)	11

NEW AND FORTHCOMING BOOKS.

R. S. GUNDRY.

China, Present and Past: Foreign Intercourse, Progress and Resources, The Missionary Question, &c. By R. S. GUNDRY, Author of "China and her Neighbours." Demy 8vo.

OSWALD CRAWFURD.

A Year of Sport and Natural History. Shooting, Hunting, Coursing, Falconry, and Fishing. Edited by OSWALD CRAWFURD. With Chapters on Birds of Prey, Nidifications of Birds, and the Habits of British Wild Birds and Animals. With numerous Illustrations by FRANK FELLER, CECIL ALDIN, A. T. ELWES, STANLEY BERKELEY, &c. Demy 4to. 21s.

CHARLES DIXON.

The Migration of British Birds: including their Post-Glacial Emigration as Traced by the Application of a New Law of Dispersal. Being a Contribution to the Study of Migration, Geographical Distribution, and Insular Faunas. By CHARLES DIXON. With Maps. Crown 8vo.

A. E. T. WATSON.

Sketches in the Hunting Field. By A. E. T. WATSON. A New Edition, with numerous Illustrations by JOHN STURGESS. Crown 8vo. 3s. 6d.

G. F. UNDERHILL AND H. S. SWEETLAND.

Through a Field Glass. By G. F. UNDERHILL and H. S. SWEETLAND. With Illustrations by L. THACKERAY, Crown 8vo. 2s.

AUGUSTUS GRIMBLE.

Highland Sport. By AUGUSTUS GRIMBLE. With Illustrations by A. THORBURN. Large Paper Edition. £2 2s. net.

"SNAFFLE."

Gun, Rifle, and Hound, in East and West. By "SNAFFLE." With Illustrations by H. DIXON. Demy 8vo. 14s.

COLONEL POLLOK.

Incidents of Foreign Sport and Travel. By Colonel POLLOK, Author of "Sport in British Burma." With Illustrations by A. T. ELWES. Demy 8vo. 16s.

GENERAL SIR C. P. BEAUCHAMP WALKER, K.C.B.

Days of a Soldier's Life. Written during active service in the Crimean, Chinese, Austro-Prussian ('66), and Franco-German ('70-'71) Wars, by General Sir C. P. BEAUCHAMP WALKER. Demy 8vo., with Portrait. 18s.

COLONEL G. B. MALLESON, C.S.I.

Life of Warren Hastings: First Governor-General of India. By Colonel G. B. MALLESON, C.S.I. With Portrait. Demy 8vo. 18s.

LIEUT.-COLONEL COOPER-KING.

Life of George Washington. By Lieut.-Colonel COOPER-KING. With Maps and Plans. Large Crown 8vo. 6s.

FITZHUGH LEE.
General Lee, of the Confederate Army. By FITZHUGH LEE, his Nephew. With Portrait and Maps. Crown 8vo. 6s.

MARY FRANCES BILLINGTON.
Woman in India. By MARY FRANCES BILLINGTON. With an Introduction by the Marchioness of DUFFERIN AND AVA, C.I., and numerous Illustrations by HERBERT JOHNSON, and others. Dedicated by permission to H.R.H. the DUCHESS of CONNAUGHT. Demy 8vo. 14s.

CHARLES G. HARPER.
The Marches of Wales: Notes and Impressions on the Welsh Borders, from the Severn Sea to the Sands o' Dee. By CHARLES G. HARPER. With 114 Illustrations. Demy 8vo. 16s.

PERROT AND CHIPIEZ.
The History of Art in Primitive Greece. (Mycenian Art.) By GEORGES PERROT and CHARLES CHIPIEZ. With 553 Illustrations. Two vols. Imperial 8vo. 42s.

CHARLES DICKENS AND GEORGE CRUIKSHANK.
The Adventures of Oliver Twist: or, the Parish Boy's Progress. By CHARLES DICKENS. An Edition de Luxe. With Twenty-six Water-colour Drawings by GEORGE CRUIKSHANK. Imperial 8vo. 42s. net.

V. MARMERY.
The Progress of Science: its Origin, Course, Promoters and Results. By V. MARMERY. Demy 8vo. 7s. 6d.

W. J. LINEHAM.
A Text-book of Mechanical Engineering. By WILFRID J. LINEHAM, Head of the Engineering Department at the Goldsmiths' Institute. With numerous Illustrations. Crown 8vo. 10s. 6d. net.

GEORGE V. C. HOLMES.
Naval Architecture and Shipbuilding. By GEORGE V. C. HOLMES, Author of "Marine Engines and Boilers." With Illustrations. Crown 8vo.

HENRY ADAMS, M.I.C.E.
Machine Construction and Drawing. (Elementary.) A Key to the Examinations of the Science and Art Department. By HENRY ADAMS, M.I.C.E., Author of "Building Construction." Crown 8vo. 2s. 6d.

H. H. STATHAM.
Architecture for General Readers: to which is added an Historical Sketch of Architecture. By H. HEATHCOTE STATHAM. With hundreds of Illustrations by the Author.

HENRY ANGEL.
Practical Plane and Solid Geometry. By HENRY ANGEL, Lecturer at the Birkbeck Institute. Crown 8vo.

R. G. HATTON.
Figure Drawing and Composition. By R. G. HATTON, Author of "Textbook of Elementary Design." Illustrated. Crown 8vo.

CATALOGUE OF BOOKS

PUBLISHED BY

CHAPMAN & HALL, LIMITED.

―――◆―――

Agriculture, Farming, Horticulture, &c.

Agricultural Science (Lectures on), AND OTHER PROCEEDINGS OF THE INSTITUTE OF AGRICULTURE, SOUTH KENSINGTON, 1883-84. Crown 8vo., sewed, 2s.

Agricultural Zoology. By Dr. J. RITZEMA BOS. Translated by Professor J. R. AINSWORTH DAVIS, B.A., F.C.P. With an Introduction by MISS E. A. ORMEROD, F.R.Met.S., F.R.M.S., etc. With 149 Illustrations. Crown 8vo., 6s.

About Orchids: A Chat. By FREDERICK BOYLE. With Coloured Illustrations. Large crown 8vo., 8s.

Food Grains of India. By Professor A. H. CHURCH, M.A. Oxon. With numerous Woodcuts. Small 4to., 6s.

Animal Plagues: THEIR HISTORY, NATURE, AND PREVENTION. By GEORGE FLEMING, F.R.C.S. 8vo., cloth, 15s.

Practical Lessons in Botany. Adapted for Beginners in all Classes. By the Rev. Professor HENSLOW. Illustrated. Crown 8vo., sewn, 6d.

The Pleasures and Profits of our Little POULTRY FARM. By Miss G. HILL. Small 8vo., 3s.

Dairy Farming. To which is added a Description of the Chief Continental Systems. By JAMES LONG. With numerous Illustrations. Crown 8vo., 9s.

Illustrations of the Principal Natural ORDERS OF THE VEGETABLE KINGDOM, PREPARED FOR THE SCIENCE AND ART DEPARTMENT, SOUTH KENSINGTON. By D. OLIVER, LL.D., F.L.S., F.R.S., &c. New Edition, revised by Author. With 109 Coloured Plates. Royal 8vo., 16s.

British Bee Farming: Its Profits and Pleasures. By JAMES F. ROBINSON. Large crown 8vo., 5s.

Farming for Pleasure and Profit. By ARTHUR ROLAND. Edited by WILLIAM ABLETT. 8 vols. Crown 8vo., 5s. each.

DAIRY - FARMING, MANAGEMENT OF COWS, etc.

POULTRY-KEEPING.

TREE-PLANTING, FOR ORNAMENTATION OR PROFIT.

STOCK-KEEPING AND CATTLE-REARING.

DRAINAGE OF LAND, IRRIGATION, MANURES, etc.

ROOT-GROWING, HOPS, etc.

MANAGEMENT OF GRASS LANDS, LAYING DOWN GRASS, ARTIFICIAL GRASSES, etc.

MARKET GARDENING, HUSBANDRY FOR FARMERS AND GENERAL CULTIVATORS.

Prairie Experiences in Handling CATTLE AND SHEEP. By Major SHEPHERD, R.E. With Illustrations and Map. Demy 8vo., 10s. 6d.

Holt Castle; or, Threefold Interest in Land. By Prof. TANNER, F.C.S. Cr. 8vo., 4s. 6d.

Jack's Education; or, How He Learnt Farming. By Professor TANNER, F.C.S. Second Edition. Crown 8vo., 3s. 6d.

Principles of Agricultural Practice AS AN INSTRUCTIONAL SUBJECT. By Prof. JOHN WRIGHTSON, M.R.A.C., F.C.S., &c., President of the College of Agriculture, Downton. With Geological Map. Second Edition. Crown 8vo., 5s.

Fallow and Fodder Crops. By Prof. JOHN WRIGHTSON, M.R.A.C., F.C.S., &c., President of the College of Agriculture, Downton. Crown 8vo., 5s.

Art.

Written Design. By T. R. ABLETT. Oblong, sewed, 6*d*.

Practical Plane and Solid Geometry. By HENRY ANGEL, Lecturer at the Birkbeck Institute. Crown 8vo.

Key to Examinations of Science and ART DEPARTMENT. (Subject I.)

Alfred Stevens (Sculptor). A Biographical Sketch. By W. ARMSTRONG. Fully illustrated. Imp. 4to., handsomely bound, 10*s*. 6*d*.

Charts for Model Drawing. By T. C. BARFIELD. 8*s*.

Principles of the Science of Colour. By W. BENSON. 4to., 15*s*.

The Industrial Arts of India. By Sir GEORGE C. M. BIRDWOOD, C.S.I. With Map and 174 Illustrations. New Edition. Demy 8vo., 14*s*.

Elements of Geometrical Drawing. By THOMAS BRADLEY, Royal Military Academy, Woolwich. In Two Parts, with Sixty Plates. Oblong folio, half bound, each Part 16*s*.

Linear Perspective, for the Use of Schools of Art. By R. BURCHETT. New Edition. With Illustrations. Post 8vo., cloth, 7*s*.

Practical Geometry: The Course of Construction of Plane Geometrical Figures. By R. BURCHETT. With 137 Diagrams. Eighteenth Edition. Post 8vo., cloth, 5*s*.

Definition of Geometry. By R. BURCHETT. 18mo., sewed, 5*d*.

English Porcelain: A Handbook to the China made in England during the 18th Century. By Prof. A. H. CHURCH, M.A. Oxon. With numerous Woodcuts. Large crown 8vo., 3*s*.

English Earthenware: A Handbook to the Wares made in England during the 17th and 18th Centuries. By Prof. A. H. CHURCH, M.A. Oxon. With numerous Woodcuts. Large crown 8vo., 3*s*.

Precious Stones: Considered in their Scientific and Artistic relations. By Prof. A. H. CHURCH, M.A. Oxon. With a Coloured Plate and Woodcuts. Second Edition. Large crown 8vo., 2*s*. 6*d*.

College and Corporation Plate. A Handbook for the Reproduction of Silver Plate. By WILFRED JOSEPH CRIPPS, M.A., F.S.A. With numerous Illustrations. Large crown 8vo., cloth, 2*s*. 6*d*.

Interior Architecture. Doors, Vestibules, Staircases, Anterooms, Drawing. Dining, and Bed Rooms, Libraries, Bank and Newspaper Offices, Shop Fronts and Interiors. By E. DAUBOURG. Half-imperial, cloth, £2 12*s*. 6*d*.

Tapestry. By ALFRED DE CHAMPEAUX. With numerous Woodcuts. Cloth, 2*s*. 6*d*.

Art in the Modern State. By Lady DILKE. With facsimile. Demy 8vo., 9*s*.

Drawing Book of the Government SCHOOL OF DESIGN. By WILLIAM DYCE, R.A. Fifty selected Plates. Folio, sewed, 5*s*.; mounted, 18*s*.

Elementary Outlines of Ornament. By WILLIAM DYCE, R.A. Plates I. to XXII., containing 97 Examples, adapted for Practice of Standards I. to IV. Small folio, sewed, 2*s*. 6*d*.

Selection from Dyce's Drawing Book. Fifteen Plates. Sewed, 1*s*. 6*d*.; mounted on cardboard, 6*s*. 6*d*.

Text to Dyce's Drawing Book. By WILLIAM DYCE, R.A. Crown 8vo., sewed, 6*d*.

Musical Instruments. By CARL ENGEL. With numerous Woodcuts. Large crown 8vo., cloth, 2*s*. 6*d*.

Maiolica. By C. D. E. FORTNUM, F.S.A. With numerous Woodcuts. Large crown 8vo., cloth, 2*s*. 6*d*.

Bronzes. By C. D. E. FORTNUM, F.S.A. With numerous Woodcuts. Large crown 8vo., cloth, 2*s*. 6*d*.

Japanese Pottery. Being a Native Report, with an Introduction and Catalogue. By A. W. FRANKS. With numerous Illustrations and Marks. Large crown 8vo., cloth, 2*s*. 6*d*.

Ironwork: From the Earliest Time to the End of the Mediæval Period. By J. STARKIE GARDNER. With 57 Illustrations. Large crown 8vo., 3*s*.

French Pottery. By PAUL GASNAULT and ED. GARNIER. With Illustrations and Marks. Large crown 8vo., 3*s*.

A Practical Handbook of Drawing FOR MODERN METHODS OF REPRODUCTION. By CHARLES G. HARPER. With many Illustrations showing comparative results. Crown 8vo., 7*s*. 6*d*.

ART—CONTINUED.

The Decoration of Metals: Chasing, REPOUSSÉ AND SAW PIERCING. By JOHN HARRISON. With 180 Illustrations. Crown 8vo., 3s. 6d.

Elementary Design: Being a Theoretical and Practical Introduction in the Art of Decoration. By RICHARD G. HATTON, Durham College of Science, Newcastle-on-Tyne. With 110 Illustrations. Crown 8vo., 2s. 6d.

Figure Drawing and Composition. Being a number of Hints for the Student and Designer upon the Treatment of the Human Figure. By R. G. HATTON, author of "Text-book of Elementary Design." With 500 Diagrams. Crown 8vo.

Industrial Arts of Scandinavia in the PAGAN TIME. By HANS HILDEBRAND. With numerous Woodcuts. Large crown 8vo., 2s. 6d.

Twelve Heads After Holbein. Selected from Drawings in Her Majesty's Collection at Windsor. Reproduced in Autotype in portfolio. £1 16s.

Industrial Arts: Historical Sketches. With numerous Illustrations. Large crown 8vo., 3s.

Theory and Practice of Design: An Advanced Text Book on Decorative Art. By FRANK G. JACKSON, Master in the Birmingham Municipal School of Art. With 700 Illustrations. Large crown 8vo., 9s.

Decorative Design. An Elementary Text Book of Principles and Practice. By FRANK G. JACKSON. With numerous Illustrations. Second Edition. Crown 8vo., 7s. 6d.

Handbook to Perspective. By HENRY A. JAMES, M.A. Crown 8vo., 2s. 6d.

Perspective Charts, for use in Class Teaching. By HENRY A. JAMES, M.A. 2s.

Hints to Amateurs. A Handbook on Art. By LOUISE JOPLING. With Diagrams. Crown 8vo., 1s. 6d.

The Street of Human Habitations. By Mrs. RAY S. LINEHAM. Fully Illustrated. Crown 8vo., 6s.

Russian Art and Art Objects in Russia. A Handbook to the Reproduction of Goldsmiths' Work and other Art Treasures. By ALFRED MASKELL. With Illustrations. Large crown 8vo., 4s. 6d.

Ivories: Ancient and Mediæval. By WILLIAM MASKELL. With numerous Woodcuts. Large crown 8vo., cloth, 2s. 6d.

Handbook to the Dyce and Forster COLLECTIONS. By WILLIAM MASKELL. With Illustrations. Large crown 8vo., cloth, 2s. 6d.

Life in Ancient Egypt and Assyria. By G. MASPÉRO, late Director of Archæology in Egypt, and Member of the Institute of France. Translated by A. P. MORTON. With 188 Illustrations. Third Thousand. Crown 8vo., 5s.

Raphael: His Life, Works, and Times. By EUGENE MUNTZ. Illustrated with about 200 Engravings. A New Edition, revised from the Second French Edition by W. ARMSTRONG, B.A. Oxon. Imperial 8vo., 25s.

Glass. By ALEXANDER NESBITT. With numerous Woodcuts. Large crown 8vo., cloth, 2s. 6d.

Elementary Drawing: A Few Suggestions for Students and Teachers. By H. FOSTER NEWEY, Birmingham School of Art. Illustrated. Crown 8vo., 2s. 6d.

A History of Ancient Art in Primitive GREECE. By GEORGES PERROT and CHARLES CHIPIEZ. With 553 Illustrations. 2 vols. Imperial 8vo. 42s.

A History of Ancient Art in Persia. By GEORGES PERROT and CHARLES CHIPIEZ. With 254 Illustrations, and 12 Steel and Coloured Plates. Imperial 8vo, 21s.

A History of Ancient Art in Phrygia — LYDIA, AND CARIA — LYCIA. By GEORGES PERROT and CHARLES CHIPIEZ. With 280 Illustrations. Imperial 8vo., 15s.

A History of Ancient Art in Sardinia, JUDÆA, SYRIA, AND ASIA MINOR. By GEORGES PERROT and CHARLES CHIPIEZ. With 395 Illustrations. 2 vols. Imperial 8vo., 36s.

A History of Ancient Art in Phœnicia AND ITS DEPENDENCIES. By GEORGES PERROT and CHARLES CHIPIEZ. With 654 Illustrations. 2 vols. Imperial 8vo., 42s.

A History of Art in Chaldæa and ASSYRIA. By GEORGES PERROT and CHARLES CHIPIEZ. With 452 Illustrations. 2 vols. Imperial 8vo., 42s.

ART—CONTINUED.

A History of Art in Ancient Egypt. By GEORGES PERROT and CHARLES CHIPIEZ. With 600 Illustrations. 2 vols. Imperial 8vo., 42s.

Gold and Silver Smith's Work. By J. H. POLLEN. With numerous Woodcuts. Large crown 8vo., cloth, 2s. 6d.

Ancient and Modern Furniture and Woodwork. By J. H. POLLEN. With numerous Woodcuts. Large crown 8vo., cloth, 2s. 6d.

The Art of the Saracens in Egypt. By STANLEY LANE POOLE, B.A., M.R.A.S. With 108 Woodcuts. Large crown 8vo., 4s.

Ten Lectures on Art. By E. J. POYNTER, R.A. Third Edition. Large crown 8vo., 9s.

Sciography, or Parallel and Radial PROJECTION OF SHADOWS. Being a Course of Exercises for the use of Students in Architectural and Engineering Drawing, and for Candidates preparing for the Examinations in this subject and in Third Grade Perspective conducted by the Science and Art Department. By ROBERT PRATT, Headmaster School of Science and Art, Barrow-in-Furness. Oblong quarto, 7s. 6d.

Outlines of Historic Ornament. Translated from the German. Edited by GILBERT REDGRAVE. With numerous Illustrations. Crown 8vo., 4s.

Manual of Design. By RICHARD REDGRAVE, R.A. With Woodcuts. Large crown 8vo., cloth, 2s. 6d.

Elementary Manual of Colour, with a Catechism on Colour. By RICHARD REDGRAVE, R.A. 24mo., cloth, 9d.

A Descriptive Catalogue of the HISTORICAL COLLECTION OF WATER-COLOUR PAINTINGS IN THE SOUTH KENSINGTON MUSEUM. By SAMUEL REDGRAVE. With numerous Chromo-lithographs and other Illustrations. Royal 8vo., £1 1s.

The Industrial Arts in Spain. By JUAN F. RIANO. With numerous Woodcuts. Large crown 8vo., cloth, 4s.

Italian Sculpture of the Middle Ages AND PERIOD OF THE REVIVAL OF ART. By J. C. ROBINSON. With 20 Engravings. Royal 8vo., cloth, 7s. 6d.

Textile Fabrics. By the Very Rev. Canon ROCK, D.D. With numerous Woodcuts. Large crown 8vo., cloth 2s. 6d.

Egyptian Art. An Elementary Handbook for the use of Students. By CHARLES RYAN, late Head Master of the Ventnor School of Art. With 56 Illustrations. Crown 8vo., 2s. 6d.

The Sculptor and Art Student's Guide to the Proportions of the Human Form, with Measurements in feet and inches of Full-grown Figures of Both Sexes and of Various Ages. By Dr. G. SCHADOW. Plates reproduced by J. SUTCLIFFE. Oblong folio, 31s. 6d.

Wood-Carving in Practice and THEORY, AS APPLIED TO HOME ARTS. With Notes on Designs having special application to Carved Wood in different Styles. By F. L. SCHAUERMANN. Containing 124 Illustrations. Second Edition. Large crown 8vo., 5s.

The Mythology of Greece and Rome, with Special Reference to its Use in Art. From the German. By O. SEEMAN. Edited by G. H. BIANCHI. 64 Illustrations. New Edition. Crown 8vo., 5s.

Persian Art. By Major R. MURDOCK SMITH, R.E. With Map and Woodcuts. Second Edition. Large crown 8vo., 2s.

Architecture for General Readers, to which is added an Historical Sketch of Architecture. By H. HEATHCOTE STATHAM With hundreds of Illustrations by the author. Large crown 8vo.

Early Christian Art in Ireland. By MARGARET STOKES. With 106 Woodcuts. Crown 8vo., 4s.

Elementary Art Teaching: An Educational and Technical Guide for Teachers and Learners, including Infant Schoolwork; The Work of the Standards; Freehand; Geometry; Model Drawing, Nature Drawing; Colours; Light and Shade; Modelling and Design. By EDWARD R. TAYLOR, Head Master of the Birmingham Municipal School of Art. With over 600 Diagrams and Illustrations. 8vo., 10s. 6d.

The Barbizon School of Painters: Corot, Rousseau, Diaz, Millet, and Daubigny. By D. C. THOMSON. With 130 Illustrations, including 36 Full-page Plates, of which 18 are Etchings. 4to., cloth, 42s.

Drawing-Book. By G. WALLIS. Sewed, 3s. 6d.; mounted, 8s.

CHAPMAN & HALL, LIMITED. 9

ART—*CONTINUED*.

The Principles of Ornament. By JAMES WARD. Edited by GEORGE AITCHINSON, A.R.A. Large crown 8vo., 7s. 6d.

Elementary Principles of Ornament. By JAMES WARD. With 122 Illustrations in the Text. Large crown 8vo., 5s.

Church Embroidery—Designs for. By A. R. Letterpress by the Hon. Mrs. WIEL. With numerous Illustrations. 4to., 12s. net.

Analysis of Ornament: The Characteristics of Styles. An Introduction to the History of Ornamental Art. By R. N. WORNUM. With many Illustrations. Ninth Edition. Royal 8vo., cloth, 8s.

Industrial Arts of Denmark, from THE EARLIEST TIMES TO THE DANISH CONQUEST OF ENGLAND. By J. J. A. WORSAAE. With Maps and Woodcuts. Large crown 8vo., 3s. 6d.

Biography and Reminiscences.

Alfred Stevens (SCULPTOR). A Biographical Sketch. By W. ARMSTRONG. Fully illustrated. Imp. 4to., handsomely bound, 10s. 6d.

From Sinner to Saint; or, Character Transformations. By JOHN BURN BAILEY. Crown 8vo., 6s.

Modern Methuselahs; or, Short Biographical Sketches of a few advanced Nonagenarians or actual Centenarians. By JOHN BURN BAILEY. Demy 8vo., 10s. 6d.

A Journalist's Jottings. By W. BEATTY-KINGSTON. 2 vols. Demy 8vo., 24s.

A Wanderer's Notes. By W. BEATTY-KINGSTON. 2 vols. Demy 8vo., 24s.

Music and Manners: Personal Reminiscences and Sketches of Character. By W. BEATTY-KINGSTON. 2 vols. Demy 8vo., 30s.

Memoir of Benjamin Lord Bloomfield, G.C.B., &c. By GEORGIANA LADY BLOOMFIELD. With Portraits. 2 vols. Demy 8vo., 28s.

A Girl's Life Eighty Years Ago. Selections from the Letters of Eliza Southgate Bowne, with an Introduction by CLARENCE COOK. Illustrated with Portraits and Views. Crown 4to., 12s.

Frederick the Great. By Col. C. B. BRACKENBURY. With Maps and Portrait. Large crown 8vo., 4s.

Musical Celebrities: Portraits and Biographies. By F. F. BUFFEN. Second Series. Crown 4to., 21s.

The Life of Sir Richard Francis Burton. By Lady ISABEL BURTON. With Portraits, numerous Coloured and other Illustrations, and Maps. 2 vols. Demy 8vo., 42s.

Life of Frederick Schiller and Examination of his Works. By THOMAS CARLYLE. With Supplement of 1872. Portrait and Plates. Demy 8vo., 9s. and 8s.; crown 8vo., 2s. 6d., 2s., and 1s.

Oliver Cromwell's Letters and SPEECHES. By THOMAS CARLYLE. With Portraits. 5 vols., demy 8vo., 9s. each; 3 vols., demy 8vo., 8s. each; 3 vols., crown 8vo., 2s. 6d. each; 5 vols., crown 8vo., 1s. each; 1 vol., crown 8vo., 2s. 6d.

Life of John Sterling. By THOMAS CARLYLE. With Portrait. Demy 8vo., 9s. and 8s.; crown 8vo., 2s. 6d. and 1s.

History of Frederick the Second. By THOMAS CARLYLE. 10 vols., demy 8vo., 9s. each; 6 vols., demy 8vo., 8s. each; 5 vols., crown 8vo., 2s. 6d. each; 10 vols., crown 8vo., 1s. each.

Early Kings of Norway. By THOMAS CARLYLE. With Portrait Illustrations. Demy 8vo., 9s. and 8s.; crown 8vo., 2s. 6d. and 1s.

Life and Letters of Charlotte Elizabeth, Princess Palatine and mother of Philippe d'Orléans, Regent of France, 1652-1722. With Portraits. Demy 8vo., 10s. 6d.

George Washington. By Lieut.-Colonel COOPER-KING. With Portrait and Maps. Large crown 8vo., 6s.

BIOGRAPHY AND REMINISCENCES—*CONTINUED.*

Memoirs of a Royalist. By the Count DE FALLOUX. Edited by C. B. PITMAN. 2 vols. With Portraits. Demy 8vo., 32s.

The Salon of Madame Necker. By VICOMTE D'HAUSSONVILLE. 2 vols. Crown 8vo., 18s.

Recollections of Forty Years. By FERDINAND DE LESSEPS. 2 vols. Demy 8vo., 24s.

Experiences of a Woolwich Professor DURING FIFTEEN YEARS AT THE ROYAL MILITARY ACADEMY. By Major-General A. W. DRAYSON. Demy 8vo., 8s.

Englishman in Paris: Notes and Recollections during the Reign of Louis Philippe and the Empire. Eighth Thousand. Crown 8vo., 7s. 6d.

Life and Letters of Edward Livingstone Youmans. By JOHN FISKE. Comprising Correspondence with Spencer, Huxley, Tyndall, and others. Crown 8vo., 8s.

Henry Irving: A Record of Twenty Years at the Lyceum. By PERCY FITZGERALD, M.A., F.S.A. With Portrait. Demy 8vo., 14s.

The Life of Charles Dickens. By JOHN FORSTER. Original Edition. Vol. I., 8vo., cloth, 12s. Vol. II., 8vo., cloth, 14s. Vol. III., 8vo., cloth, 16s.

Uniform with the Illustrated Library Edition of Dickens's Works. 2 vols. Demy 8vo., 20s.

Uniform with the "Library" Edition and the "Popular Library" Edition. 10s. 6d. each.

Uniform with the "C. D." Edition. With numerous Illustrations. 2 vols. 7s.

Uniform with the Crown Edition. Crown 8vo., 5s.

Uniform with the Household Edition. Illustrations by F. BARNARD. Crown 4to., cloth, 5s.

Uniform with the Pictorial Edition. With 40 Illustrations by F. BARNARD and others. Royal 8vo., 3s. 6d.

Letters from the Crimea, the Danube, AND ARMENIA. By General GORDON. Edited by DEMETRIUS C. BOULGER. Second Edition. Crown 8vo., 5s.

Secrets of the Prison House. By Major ARTHUR GRIFFITHS, H.M. Inspector of Prisons. With numerous Illustrations by GEORGE D. ROWLANDSON. 2 vols. Demy 8vo., 30s.

French Revolutionary Generals. By Major ARTHUR GRIFFITHS, H.M. Inspector of Prisons. Large crown 8vo., 6s.

Swift: THE MYSTERY OF HIS LIFE AND LOVE. By the Rev. JAMES HAY. Crown 8vo., 6s.

Behind the Scenes of the Comédie FRANCAISE, AND OTHER RECOLLECTIONS. By ARSÈNE HOUSSAYE. Translated from the French. Demy 8vo., 14s.

Turenne. By H. M. HOZIER. With Portrait and two Maps. Large crown 8vo., 4s.

Creators of the Age of Steel. Memoirs of Sir W. Siemens, Sir H. Bessemer, Sir J. Whitworth, Sir J. Brown, and other Inventors. By W. T. JEANS. Second Edition. Crown 8vo., 7s. 6d.

The Life of Miguel de Cervantes SAAVEDRA: a Biographical, Literary, and Historical Study, with a Tentative Bibliography from 1585 to 1892, and an Annotated Appendix on the "Canto de Calíope." By JAMES FITZMAURICE KELLY. Demy 8vo., 16s.

Convivial Caledonia: Inns and Taverns of Scotland, and some Famous People who have Frequented Them. By ROBERT KEMPT. Crown 8vo., 2s. 6d.

General Lee of the Confederate Army. By FITZHUGH LEE, his Nephew. With Portrait and Maps. Crown 8vo., 6s.

A Waterbiography. By R. C. LESLIE. With Illustrations by the Author. Crown 8vo., 7s. 6d.

A Sea Painter's Log. By R. C. LESLIE. With 12 Full-page Illustrations by the Author. Large crown 8vo., 12s.

H. M. Stanley: HIS LIFE, WORKS, AND EXPLORATIONS. By the Rev. H. W. LITTLE. Demy 8vo., 10s. 6d.

The Life of Warren Hastings, First Governor-General of India. By Col. G. B. MALLESON, C.S.I. With Portrait. Demy 8vo., 18s.

Loudon: A Sketch of the Military Life of Gideon Ernest, Freiherr von Loudon. By Col. G. B. MALLESON, C.S.I. With Portrait and Maps. Large crown 8vo., 4s.

Reminiscences of a Regicide. Edited from the Original MSS. of SERGENT MARCEAU, Member of the Convention, and Administrator of Police in the French Revolution of 1789. By M. C. M. SIMPSON. Demy 8vo., with Illustrations and Portraits, 14s.

BIOGRAPHY AND REMINISCENCES—CONTINUED.

Raphael: his Life, Works, and Times. By EUGENE MUNTZ. Illustrated with about 200 Engravings. A New Edition, revised from the Second French Edition. By W. ARMSTRONG, B.A. Imperial 8vo., 25s.

Life of Richard Cobden. By the Right Hon. JOHN MORLEY, M.P. With Portrait. New Edition. Crown 8vo., 7s. 6d. Popular Edition, with Portrait, 4to., sewed, 1s.; cloth, 2s.

Memoir of Lieutenant Rudolph de LISLE, R.N., of the Naval Brigade. By the Rev. H. N. OXENHAM, M.A. Third Edition. Crown 8vo., 7s. 6d.

The Earl of Peterborough and Monmouth (Charles Mordaunt): A Memoir. By Colonel FRANK RUSSELL, Royal Dragoons. With Illustrations. 2 vols. Demy 8vo., 32s.

The Life of the Right Hon. W. E. Forster. By Sir T. WEMYSS REID. With Portraits. Fourth Edition. 2 vols. Demy 8vo., 32s.
Fifth Edition, in one volume, with new Portrait. Demy 8vo., 10s. 6d.

Recollections of My Youth. By ERNEST RENAN. Translated from the French, and Revised by MADAME RENAN. Second Edition. Crown 8vo., 3s. 6d.

Elisabeth of Roumania: A Study. With Two Tales from the German of Carmen Sylva, Her Majesty Queen of Roumania. By BLANCHE ROOSEVELT. With Two Portraits and Illustrations. Demy 8vo., 12s.

Early Days Recalled. By Mrs. JANET Ross. With Illustrations and Portrait. Crown 8vo., 5s.

Friedrich Frobel: A Short Sketch of his Life, including Fröbel's Letters from Dresden and Leipzig to his Wife, now first Translated into English. By EMILY SHIRREFF. Crown 8vo., 2s.

Life of Suvoroff. By Lieut.-Col. SPALDING. Crown 8vo., 6s.

Parliamentary Generals of the Great CIVIL WAR. By Major WALFORD, R.A. With Maps. Large crown 8vo., 4s.

Days of a Soldier's Life. Written during active service in the Crimean, Chinese, Austro-Prussian ('66), and Franco-German ('70-'71) Wars. By General Sir C. P. BEAUCHAMP WALKER. Demy 8vo., with Portrait. 18s.

Parallel Lives of Ancient and Modern HEROES. By C. D. YOUNGE. New Edition. 12mo., cloth, 4s. 6d.

Cookery, &c.

Hilda's "Where is it?" of Recipes. Containing many old CAPE, INDIAN, and MALAY DISHES and PRESERVES; also Directions for Polishing Furniture, Cleaning Silk, &c.; and a Collection of Home Remedies in Case of Sickness. By HILDAGONDA J. DUCKITT. Fifth Thousand. Crown 8vo., 4s. 6d.

Dinners in Miniature. By Mrs. EARL. Crown 8vo., 2s. 6d.

The Royal Confectioner: English and Foreign. By C. E. FRANCATELLI. With Illustrations. Sixth Thousand. Crown 8vo., 5s.

The Pytchley Book of Refined Cookery AND BILLS OF FARE. By Major L——. Fifth Edition. Large crown 8vo., 8s.

Breakfasts, Luncheons, and Ball SUPPERS. By Major L——. Crown 8vo., 4s.

Table Decoration. By WILLIAM LOW. With 19 Full Illustrations. Demy 8vo., 6s.

Official Handbook of the National TRAINING SCHOOL FOR COOKERY. Containing Lessons on Cookery, forming the Course of Instruction in the School. Compiled by "R. O. C." Twenty-fourth Thousand. Large crown 8vo., 6s.

Breakfast and Savoury Dishes. By "R. O. C." Ninth Thousand. Crown 8vo., 1s.

Sick-Room Cookery. Compiled by "R. O. C." Crown 8vo., sewed, 6d.

How to Cook Fish. Compiled by "R. O. C." Crown 8vo., sewed, 3d.

St. James's Cookery Book. By LOUISA ROCHFORT. Crown 8vo., 3s. 6d.

The Kingswood Cookery Book. By H. F. WICKEN. Crown 8vo., 2s.

Fiction.

A Romance of N'Shabe: Being a Record of Startling Adventures in South Central Africa. By ANDREW A. ANDERSON. With Illustrations. Crown 8vo., 5s.

The Story of Allan Gordon. By Captain LINDSAY ANDERSON. With Illustrations. Crown 8vo., 2s. 6d.

Among Typhoons and Pirate Craft. By Captain LINDSAY ANDERSON. With Illustrations by STANLEY WOOD. Crown 8vo., 2s. 6d.

A Cruise in an Opium Clipper. By Captain LINDSAY ANDERSON. With Illustrations. Crown 8vo., 2s. 6d.

The Prophet John: A Romance. By FREDERICK BOYLE. Crown 8vo., 5s.

The Orchid Seekers: A Story of Adventure in Borneo. By FREDERICK BOYLE and ASHMORE RUSSAN. Illustrated by ALFRED HARTLEY. Crown 8vo., 7s. 6d.

The Lazy Tour of Two Idle Apprentices; No Thoroughfare; Perils of certain English Prisoners. By WILKIE COLLINS and CHARLES DICKENS. With 8 Illustrations. Crown 8vo., 5s.

CHARLES DICKENS'S WORKS.

Pickwick Papers.
Martin Chuzzlewit.
Dombey and Son.
Nicholas Nickleby.
David Copperfield.
Bleak House.
Little Dorrit.
Our Mutual Friend.
Barnaby Rudge.
Old Curiosity Shop.
Edwin Drood and Other Stories.
Christmas Stories, from "Household Words."
Sketches by "Boz."
Christmas Books.
Oliver Twist.
Great Expectations.
Tale of Two Cities.
Hard Times.
Uncommercial Traveller.

** *For detailed List of the different editions of Charles Dickens's Works see pages 27–31.*

Innocencia: A Story of the Prairie Regions of Brazil. By SYLVIO DINARTE. Translated from the Portuguese and Illustrated by JAMES W. WELLS, F.R.G.S. Crown 8vo., 6s.

South African Sketches. By Colonel A. B. ELLIS. Crown 8vo., 6s.

Undine: a Romance translated from the German. By DE LA MOTTE FOUQUÉ. With an Introduction by JULIA CARTWRIGHT. Illustrated by HEYWOOD SUMNER. Crown 4to., 5s.

The New Academe: An Educational Romance. By EDWARD HARTINGTON. Crown 8vo., 5s.

Queen of Beauty; or, The Adventures of Prince Elfreston. By RE HENRY. Illustrated by JOHN JELLICOE. Small 4to., 6s.

Wanneta, the Sioux. By WARREN K. MOOREHEAD. With Illustrations from Life. Large crown 8vo., 6s.

A Partner from the West. By ARTHUR PATERSON. Crown 8vo., 5s.

The Goldsmith's Ward: A Tale of London City in the Fifteenth Century. By Mrs. R. H. READE. With 27 Illustrations by W. BOWCHER. Crown 8vo., 6s.

Miss Parson's Adventure, and other Stories. By W. CLARK RUSSELL, W. E. NORRIS, JULIAN HAWTHORNE, Mrs. L. B. WALFORD, J. M. BARRIE, F. C. PHILIPS, Mrs. ALEXANDER, and WILLIAM WESTALL. With 16 Illustrations. Crown 8vo., 5s.

Karma. By A. P. SINNETT. New Edition. Crown 8vo., 3s.

The Chronicles of Barsetshire. By ANTHONY TROLLOPE. A Uniform Edition, in 8 vols., large crown 8vo., handsomely printed, each vol. containing Frontispiece. 6s. each :—

    THE WARDEN AND BARCHESTER TOWERS. 2 vols.
    DR. THORNE.
    FRAMLEY PARSONAGE.
    THE SMALL HOUSE AT ALLINGTON. 2 vols.
    LAST CHRONICLE OF BARSET. 2 vols.

A Princess of Chalco. By A. WALL. With Illustrations. Crown 8vo., 6s.

FICTION—*CONTINUED.*

Supplejack: a Romance of Maoriland. By R. WARD. With 8 Illustrations. Crown 8vo., 6s.

THREE & SIXPENCE EACH.

Stories from "Black and White." By GRANT ALLEN, Mrs. LYNN LINTON, J. M. BARRIE, Mrs. OLIPHANT, W. CLARK RUSSELL, THOMAS HARDY, W. E. NORRIS, and JAMES PAYN. With numerous Illustrations. Crown 8vo.

From the Frontier: Sketches and Stories of Savage Life. By FREDERICK BOYLE. Crown 8vo.

Rachel and Maurice, and other Tales. By the Hon. MARGARET COLLIER, Madame Galletti di Cadilliac. Crown 8vo.

Cross Currents: A Novel. By MARY A. DICKENS. Third Thousand.

The Secret of the Princess: A Tale of Country, Camp, Convict, and Cloister Life in Russia. By MRS. SUTHERLAND EDWARDS. Crown 8vo.

The Story of Helen Davenant. By VIOLET FANE. Crown 8vo.

The Vyvyans: or, the Murder in the Rue Bellechasse. By ANDRÉE HOPE. Crown 8vo.

A Black Squire. By Mrs. ALFRED HUNT. Crown 8vo.

'Midst the Wild Carpathians. By MAURUS JOKAI. Translated by R. NISBET BAIN. Crown 8vo.

A Human Document. By W. H. MALLOCK. Sixth Thousand. Crown 8vo.

The Star of Fortune: a Story of the Indian Mutiny. By J. E. MUDDOCK. Crown 8vo.

A Deputy Providence. By HENRY MURRAY. Crown 8vo.

The Queen of Spades and other Stories. By A. S. PUSHKIN. With a Biography. Translated from the Russian by Mrs. SUTHERLAND EDWARDS. Illustrated. Crown 8vo.

THREE & SIXPENCE EACH—*continued.*

In Low Relief: A Bohemian Transcript. By MORLEY ROBERTS. Crown 8vo.

Clove Pink: a Study from Memory. By ANNA C. STEELE. Second Edition. Crown 8vo.

The Mystery of the Patrician Club. By ALBERT D. VANDAM. Crown 8vo.

GEORGE MEREDITH'S WORKS.

A Uniform Edition. Crown 8vo., 3s. 6d. each.

Lord Ormont and his Aminta.

One of our Conquerors.

Diana of the Crossways.

Evan Harrington.

The Ordeal of Richard Feverel.

The Adventures of Harry Richmond.

Sandra Belloni.

Vittoria.

Rhoda Fleming.

Beauchamp's Career.

The Egoist.

The Shaving of Shagpat; and Farina.

The 6s. Edition is also to be had.

TWO SHILLINGS EACH.

Eline Vere. By LOUIS COUPERUS. Translated from the Dutch by J. T. GREIN. Crown 8vo.

Cross Currents: A Novel. By MARY A. DICKENS. Third Thousand.

The Story of Helen Davenant. By VIOLET FANE. Crown 8vo.

Pretty Michal. By MAURUS JOKAI. Translated by R. NISBET BAIN. Cr. 8vo.

FICTION—*CONTINUED.*

TWO SHILLINGS EACH—*continued.*

A Deputy Providence. By HENRY MURRAY. Crown 8vo.

The Queen of Spades and other Stories. By A. S. PUSHKIN. With a Biography. Translated from the Russian by Mrs. SUTHERLAND EDWARDS. Illustrated. Crown 8vo.

In Low Relief: A Bohemian Transcript. By MORLEY ROBERTS. Crown 8vo.

Through a Field Glass. By G. F. UNDERHILL and H. S. SWEETLAND. With Illustrations by L. THACKERAY. Crown 8vo.

ONE SHILLING EACH.

The Waif from the Waves: A Story of Three Lives, touching this World and Another. By the Rev. Canon KNOX LITTLE. Fifth Thousand. Crown 8vo., in cloth, 1s. 6d.

The Child of Stafferton: A Chapter from a Family Chronicle. By the Rev. Canon KNOX-LITTLE. Twelfth Thousand. Crown 8vo., in cloth, 1s. 6d.

The Broken Vow: A Story of Here and Hereafter. By the Rev. Canon KNOX LITTLE. Eighteenth Thousand. Crown 8vo., in cloth, 1s. 6d.

History and Politics.

Frederick the Great. By Colonel C. B. BRACKENBURY. With Maps and Portrait. Large crown 8vo., 4s.

The British Army. By the Author of "Greater Britain." Demy 8vo., 12s.

Court Life in Egypt. By A. J. BUTLER. Second Edition. Illustrated. Large crown 8vo., 12s.

History of Frederick the Second. By THOMAS CARLYLE. 10 vols. Demy 8vo., 9s. each; 6 vols., demy 8vo., 8s. each; 5 vols., crown 8vo., 2s. 6d. each; 10 vols., Crown 8vo., 1s. each.

Oliver Cromwell's Letters and Speeches. By THOMAS CARLYLE. With Portraits. 5 vols., demy 8vo., 9s. each; 3 vols., demy 8vo., 8s. each; 3 vols., crown 8vo., 2s. 6d. each; 5 vols., crown 8vo., 1s. each; 1 vol., crown 8vo., 2s. 6d.

On Heroes, Hero Worship, and the Heroic in History. By THOMAS CARLYLE. Demy 8vo., 7s. 6d., 8s.; crown 8vo., 2s. 6d., 2s., 1s.

The French Revolution. A History. By THOMAS CARLYLE. 3 vols., demy 8vo., 9s. each; 2 vols., demy 8vo., 8s. each; 2 vols., crown 8vo., 2s. 6d. each; 3 vols., crown 8vo., 1s. each; 1 vol., crown 8vo., 2s.

Early Kings of Norway; Essay on the Portraits of John Knox. By THOMAS CARLYLE. With Portrait Illustrations. Demy 8vo., cloth, 9s. and 8s.; crown 8vo., 2s. 6d., and 1s.

Ireland in the Days of Dean Swift. By J. B. DALY, LL.D. Crown 8vo., 5s.

Germany and the Germans: Social Life, Culture, Religious Life, etc., etc. By WILLIAM HARBUTT DAWSON. In 2 vols. Demy 8vo., 26s.

Paddy at Home; OR, IRELAND AND THE IRISH AT THE PRESENT TIME, AS SEEN BY A FRENCHMAN. By Baron E. DE MANDAT-GRANCEY. Fifth Edition. Crown 8vo., 1s.; in cloth, 1s. 6d.

Siberia as it is. By H. DE WINDT. With numerous Illustrations. Demy 8vo., 18s.

A Child's History of England. By CHARLES DICKENS. Illustrated. Demy 8vo., 10s.; post 8vo., 8s.; crown 8vo., 5s.; 4to., 3s.; royal 8vo., 3s. 6d.; crown 8vo., 3s. 6d.; crown 8vo., 2s. 6d.; small fcap. 8vo., 1s. 6d.

The History of Ancient Civilisation. A Handbook based upon M. Gustave Ducoudray's "Histoire Sommaire de la Civilisation." Edited by Rev. J. VERSCHOYLE, M.A. With Illustrations. Large crown 8vo., 6s.

CHAPMAN & HALL, LIMITED.   15

HISTORY AND POLITICS—*CONTINUED*.

The History of Modern Civilisation. By GUSTAVE DUCOUDRAY. With Illustrations. Large crown 8vo., 9s.

Old Court Life in Spain. By FRANCES MINTO ELLIOT. 2 vols. Demy 8vo., 24s.

History of the Gold Coast of West Africa. By A. B. ELLIS, Colonel 1st West India Regiment. Demy 8vo., 10s. 6d.

The Yoruba-Speaking Peoples of the SLAVE COAST OF WEST AFRICA; their Religion, Manners, Customs, Laws, Language, &c. By A. B. ELLIS. With an Appendix and Map. Demy 8vo., 10s. 6d.

The Ewe-Speaking People of the SLAVE COAST OF WEST AFRICA. By A. B. ELLIS. With Map. Demy 8vo., 10s. 6d.

The Tshi-Speaking Peoples of the Gold COAST: their Religion, Manners, Customs, Laws, Language, &c. By A. B. ELLIS. With Map. Demy 8vo., 10s. 6d.

Politics and Letters. By T. H. S. ESCOTT. Demy 8vo., 9s.

England: Its People, Polity, and Pursuits. By T. H. S. ESCOTT. New and Revised Edition. Eighth Thousand. Demy 8vo., 3s. 6d.

The Present Position of European POLITICS. By the Author of "Greater Britain." Demy 8vo., 12s.

Chronicles of Bow Street Police Office. By PERCY FITZGERALD, F.S.A. New and Cheaper Edition.

The History of Pickwick. An Account of its Characters, Localities, Allusions, and Illustrations. By PERCY FITZGERALD, F.S.A. With a Bibliography. Demy 8vo., 8s.

Italy: Present and Future. By ANTONIO GALLENGA. 2 vols. Demy 8vo., 21s.

An Election Manual. Containing the Parliamentary Elections (Corrupt and Illegal Practices) Act, 1883, with Notes. By Sir J. E. GORST, Q.C., M.P. Third Edition. Crown 8vo., 1s. 6d.

Our South African Empire. By WILLIAM GRESWELL, M.A., F.R.C.I. With Map. 2 vols. Crown 8vo., 21s.

The Great Republic. By Sir LEPEL HENRY GRIFFIN, K.C.S.I. Second Edition. Crown 8vo., 4s. 6d.

China and Her Neighbours. France in Indo-China, Russia and China, India and Thibet, &c. By R. S. GUNDRY. With Maps. Demy 8vo., 9s.

China, Present and Past: Foreign Intercourse, Progress and Resources, The Missionary Question, &c. By R. S. GUNDRY. Demy 8vo.

Chronicles of an Old Inn: or, a Few Words about Gray's Inn. By ANDRÉE HOPE. Crown 8vo., 5s.

Middlesex County Records. Indictments, Recognizances, Coroners' Inquisitions, Post Mortem, Orders, Memoranda, and Certificates of Convictors of Conventiclers, *temp.* 19 Charles II. to 4 James II. By J. CORDY JEAFFRESON, B.A. 4 vols. With Portraits, Illustrations, and Facsimiles. Demy 8vo., 25s. each.

Russian Characteristics. By E. B. LANIN. Reprinted, with Revisions, from *The Fortnightly Review*. Demy 8vo., 14s.

Egypt under Ismail: A Romance of History. By J. C. MCCOAN. With Portrait and Appendix of Official Documents. Crown 8vo., 7s. 6d.

British East Africa. A History of the Formation and Work of the Imperial British East Africa Company. Compiled with the Authority of the Directors from Official Documents and the Records of the Company. By P. L. M'DERMOTT. With Maps and Illustrations. Crown 8vo., 6s.

Our Ocean Railways; or, The Rise, Progress, and Development of Ocean Steam Navigation, etc., etc. By A. F. MACDONALD. With Maps and Illustrations. Large crown 8vo., 6s.

The Emancipation of South America. By General DON BARTOLOME MITRE. Being a Condensed Translation, by WILLIAM PILLING, of "The History of San Martin." Demy 8vo., with Maps, 12s.

History of England from the Year 1830 TO THE RESIGNATION OF THE GLADSTONE MINISTRY, 1874. By W. NASSAU MOLESWORTH. Twelfth Thousand. 3 vols. Crown 8vo., 18s.

Poland: AN HISTORICAL SKETCH. By Field-Marshal Count VON MOLTKE. With Biographical Notice by E. S. BUCHHEIM. Crown 8vo., 4s. 6d. and 1s.

Tonkin; or, France in the Far East. By C. B. NORMAN. With Maps. Demy 8vo., 14s.

HISTORY AND POLITICS—*CONTINUED*.

The Victories of the British Army in the Peninsula and the South of France from 1808 to 1814. An Epitome of Napier's History of the Peninsular War, and Gurwood's Collection of the Duke of Wellington's Despatches. By ROBERT O'BYRNE, F.R.G.S. Crown 8vo., 5*s*.

Toryism and the Tory Democracy. By STANDISH O'GRADY. Crown 8vo., 5*s*.

The Radical Programme. From the *Fortnightly Review*, with Additions. With a Preface by the Right Hon. J. CHAMBERLAIN, M.P. Thirteenth Thousand. Crown 8vo. Paper Covers, 1*s*.

History of the People of Israel. By ERNEST RENAN.
FIRST DIVISION. Till the Time of King David. Demy 8vo., 14*s*.
SECOND DIVISION. From the Reign of David up to the Capture of Samaria. Demy 8vo., 14*s*.
THIRD DIVISION. From the Time of Hezekiah till the Return from Babylon. Demy 8vo., 14*s*.

The Future of Science: Ideas of 1848. By ERNEST RENAN. Demy 8vo., 18*s*.

A History of Vagrants and Vagrancy and Beggars and Begging. By C. J. RIBTON-TURNER. With Illustrations. Demy 8vo., 21*s*.

The Republic as a Form of Government; or, The Evolution of Democracy in America. By JOHN SCOTT. Crown 8vo., 7*s*. 6*d*.

The First Technical College: a Sketch of the History of "The Andersonian" and the Institutions descended from it, 1796-1894. By A. HUMBOLDT SEXTON. With Portraits and Illustrations. Cr. 8vo. 3*s*. 6*d*.

Castle St. Angelo. By W. W. STORY. With Illustrations. Crown 8vo., 10*s*. 6*d*.

Galileo and His Judges. By F. R. WEGG-PROSSER. Demy 8vo., 5*s*.

Literature, Belles-Lettres, and Poetry.

Songs and Verses. By H. CUMBERLAND BENTLEY. Illustrated by FINCH MASON, and dedicated to J. G. WHYTE MELVILLE. Crown 8vo., 4*s*.

Sartor Resartus. By THOMAS CARLYLE. With a Portrait. Demy, 7*s*. 6*d*. and 8*s*.; crown 8vo., 2*s*. 6*d*., 2*s*. and 1*s*.; 4to., sewed, 6*d*.

Life of Frederick Schiller and Examination of his Works. By THOMAS CARLYLE. With Supplement of 1872. Portrait and Plates. Demy, 9*s*. and 8*s*.; crown, 2*s*. 6*d*., 2*s*. and 1*s*.

Critical and Miscellaneous Essays. By THOMAS CARLYLE. With Portrait. 6 vols. Demy, 9*s*. each; 3 vols., demy 8vo., 8*s*. each; 4 vols., crown 8vo., 2*s*. 6*d*. each; 2 vols., crown, 2*s*. each; 7 vols., crown 8vo., 1*s*. each; 4to., sewed, 6*d*.

On Heroes, Hero Worship, and the Heroic in History. By THOMAS CARLYLE. Demy 8vo., 7*s*. 6*d*. and 8*s*.; crown 8vo., 2*s*. 6*d*., 2*s*. and 1*s*.; 4to., sewed, 6*d*.

Past and Present. By THOMAS CARLYLE. Demy 9*s*. and 8*s*.; crown 8vo., 2*s*. 6*d*., 2*s*. and 1*s*.

Latter-day Pamphlets. By THOMAS CARLYLE. Demy 8vo., 9*s*. and 8*s*.; crown 8vo., 2*s*. 6*d*., 2*s*. and 1*s*.

Translations from the German. By THOMAS CARLYLE. 3 vols., demy, 9*s*. each; 3 vols., demy 8vo., 8*s*. each; 3 vols., 2*s*. 6*d*. each; 5 vols., 1*s*. each.

Essay on the Portraits of John Knox. By THOMAS CARLYLE. With Portrait Illustrations. Demy 8vo., 9*s*. and 8*s*.; crown 8vo., 2*s*. 6*d*. and 1*s*.

The Canterbury Tales. Selections from the Tales of Geoffrey Chaucer rendered into Modern English. By FRANK PITT TAYLOR. Crown 8vo., 6*s*.

English of Shakespeare. Illustrated in a Philological Commentary on "Julius Cæsar." By GEORGE LILLIE CRAIK. Eighth Edition. Post 8vo., cloth, 5*s*.

CHAPMAN & HALL, LIMITED. 17

LITERATURE, &c.—CONTINUED.

Outlines of the History of the English Language. By GEORGE LILLIE CRAIK. Eleventh Edition. Post 8vo., cloth, 2s. 6d.

Studies at Leisure. By W. L. COURTNEY, M.A., LL.D., of New College, Oxford. Crown 8vo., 6s.

Studies New and Old. By W. L. COURTNEY, M.A., LL.D., of New College, Oxford. Crown 8vo., 6s.

Some French Writers. By EDWARD DELILLE. Contents: Bourget, Pierre Loti, Baudelaire, Guy de Maupassant, Verlaine, Maurice Barres, &c. Crown 8vo., 5s.

Handbook to the Dyce and Forster Collections in the South Kensington Museum. With Portraits and Facsimiles. 2s. 6d.

Autumn Songs. By VIOLET FANE. Crown 8vo., 6s.

Life and Works. By W. S. LANDOR. 8 vols.;
Vol. I. Out of Print.
Vol. II. Out of Print.
Vol. III. CONVERSATIONS OF SOVEREIGNS AND STATESMEN, AND FIVE DIALOGUES OF BOCCACCIO AND PETRARCA. Demy 8vo., 14s.

Life and Works. By W. S. LANDOR—Continued.
Vol. IV. DIALOGUES OF LITERARY MEN. Demy 8vo., 14s.
Vol. V. DIALOGUES OF LITERARY MEN (continued). FAMOUS WOMEN. LETTERS OF PERICLES AND ASPASIA. And Minor Prose Pieces. Demy 8vo., 14s.
Vol. VI. MISCELLANEOUS CONVERSATIONS. Demy 8vo., 14s.
Vol. VII. GEBIR, ACTS AND SCENES AND HELLENICS. Poems. Demy 8vo., 14s.
Vol. VIII. MISCELLANEOUS POEMS AND CRITICISMS ON THEOCRITUS, CATULLUS, AND PETRARCH. Demy 8vo., 14s.

Dante for Beginners: a Sketch of the "Divina Commedia." By ARABELLA SHORE. With Translations, Biographical and Critical Notices, and Illustrations. With Portrait. Crown 8vo., 6s.

Essays, Speculative and Suggestive. By JOHN ADDINGTON SYMONDS. New Edition. Demy 8vo., 9s.

Cosmopolitan Essays. By Sir RICHARD TEMPLE, Bart., M.P., G.C.S.I. With Maps. Demy 8vo., 16s.

Military.

Frederick the Great. By Col. C. B. BRACKENBURY. With Maps and Portrait. Large crown 8vo., 4s.

The British Army. By the Author of "Greater Britain." Demy 8vo., 12s.

Historical Record of the First or Royal Regiment of Dragoons. By General DE AINSLIE. Illustrated. Royal 8vo., 21s.

History of Frederick the Second. By THOMAS CARLYLE. 10 vols., demy 8vo., 9s. each; 6 vols., demy 8vo., 8s. each; 5 vols., 2s. 6d. each; 10 vols., 1s. each.

George Washington. By Lieut.-Colonel COOPER-KING. Large crown 8vo. With Portrait and Maps. 6s.

Practical Military Surveying and Sketching. By Major-General A. W. DRAYSON. Fifth Edition. Post 8vo., 4s. 6d.

History of the 1st West India Regiment. By Colonel A. B. ELLIS. With Coloured Illustrations. Demy 8vo., 14s.

With the Camel Corps up the Nile. By Count GLEICHEN. With numerous Sketches by the Author. Third Edition. Large crown 8vo., 9s.

Letters from the Crimea, the Danube, and Armenia. By General GORDON. Edited by DEMETRIUS C. BOULGER. Second Edition. Crown 8vo., 5s.

French Revolutionary Generals. By Major ARTHUR GRIFFITHS. Large crown 8vo., 6s.

Turenne. By H. M. HOZIER. With Portrait and Two Maps. Large crown 8vo., 4s.

General Lee of the Confederate Army. By FITZHUGH LEE, his Nephew. With Portrait and Maps. Crown 8vo., 6s.

On Active Service. By W. W. LLOYD, late 24th Regiment. Printed in Colours. Oblong 4to., 5s.

Sketches of Indian Life. By W. W. LLOYD, late 24th Regiment. Printed in Colours. 4to., 6s.

MILITARY—CONTINUED.

The Life of Warren Hastings, First Governor-General of India. By Colonel G. B. MALLESON, C.S.I. With Portrait. Demy 8vo., 18s.

Prince Eugene of Savoy. By Colonel G. B. MALLESON, C.S.I. With Portrait and Maps. Large crown 8vo., 6s.

Loudon: A Sketch of the Military Life of Gideon Ernest, Freicherr von Loudon. By Colonel G. B. MALLESON, C.S.I. With Portrait and Maps. Large crown 8vo., 4s.

The Victories of the British Army in THE PENINSULA AND THE SOUTH OF FRANCE from 1808 to 1814. An Epitome of Napier's History of the Peninsular War, and Gurwood's Collection of the Duke of Wellington's Despatches. By ROBERT O'BYRNE, F.R.G.S. Crown 8vo., 5s.

The Earl of Peterborough and Monmouth (Charles Mordaunt): A Memoir. By Colonel FRANK RUSSELL, Royal Dragoons. With Illustrations. 2 vols. Demy 8vo., 32s.

Life in the Army: Every-day Incidents in Camp, Field, and Quarters. By R. SIMKIN. Printed in Colours. Oblong 4to., 5s.

Life of Suvoroff. By Lieut.-Col. SPALDING. Crown 8vo., 6s.

Martial Law and Custom of War; or, Military Law and Jurisdiction in Troublous Times. By Lieut.-Col. TOVEY, R.E. Crown 8vo., 6s.

Parliamentary Generals of the Great CIVIL WAR. By Major WALFORD, R.A. With Maps. Large crown 8vo., 4s.

Days of a Soldier's Life. Written during active service in the Crimean, Chinese, Austro-Prussian ('66), and Franco-German ('70-'71) Wars. By General Sir C. P. BEAUCHAMP WALKER. With Portrait. Demy 8vo. 18s.

The Young Officer's "Don't." Crown 8vo., 1s.

Miscellaneous.

The Carlyle Birthday Book. By THOMAS CARLYLE. Second Edition. Small fcap. 8vo., 3s.

Character in the Face. Physiognomical Sketches. Our Looks and what they Mean. Crown 8vo., 5s.

The Charles Dickens Birthday Book. With Five Illustrations. In a handsome fcap. 4to. volume, 12s.

The Humour and Pathos of Charles DICKENS. By CHARLES KENT. With Portrait. Crown 8vo., 6s.

Animal Plagues: THEIR HISTORY, NATURE, AND PREVENTION. By GEORGE FLEMING, F.R.C.S. 8vo., cloth, 15s.

Practical Horse-Shoeing. By GEORGE FLEMING, F.R.C.S. With 37 Illustrations. Fifth Edition, enlarged. 8vo., sewed, 2s.

Rabies and Hydrophobia: THEIR HISTORY, NATURE, CAUSES, SYMPTOMS, AND PREVENTION. By GEORGE FLEMING, F.R.C.S. With 8 Illustrations. 8vo., cloth, 15s.

A Travelling Atlas of the English COUNTIES. By SIDNEY HALL. Fifty Maps, coloured. New Edition, including the Railways, corrected up to the present date. Demy 8vo., in roan tuck, 10s. 6d.

English Composition Exercises. By J. M. LAINÉ, M.A. Crown 8vo., 2s. 6d.

The Tarot of the Bohemians. The most Ancient Book in the World. For the exclusive use of the Initiates. An Absolute Key to Occult Science. By PAPUS. With numerous Illustrations. Large crown 8vo., 7s. 6d.

The Dickens' Dictionary. A Key to the Characters and Principal Incidents in the Tales of Charles Dickens. By GILBERT PIERCE and W. A. WHEELER. New Edition. Large crown 8vo., 5s.

Austrian Health Resorts Throughout THE YEAR. By W. FRASER RAE. A New and Enlarged Edition. Crown 8vo., 5s.

A Birthday Book. By Lady GWENDOLEN RAMSDEN. Containing 46 Illustrations from Original Drawings. Royal 8vo., 21s.

Home Education in Relation to the KINDERGARTEN. By EMILY SHIRREFF. Two Lectures. Crown 8vo., 1s. 6d.

Coach Trimming. By GEORGE A. THRUPP and WILLIAM FARR. With 60 Illustrations. Crown 8vo., 2s. 6d.

CHAPMAN & HALL, LIMITED. 19

Music, Drama, &c.

Music and Manners: Personal Reminiscences and Sketches of Character. By W. BEATTY-KINGSTON. 2 vols. Demy 8vo., 30s.

Musical Celebrities: Portraits and Biographies. By F. F. BUFFEN. Second Series. Crown 4to., 21s.

English of Shakespeare. Illustrated in a Philological Commentary on "Julius Cæsar." By GEORGE LILLIE CRAIK. Eighth Edition. Post 8vo., cloth, 5s.

Musical Instruments. By CARL ENGEL. With numerous Woodcuts. Large crown 8vo., cloth, 2s. 6d.

Henry Irving. A Record of Twenty Years at the Lyceum. By PERCY FITZGERALD, M.A., F.S.A. With Portrait. Demy 8vo., 14s.

The French Stage in the Eighteenth CENTURY. By FREDERICK HAWKINS. With Portraits. 2 vols. Demy 8vo., 30s.

Annals of the French Stage: FROM ITS ORIGIN TO THE DEATH OF RACINE. By FREDERICK HAWKINS. Four Portraits. 2 vols. Demy 8vo., 28s.

Behind the Scenes of the Comédie FRANCAISE, AND OTHER RECOLLECTIONS. By ARSÉNE HOUSSAYE. Translated from the French. Demy 8vo., 14s.

Half a Century of Music in England, 1837—1887. By F. HUEFFER. Demy 8vo., 8s.

Acrobats and Mountebanks. By H. LE ROUX. With over 200 Illustrations by J. GARNIER. Royal 8vo., 16s.

Form and Design in Music: A Brief Outline of the Æsthetic Conditions of the Art, addressed to General Readers. By H. H. STATHAM. With Musical Examples. Demy 8vo., 2s. 6d.

My Thoughts on Music and Musicians. By H. H. STATHAM. Illustrated with Frontispiece of the Entrance-front of Handel's Opera House and Musical Examples. Demy 8vo., 18s.

Natural History.

Agricultural Zoology. By Dr. J. RITZEMA BOS. Translated by Professor J. R. AINSWORTH DAVIS, B.A., F.C.P. With an Introduction by Miss E. A. ORMEROD, F.R.Met.S., F.R.M.S., etc. With 149 Illustrations. Crown 8vo., 6s.

Log-Book of a Fisherman and Zoologist. By FRANK BUCKLAND. With Illustrations. Sixth Thousand. Cr. 8vo., 3s. 6d.

A Year of Sport and Natural History: Shooting, Hunting, Coursing, Falconry, and Fishing. Edited by OSWALD CRAWFURD. With Chapters on Birds of Prey, Nidifications of Birds, and the Habits of British Wild Birds and Animals. With numerous Illustrations by FRANK FELLER, CECIL ALDIN, A. T. ELWES, STANLEY BERKELEY, &c. Demy 4to., 21s.

The Migration of British Birds, including their Post Glacial Emigration as traced by the Application of a New Law of Dispersal. Being a Contribution to the Study of Migration, Geographical Distribution, and Insular Faunas. By CHARLES DIXON. With Maps. Crown 8vo.

The Nests and Eggs of Non-Indigenous British Birds; or, such species that do not Breed within the British Archipelago. By CHARLES DIXON. With Coloured Frontispiece. Crown 8vo., 6s.

Jottings about Birds. By CHARLES DIXON. With Coloured Frontispiece by J. SMIT. Crown 8vo., 6s.

The Nests and Eggs of British Birds: When and Where to Find Them. Being a Handbook to the Oology of the British Islands. By CHAS. DIXON. Cr. 8vo., 6s.
*** *A Large Paper Edition, containing 157 Coloured Illustrations, Demy 8vo., 15s. net.*

The Game Birds and Wild Fowl of THE BRITISH ISLANDS. By CHARLES DIXON. Illustrated by A. T. ELWES. Demy 8vo., 18s.

The Migration of Birds: An Attempt to Reduce the Avian Season-flight to Law. By CHARLES DIXON. Crown 8vo., 6s.

The Birds of Our Rambles: A Companion for the Country. By CHARLES DIXON. With Illustrations by A. T. ELWES. Large crown 8vo., 7s. 6d.

Idle Hours with Nature. By CHARLES DIXON. With Frontispiece. Cr. 8vo., 6s.

Annals of Bird Life: A Year-Book of British Ornithology. By CHARLES DIXON. With Illustrations. Crown 8vo., 7s. 6d.

Birds in a Village. By W. H. HUDSON, C.M.Z.S., Joint Author of "Argentine Ornithology." Square crown 8vo., 7s. 6d.

NATURAL HISTORY—*CONTINUED.*

Idle Days in Patagonia. By W. H. HUDSON, C.M.Z.S. Joint Author of "Argentine Ornithology." With numerous Illustrations by J. SMIT and A. HARTLEY. Demy 8vo., 14*s.*

The Naturalist in La Plata. By W. H. HUDSON, C.M.Z.S. With numerous Illustrations by J. SMIT. Third and Cheaper Edition. Demy 8vo.

Creatures of Other Days. By the Rev. H. N. HUTCHINSON, F.G.S. With a Preface by Sir W. H. FLOWER, K.C.B., F.R.S., and numerous Illustrations by J. SMIT and others. Large Demy 8vo., 14*s.*

Extinct Monsters. A Popular Account of some of the larger forms of Ancient Animal Life. By the Rev. H. N. HUTCHINSON, F.G.S. With numerous Illustrations by J. SMIT and others. Third Thousand, Revised and Enlarged. Demy 8vo., 12*s.*

Economic Entomology. APTERA. By ANDREW MURRAY, F.L.S. With numerous Illustrations. Large crown 8vo., 3*s.* 6*d.*

The Typical Parts in the Skeletons of A CAT, DUCK, AND CODFISH. With comparative descriptions arranged in a Tabular Form. By E. TULLEY NEWTON, F.G.S. New Edition. Demy 8vo., 1*s.*

The Habits of the Salmon. By Major TRAHERNE. Crown 8vo., 3*s.* 6*d.*

Science and Technology.

Building Construction. Key to Examinations of Science and Art Department. By HENRY ADAMS, M.Inst.C.E., M.I.Mech.E., F.S.I., etc. Professor of Engineering at the City of London College. Crown 8vo., 4*s.*

Machine Construction and Drawing: A Key to the Examinations of the Science and Art Department. Subject II. (advanced). By HENRY ADAMS, M.Inst.C.E. Crown 8vo., 2*s.* 6*d.*

Mechanics and Experimental Science. As required for the Matriculation Examination of the University of London. By EDWARD AVELING, D.Sc., Fellow of University College, London.
MECHANICS. With numerous Woodcuts. Crown 8vo., 6*s.* Key to Problems in ditto. Crown 8vo., 3*s.* 6*d.*
CHEMISTRY. With numerous Woodcuts. Crown 8vo., 6*s.* Key to Problems in ditto. Crown 8vo., 2*s.* 6*d.*
MAGNETISM AND ELECTRICITY. With numerous Woodcuts. Crown 8vo., 6*s.*
LIGHT AND HEAT. With numerous Woodcuts. Crown 8vo., 6*s.* Key to the last two volumes in one vol. Crown 8vo., 5*s.*

The Beam: or, Technical Elements of Girder Construction. By W. L. BAKER, A.M.I.C.E. Crown 8vo., 4*s.*

The Chemistry of Foods. By JAMES BELL, Ph.D., &c., Principal of the Somerset House Laboratory. With Microscopic Illustrations. PART I. TEA, COFFEE, COCOA, SUGAR, ETC. Large crown 8vo., 2*s.* 6*d.* PART II. MILK, BUTTER, CHEESE, CEREALS, PREPARED STARCHES, ETC. Large crown 8vo., 3*s.*

Elements of Human Physiology for THE HYGIENE EXAMINATIONS OF THE SCIENCE AND ART DÉPARTMENT. By Dr. J. H. E. BROCK, Assistant Examiner in Hygiene, Science and Art Department. Crown 8vo., 1*s.* 6*d.*

Plain Words About Water. By Professor A. H. CHURCH, M.A. Oxon. Illustrated. Crown 8vo., sewed, 6*d.*

Food: Some Account of its Sources, Constituents, and Uses. By Professor A. H. CHURCH, M.A. Oxon. A New and Revised Edition. Large crown 8vo., cloth, 3*s.*

Sketch of the First Principles of PHYSIOGRAPHY. By JOHN DOUGLAS. With Maps and numerous Illustrations. Crown 8vo., 6*s.*

Thirty Thousand Years of the Earth's PAST HISTORY. By Major-General A. W. DRAYSON. Large crown 8vo., 5*s.*

Practical Metallurgy: An Elementary Text-Book. By A. R. GOWER, Royal School of Mines. With Illustrations. Crown 8vo., 3*s.*

Naval Architecture and Shipbuilding. By GEORGE C. V. HOLMES, Secretary of the Institution of Naval Architects.
[*In the Press.*

Marine Engines and Boilers. By GEORGE C. V. HOLMES. With 69 Woodcuts. Large crown 8vo., 3*s.*

The Sea Boat: How to Build, Rig, and Sail Her. By R. C. LESLIE. With numerous Illustrations by the Author. Crown 8vo., 4*s.* 6*d.*

SCIENCE AND TECHNOLOGY—*CONTINUED.*

A Text-Book of Mechanical Engineering. By WILFRED J. LINEHAM, Head of the Engineering Department at the Goldsmiths' Institute. With 700 Illustrations and 18 folding Plates. Cr. 8vo. 10s. 6d. *net.*

Practical Manual of Chemical Assaying, as applied to the Manufacture of Iron. By L. L. DE KONINCK and E. DIETZ. Edited, with notes, by ROBERT MALLET. Post 8vo., cloth, 6s.

Advanced Physiography (Physiographic Astronomy). Designed to meet the Requirements of Students preparing for the Elementary and Advanced Stages of Physiography in the Science and Art Department Examinations, and as an Introduction to Physical Astronomy. By JOHN MILLS. Crown 8vo., 4s. 6d.

Elementary Physiographic Astronomy. By JOHN MILLS, formerly Assistant to the Solar Physics Committee. Crown 8vo., 1s. 6d.

Alternative Elementary Physics. By JOHN MILLS. Second Edition. Crown 8vo., 2s. 6d.

Quantitative Analysis (INTRODUCTORY LESSONS ON). By JOHN MILLS and BARKER NORTH. With numerous Woodcuts. Crown 8vo., 1s. 6d.

Handbook of Quantitative Analysis. By JOHN MILLS and BARKER NORTH. Crown 8vo., 3s. 6d.

Wood-Working Positions. By W. NELSON, Organiser, Manual Instruction, Manchester School Board. Twelve Illustrations by HERBERT COLE. Royal 4to., 2s. 6d. Large size, 6s.

Handbook to the Special Loan Collection of Scientific Apparatus. 3s.

A Catalogue of Modern Works on Science and Technology. Classified under Authors and Subjects. Twenty-second Edition. With Index. Cr. 8vo., 1s.

Solutions to the Questions in Pure Mathematics—Stages 1 and 2—Set at the Science and Art Examinations from 1881 to 1886. By THOMAS T. RANKIN, C.E., Rector of the Gartsherrie Science School, and West of Scotland Mining College. Crown 8vo., 2s.

Elementary Building Construction. By GEORGE ROBSON. Illustrated by a Design for an Entrance Lodge and Gate. Fifteen Plates. Oblong folio, sewed, 8s.

Home Work in Chemistry (Inorganic): a Series of Exercises with Explanations and Worked Examples. By A. HUMBOLDT SEXTON, F.I.C., F.C.S. Third Edition. Crown 8vo., 1s.

Animal Products: Their Preparation, Commercial Uses, and Value. By T. L. SIMMONDS. With numerous Illustrations. Large crown 8vo., 3s. 6d.

Sport.

The Sea and the Rod. By F. G. AFLALO and Surgeon-General C. T. PASKE. With Illustrations. Crown 8vo., 4s. 6d.

How I became a Sportsman. By AVON. Crown 8vo. With Illustrations. 3s. 6d.

Congo Free State and its Big Game Shooting, TRAVEL AND ADVENTURES. By Captain H. BAILEY (BULA N'ZAU). Illustrated from the Author's sketches. Demy 8vo., 14s.

Songs and Verses. By H. CUMBERLAND BENTLEY. Illustrated by FINCH MASON, and dedicated to J. G. WHYTE MELVILLE. Crown 8vo., 4s.

Sport: Fox Hunting, Salmon Fishing, Covert Shooting, Deer Stalking. By the late W. BROMLEY-DAVENPORT, M.P. With numerous Illustrations by General CREALOCK, C.B. New Cheap Edition. Post 8vo., 3s. 6d.

Log-Book of a Fisherman and Zoologist. By FRANK BUCKLAND. With Illustrations. Sixth Thousand. Cr. 8vo., 3s. 6d.

English and American Yachts. By EDWARD BURGESS. Illustrated with 50 beautiful Photogravure Engravings. Oblong folio, 42s.

A Year of Sport and Natural History: Shooting, Hunting, Coursing, Falconry, and Fishing. Edited by OSWALD CRAWFURD. With Chapters on Birds of Prey, Nidifications of Birds, and the Habits of British Wild Birds and Animals. With numerous Illustrations by FRANK FELLER, CECIL ALDIN, A. T. ELWES, STANLEY BERKELEY, &c. Demy 4to., 21s., *net.*

A Mirror of the Turf; or, The Machinery of Horse-racing Revealed, showing the Sport of Kings as it is to-day. By LOUIS HENRY CURZON. Crown 8vo., 8s.

The Racehorse in Training, with Hints on Racing and Racing Reform. By WILLIAM DAY. Fifth Thousand. Demy 8vo., 9s.

SPORT—*CONTINUED*.

The Highlands of Central India: Notes on their Forests and Wild Tribes, Natural History and Sports. By Captain FORSYTH. With Map and Coloured Illustrations. A New Edition. Demy 8vo., 12s.

The Hunter's Arcadia. By PARKER GILLMORE. With numerous Illustrations. Demy 8vo., 10s. 6d.

Shooting and Salmon Fishing: HINTS AND RECOLLECTIONS. By A. GRIMBLE. Second Edition. With Illustrations. Demy 8vo., 16s.

Highland Sport. By AUGUSTUS GRIMBLE. With Twelve Illustrations by A. Thornburn. Large Paper Edition, 42s. net.

Gun, Rifle, and Hound in the East AND WEST. By "SNAFFLE." With Illustration by HARRY DIXON. Demy 8vo. 14s.

Travels, Sports, and Politics in the East of Europe. By the Marquis of HUNTLY. With Illustrations. Large crown 8vo., 12s.

Norwegian Sketches: Fishing in Strange Waters. By EDWARD KENNARD. Illustrated with 30 beautiful Sketches. Second Edition. 14s.

How to Buy a Horse. With Hints on Shoeing and Stable Management. By PELAGIUS. Third Thousand. Cr. 8vo., 1s.

Incidents of Foreign Sport and Travel. By Colonel POLLOK, Author of "Sport in British Burma." With Illustrations. Demy 8vo., 16s.

Bear Hunting in the White Mountains; or, Alaska and British Columbia Revisited. By H. W. SETON-KARR, F.R.G.S., etc. Illus. Large crown, 4s. 6d.

Ten Years' Travel and Sport in Foreign Lands; or, Travels in the Eighties. By H. W. SETON-KARR, F.R.G.S., etc. Large crown 8vo., 5s.

The Habits of the Salmon. By Major TRAHERNE. Crown 8vo., 3s. 6d.

Sketches in the Hunting Field. By A. E. T. WATSON. A New Edition, with numerous Illustrations by JOHN STURGESS. Crown 8vo., 3s. 6d.

Poachers and Poaching. By JOHN WATSON. With Frontispiece. Crown 8vo., 7s. 6d.

Sketches of British Sporting Fishes. By JOHN WATSON. With Frontispiece. Crown 8vo., 3s. 6d.

Five Months' Sport in Somali Land. By Lord WOLVERTON. With Illustrations. Demy 8vo., 7s. 6d.

Theology, Philosophy, Sociology, etc.

Handbook of Social Economy; or, The Worker's A B C. From the French. By EDMOND ABOUT. With a Biographical and Critical Introduction by W. FRASER RAE. Second Edition, revised. Crown 8vo., 4s.

Constructive Ethics: A Review of Modern Philosophy in its Three Stages of Interpretation, Criticism, and Reconstruction. By W. L. COURTNEY, M.A., LL.D., Demy 8vo., 12s.

The Yoruba-Speaking Peoples of the Slave Coast of West Africa: their Religion, Manners, Customs, Laws, Language, &c. By A. B. ELLIS, Colonel 1st West India Regiment. With an Appendix and Map. Demy 8vo., 10s. 6d.

The Ewe-Speaking People of the Slave Coast of West Africa. By A. B. ELLIS. With Map. Demy 8vo., 10s. 6d.

The Tshi-Speaking Peoples of the Gold Coast; their Religion, Manners, Customs, Laws, Language, &c. By A. B. ELLIS. With Map. Demy 8vo., 10s. 6d.

The Science of Language: LINGUISTICS PHILOLOGY, AND ETYMOLOGY. By ABEL HOVELACQUE. With Maps. Large crown 8vo., cloth, 3s. 6d.

Philistines and Israelites: A New Light on the World's History. By H. MARTYN KENNARD. Demy 4to., 6s.

Jesus Christ; God; and God and Man. Conferences delivered at Notre Dame in Paris. By PERE LACORDAIRE. Seventh Thousand. Crown 8vo., 3s. 6d.

Human Origins: Evidence from History and Science. By S. LAING. With Illustrations. Twelfth Thousand. Demy 8vo., 3s. 6d.

Problems of the Future and Essays. By S. LAING. Thirteenth Thousand. Demy 8vo., 3s. 6d.

Modern Science and Modern Thought. By S. LAING. Nineteenth Thousand. Demy 8vo., 3s. 6d.

A Modern Zoroastrian. By S. LAING. Ninth Thousand. Demy 8vo., 3s. 6d.

CHAPMAN & HALL, LIMITED. 23

THEOLOGY, &c.—*CONTINUED.*

Words of a Believer, and the Past and Future of the People. By F. LAMENNAIS. Translated from the French by L. E. MARTINEAU. With a Memoir of Lamennais. Crown 8vo., 4s.

The Elements of Political Economy. By EMILE DE LAVELEYE. Translated by W. POLLARD, B.A., St. John's College, Oxford. Crown 8vo., 6s.

Evolution; Its Nature, Its Evidences, and Its Relations to Religious Thought. By JOSEPH LE CONTE, Professor of Geology and Natural History in the University of California. A New and Revised Edition. Crown 8vo. 6s.

Philosophy, Historical and Critical. By ANDRÉ LEFEVRE. Translated, with an Introduction, by A. W. KEANE, B.A. Large crown 8vo., 3s. 6d.

Papacy, Socialism, and Democracy. By ANATOLE LEROY-BEAULIEU, Member of the Institute of France. Translated by Professor B. L. O'DONNELL. Crown 8vo., 7s. 6d.

Sociology. Based upon Ethnology. By Dr. CHARLES LETOURNEAU. Large crown 8vo., 3s. 6d.

Biology. By Dr. CHARLES LETOURNEAU. With 83 Illustrations. A New Edition. Demy 8vo., 3s. 6d.

The Claims of Christianity. By W. S. LILLY. Demy 8vo., 12s.

On Shibboleths. By W. S. LILLY. Demy 8vo., 12s.

On Right and Wrong. By W. S. LILLY. Second Edition. Demy 8vo., 12s.

Chapters on European History. By W. S. LILLY. With an Introductory Dialogue on the Philosophy of History. 2 vols. Demy 8vo., 21s.

A Century of Revolution. By W. S. LILLY. Second Edition. Demy 8vo., 12s.

Ancient Religion and Modern Thought. By W. S. LILLY. Second Edition. Demy 8vo., 12s.

The Progress of Science: Its Origin, Course, Promoters and Results. By J. V. MARMERY. Demy 8vo., 7s. 6d.

The Future of Science: Ideas of 1848. By ERNEST RENAN. Demy 8vo., 18s.

History of the People of Israel. By ERNEST RENAN.
FIRST DIVISION. Till the Time of King David. Demy 8vo., 14s.
SECOND DIVISION. From the Reign of David up to the Capture of Samaria. Demy 8vo., 14s.
THIRD DIVISION. From the time of Hezekiah till the return from Babylon. Demy 8vo., 14s.

Esoteric Buddhism. By A. P. SINNETT. Annotated and enlarged by the Author. Seventh Edition. Crown 8vo., 3s. 6d.

Aphorisms from the Writings of HERBERT SPENCER. Selected by JULIA RAYMOND GINGELL. With a Photogravure Portrait. Second Thousand. Crown 8vo., 3s.

Anthropology. By Dr. PAUL TOPINARD. With a Preface by Professor PAUL BROCA. With 49 Illustrations. Demy 8vo., 3s. 6d.

Æsthetics. By EUGENE VERON. Translated by W. H. ARMSTRONG. Large crown 8vo., 3s. 6d.

A Modern Layman's Faith Concerning the Creed and the Breed of the "Thoroughbred Man." By W. B. WOODGATE. Demy 8vo., 14s.

Travel.

Woman in India. By MARY FRANCES BILLINGTON. With a preface by the Marchioness of DUFFERIN and AVA, C.I., and numerous Illustrations by HERBERT JOHNSON and others. Demy 8vo., 14s.

Through the Heart of Asia over the Pamir to India. By GABRIEL BONVALOT. Translated from the French by C. B. PITMAN. With 250 Illustrations by ALBERT PÉPIN. Royal 8vo., 32s.

Winters in Algeria. By F. A. BRIDGMAN. With 62 Illustrations. Royal 8vo., 10s. 6d.

Two Summers in Greenland: An Artist's Adventures among Ice and Islands in Fjords and Mountains. By A. RIIS CARSTENSEN. With numerous Illustrations by the Author. Demy 8vo., 14s.

The Ancient Cities of the New World. Being Travels and Explorations in Mexico and Central America, 1857-1882. By DÉSIRÉ CHARNAY. With upwards of 200 Illustrations. Super royal 8vo., 31s. 6d.

Round the Calendar in Portugal. By OSWALD CRAWFURD. With numerous Illustrations. Royal 8vo., 18s.

TRAVEL—*CONTINUED.*

Sketches of Hindoo Life. By DEVENDRA N. DAS. Crown 8vo., 5s.

Three Months' Tour in Ireland. By MADAME DE BOVET. Translated and Condensed by Mrs. ARTHUR WALTER. With Illustrations. Crown 8vo., 6s.

Around Tonkin and Siam. By Prince HENRY D'ORLEANS. Translated by C. B. PITMAN. With 28 Illustrations. Demy 8vo., 14s.

From Pekin to Calais by Land. By H. DE WINDT. With numerous Illustrations by C. E. FRIPP from Sketches by the Author. New and Cheaper Edition. 7s. 6d.

A Ride to India Across Persia and Beluchistan. By H. DE WINDT. With numerous Illustrations. Demy 8vo., 16s.

American Notes and Pictures from Italy. By CHARLES DICKENS. With 8 Illustrations. Demy 8vo., 10s.; post 8vo., 8s.; crown 8vo., 5s., 3s. 6d., 2s. 6d. and 2s.; 4to., 3s.; royal 8vo., 3s. 6d.; fcap. 8vo., 1s. 6d.

Gibraltar. By HENRY M. FIELD. With numerous Illustrations. Demy 8vo., 7s. 6d.

The Highlands of Central India: Notes on their Forests and Wild Tribes, Natural History and Sports. By Captain FORSYTH. With Map and Coloured Illustrations. A new Edition. Demy 8vo., 12s.

Round About the Crooked Spire. By ALBERT J. FOSTER, M.A. With Illustrations. Crown 8vo., 5s.

With the Camel Corps up the Nile. By Count GLEICHEN. With numerous Sketches by the Author. Third Edition. Large crown 8vo., 9s.

A Land of Mosques and Marabouts. By the Hon. Mrs. GREVILLE-NUGENT. Illustrated. Demy 8vo., 14s.

The Marches of Wales: Notes and Impressions on the Welsh Borders, from the Severn Sea to the Sands o' Dee. By CHARLES G. HARPER. With 114 Illustrations. Demy 8vo., 16s.

A Week's Tramp in Dickens-Land. By W. R. HUGHES, F.L.S. With upwards of 100 Illustrations by F. G. KITTON, HERBERT RAILTON, and others. Second Edition. Demy 8vo., 7s. 6d.

Travels, Sports, and Politics in the East of Europe. By the Marquis of HUNTLY. With Illustrations. Large crown 8vo., 12s.

Life Aboard a British Privateer in the Time of Queen Anne. Being the Journals of Captain Woodes Rogers, Master Mariner. With Notes and Illustrations by R. C. LESLIE. A New and Cheaper Edition. Large crown 8vo., 3s. 6d.

Travels in Africa. By Dr. WM. JUNKER. Translated from the German by Professor KEANE.

Vol. I. DURING THE YEARS 1875 TO 1878. Containing 38 Full-page Plates and 125 Illustrations in the Text and Map. Demy 8vo., 21s.

Vol. II. DURING THE YEARS 1879 TO 1883. Containing numerous Full-page Plates and Illustrations in the Text and Map. Demy 8vo., 21s.

Vol. III. DURING THE YEARS 1882 TO 1886. Containing numerous Full-page Plates and Illustrations in the Text and Maps. Demy 8vo., 21s.

Across the Border; or, Pathan and Biloch. By E. E. OLIVER, Under-Secretary to the Public Works Department, Punjaub. With numerous Illustrations by J. L. KIPLING, C.I.E. Demy 8vo., 14s.

Round about New Zealand. Being Notes from a Journal of Three Years' Wandering in the Antipodes. By E. W. PAYTON. With Twenty Original Illustrations by the Author. Large crown 8vo., 12s.

Incidents of Foreign Sport and Travel. By Colonel POLLOK, Author of "Sport in British Burma." With Illustrations by A. T. ELWES. Demy 8vo., 16s.

A Suburb of Yedo. By the late THEOBALD A. PURCELL. Illustrated. Crown 8vo., 2s. 6d.

Spanish Cities: with Glimpses of Gibraltar and Tangiers. By C. A. STODDARD. With 18 Illustrations. Large crown 8vo., 7s. 6d.

Across Russia from the Baltic to the Danube. By C. A. STODDARD. With numerous Illustrations. Large crown 8vo., 7s. 6d.

With Stanley's Rear Column. By J. ROSE TROUP. With Portraits and Illustrations. Second Edition. Demy 8vo., 16s.

Untrodden Paths in Roumania. By Mrs. WALKER. With 77 Illustrations. Demy 8vo., 10s. 6d.

Eastern Life and Scenery, with Excursions to Asia Minor, Mitylene, Crete, and Roumania. By Mrs. WALKER. 2 vols., with Frontispiece to each vol. Crown 8vo., 21s.

A Month in Yorkshire. By WALTER WHITE. With a Map. Fifth Edition. Post 8vo., 4s.

A Londoner's Walk to the Land's End, and a Trip to the Scilly Isles. By WALTER WHITE. With 4 Maps. Third Edition. Post 8vo., 4s.

THOMAS CARLYLE'S WORKS.

THE ASHBURTON EDITION.
Handsomely printed, containing all the Portraits and Illustrations, in Twenty Volumes, demy 8vo., 8s. each.

THE FRENCH REVOLUTION AND PAST AND PRESENT. 2 vols.
SARTOR RESARTUS; HEROES AND HERO WORSHIP. 1 vol.
LIFE OF JOHN STERLING—LIFE OF SCHILLER. 1 vol.
LATTER-DAY PAMPHLETS—EARLY KINGS OF NORWAY—ESSAY ON THE PORTRAIT OF JOHN KNOX. 1 vol.
LETTERS AND SPEECHES OF OLIVER CROMWELL. 3 vols.
HISTORY OF FREDERICK THE GREAT. 6 vols.
CRITICAL AND MISCELLANEOUS ESSAYS. 3 vols.
TRANSLATIONS FROM THE GERMAN. 3 vols.

LIBRARY EDITION.
Handsomely printed in 34 Vols., demy 8vo., £15 3s.

SARTOR RESARTUS. With a Portrait, 7s. 6d.
THE FRENCH REVOLUTION. A History. 3 vols., each 9s.
LIFE OF FREDERICK SCHILLER AND EXAMINATION OF HIS WORKS. With Supplement of 1872. Portrait and Plates, 9s.
CRITICAL AND MISCELLANEOUS ESSAYS. With Portrait. 6 vols., each 9s.
ON HEROES, HERO WORSHIP, AND THE HEROIC IN HISTORY. 7s. 6d.
PAST AND PRESENT. 9s.

OLIVER CROMWELL'S LETTERS AND SPEECHES. With Portraits. 5 vols., each 9s.
LATTER-DAY PAMPHLETS. 9s.
LIFE OF JOHN STERLING. With Portrait, 9s.
HISTORY OF FREDERICK THE SECOND. 10 vols., each 9s.
TRANSLATIONS FROM THE GERMAN. 3 vols., each 9s.
EARLY KINGS OF NORWAY; ESSAY ON THE PORTRAITS OF JOHN KNOX; AND GENERAL INDEX. With Portrait Illustrations. 8vo., cloth, 9s.

PEOPLE'S EDITION.
37 vols., small crown 8vo., 37s.; separate vols., 1s. each.

SARTOR RESARTUS. With Portrait of Thomas Carlyle.
FRENCH REVOLUTION. A History. 3 vols.
OLIVER CROMWELL'S LETTERS AND SPEECHES. 5 vols. With Portrait of Oliver Cromwell.
ON HEROES AND HERO WORSHIP AND THE HEROIC IN HISTORY.
PAST AND PRESENT.
CRITICAL AND MISCELLANEOUS ESSAYS. 7 vols.

THE LIFE OF SCHILLER AND EXAMINATION OF HIS WORKS. With Portrait.
LATTER-DAY PAMPHLETS.
WILHELM MEISTER. 3 vols.
LIFE OF JOHN STERLING. With Portrait.
HISTORY OF FREDERICK THE GREAT. 10 vols.
TRANSLATIONS FROM MUSÆUS, TIECK, AND RICHTER. 2 vols.
THE EARLY KINGS OF NORWAY; Essay on the Portraits of Knox.

Or in sets, 37 vols. in 18, 37s.

THOMAS CARLYLE'S WORKS—*Continued.*

THE HALF-CROWN EDITION.

This Edition includes the whole of Carlyle's Writings and Translations, together with the Portraits and Maps, and is complete in twenty volumes. Crown 8vo. Price 2s. 6d. each.

SARTOR RESARTUS AND LATTER-DAY PAMPHLETS. With a Portrait of Thomas Carlyle.

PAST AND PRESENT AND ON HEROES AND HERO WORSHIP.

LIFE OF JOHN STERLING AND LIFE OF SCHILLER.

CRITICAL AND MISCELLANEOUS ESSAYS, EARLY KINGS OF NORWAY, AND ESSAY ON THE PORTRAITS OF KNOX. *In four volumes.*

FRENCH REVOLUTION: A HISTORY. *In two volumes.*

OLIVER CROMWELL'S LETTERS AND SPEECHES, with Portrait of Oliver Cromwell. *In three volumes.*

HISTORY OF FREDERICK THE GREAT. *In five volumes.*

WILHELM MEISTER. *In two volumes.*

TRANSLATIONS FROM MUSÆUS, TIECK AND RICHTER. *In one volume.*

CHEAP ISSUE.

Bound in Blue Cloth.

THE FRENCH REVOLUTION. One volume. With Portrait. Crown 8vo., 2s.

SARTOR RESARTUS, HEROES AND HERO WORSHIP, PAST AND PRESENT, AND CHARTISM. One volume. Crown 8vo., 2s.

OLIVER CROMWELL'S LETTERS AND SPEECHES. Crown 8vo., 2s. 6d.

CRITICAL AND MISCELLANEOUS ESSAYS. 2 vols. 4s.

WILHELM MEISTER. One volume, 2s.

LIVES OF SCHILLER AND STERLING. With Portraits. One volume, 2s.

SIXPENNY EDITION. 4to., sewed.

SARTOR RESARTUS. Eightieth Thousand.

HEROES AND HERO WORSHIP.

ESSAYS: BURNS, JOHNSON, SCOTT, THE DIAMOND NECKLACE.

The above in 1 vol., cloth, 2s. 6d.

CHARLES DICKENS'S WORKS.
ORIGINAL EDITIONS.

In demy 8vo.

THE MYSTERY OF EDWIN DROOD. With Illustrations by S. L. FILDES, and a Portrait engraved by BAKER. Cloth, 7s. 6d.

OUR MUTUAL FRIEND. With Forty Illustrations by MARCUS STONE. Cloth, £1 1s.

THE PICKWICK PAPERS. With Forty-three Illustrations by SEYMOUR and PHIZ. Cloth, £1 1s.

NICHOLAS NICKLEBY. With Forty Illustrations by PHIZ. Cloth, £1 1s.

SKETCHES BY "BOZ." With Forty Illustrations by GEORGE CRUIKSHANK. Cloth, £1 1s.

MARTIN CHUZZLEWIT. With Forty Illustrations by PHIZ. Cloth, £1 1s.

DOMBEY AND SON. With Forty Illustrations by PHIZ. Cloth, £1 1s.

DAVID COPPERFIELD. With Forty Illustrations by PHIZ. Cloth, £1 1s.

BLEAK HOUSE. With Forty Illustrations by PHIZ. Cloth, £1 1s.

LITTLE DORRIT. With Forty Illustrations by PHIZ. Cloth, £1 1s.

THE OLD CURIOSITY SHOP. With Seventy-five Illustrations by GEORGE CATTERMOLE and H. K. BROWNE. A New Edition. Uniform with the other volumes, £1 1s.

BARNABY RUDGE: A Tale of the Riots of 'Eighty. With Seventy-eight Illustrations by GEORGE CATTERMOLE and H. K. BROWNE. Uniform with the other volumes, £1 1s.

CHRISTMAS BOOKS: Containing—The Christmas Carol; The Cricket on the Hearth; The Chimes; The Battle of Life; The Haunted House. With all the original Illustrations. Cloth, 12s.

OLIVER TWIST AND TALE OF TWO CITIES. In one volume. Cloth, £1 1s.

OLIVER TWIST. Separately. With Twenty-four Illustrations by GEORGE CRUIKSHANK. Cloth, 11s.

A TALE OF TWO CITIES. Separately. With Sixteen Illustrations by PHIZ. Cloth, 9s.

** The remainder of Dickens's Works were not originally printed in demy 8vo.

LIBRARY EDITION.

In post 8vo. With the Original Illustrations, 30 vols., cloth, £12.

	Illustrations.	Vols.	s.	d.
PICKWICK PAPERS	43	2	16	0
NICHOLAS NICKLEBY	39	2	16	0
MARTIN CHUZZLEWIT	40	2	16	0
OLD CURIOSITY SHOP AND REPRINTED PIECES	36	2	16	0
BARNABY RUDGE AND HARD TIMES	36	2	16	0
BLEAK HOUSE	40	2	16	0
LITTLE DORRIT	40	2	16	0
DOMBEY AND SON	38	2	16	0
DAVID COPPERFIELD	38	2	16	0
OUR MUTUAL FRIEND	40	2	16	0
SKETCHES BY "BOZ"	39	1	8	0
OLIVER TWIST	24	1	8	0
CHRISTMAS BOOKS	17	1	8	0
A TALE OF TWO CITIES	16	1	8	0
GREAT EXPECTATIONS	8	1	8	0
PICTURES FROM ITALY AND AMERICAN NOTES	8	1	8	0
UNCOMMERCIAL TRAVELLER	8	1	8	0
CHILD'S HISTORY OF ENGLAND	8	1	8	0
EDWIN DROOD AND MISCELLANIES	12	1	8	0
CHRISTMAS STORIES from "Household Words," &c.	14	1	8	0

Uniform with the above, 10s. 6d.

THE LIFE OF CHARLES DICKENS. By JOHN FORSTER. With Illustrations.

CHARLES DICKENS'S WORKS—*Continued.*

THE "CHARLES DICKENS" EDITION.
In crown 8vo. In 21 vols., cloth, with Illustrations, £3 16s.

	Illustrations.	s.	d.
PICKWICK PAPERS	8	4	0
MARTIN CHUZZLEWIT	8	4	0
DOMBEY AND SON	8	4	0
NICHOLAS NICKLEBY	8	4	0
DAVID COPPERFIELD	8	4	0
BLEAK HOUSE	8	4	0
LITTLE DORRIT	8	4	0
OUR MUTUAL FRIEND	8	4	0
BARNABY RUDGE	8	3	6
OLD CURIOSITY SHOP	8	3	6
A CHILD'S HISTORY OF ENGLAND	4	3	6
EDWIN DROOD AND OTHER STORIES	8	3	6
CHRISTMAS STORIES from "Household Words"	8	3	6
SKETCHES BY "BOZ"	8	3	6
AMERICAN NOTES AND REPRINTED PIECES	8	3	6
CHRISTMAS BOOKS	8	3	6
OLIVER TWIST	8	3	6
GREAT EXPECTATIONS	8	3	6
TALE OF TWO CITIES	8	3	0
HARD TIMES AND PICTURES FROM ITALY	8	3	0
UNCOMMERCIAL TRAVELLER	4	3	0

Uniform with the above.

THE LIFE OF CHARLES DICKENS. Numerous Illustrations. 2 vols.   7 0
THE LETTERS OF CHARLES DICKENS. 2 vols.   7 0

THE HALF-CROWN EDITION.
PRINTED FROM THE EDITION THAT WAS CAREFULLY CORRECTED BY THE AUTHOR, IN 1867 AND 1868.

Complete in 21 vols. Containing the whole of the original Illustrations. Crown 8vo., 2s. 6d. each.

THE PICKWICK PAPERS. With 43 Illustrations by SEYMOUR and PHIZ.
BARNABY RUDGE: A Tale of the Riots of 'Eighty. With 76 Illustrations by GEORGE CATTERMOLE and H. K. BROWNE.
OLIVER TWIST. With 24 Illustrations by CRUIKSHANK.
THE OLD CURIOSITY SHOP. With 75 Illustrations by GEORGE CATTERMOLE and H. K. BROWNE.
DAVID COPPERFIELD. With 40 Illustrations by PHIZ.
NICHOLAS NICKLEBY. With 40 Illustrations by PHIZ.
MARTIN CHUZZLEWIT. With 40 Illustrations by PHIZ.
DOMBEY AND SON. With 40 Illustrations by PHIZ.
SKETCHES BY "BOZ." With 40 Illustrations by GEORGE CRUIKSHANK.
CHRISTMAS BOOKS. With 64 Illustrations by LANDSEER, DOYLE, MACLISE, LEECH, etc.
BLEAK HOUSE. With 40 Illustrations by PHIZ.
LITTLE DORRIT. With 40 Illustrations by PHIZ.
CHRISTMAS STORIES, from "Household Words." With 24 Illustrations by DALZIEL, GREEN, MAHONEY, etc.
AMERICAN NOTES and REPRINTED PIECES. With 8 Illustrations by MARCUS STONE and F. WALKER.
HARD TIMES and PICTURES FROM ITALY. With 8 Illustrations by F. WALKER and MARCUS STONE.
A CHILD'S HISTORY OF ENGLAND. With 8 Illustrations by MARCUS STONE.
GREAT EXPECTATIONS. With 8 Illustrations by MARCUS STONE.
TALE OF TWO CITIES. With 16 Illustrations by PHIZ.
UNCOMMERCIAL TRAVELLER. With 8 Illustrations by MARCUS STONE.
OUR MUTUAL FRIEND. With 40 Illustrations by MARCUS STONE.
EDWIN DROOD and OTHER STORIES. With 12 Illustrations by LUKE FILDES.

CHARLES DICKENS'S WORKS—*Continued.*

THE ILLUSTRATED LIBRARY EDITION.

Complete in 32 Volumes. Demy 8vo., 10s. each; or set, £16.

This Edition is printed on a finer paper and in a larger type than has been employed in any previous edition. The type has been cast especially for it, and the page is of a size to admit of the introduction of all the original illustrations.

No such attractive issue has been made of the writings of Mr. Dickens, which, various as have been the forms of publication adapted to the demands of an ever widely-increasing popularity, have never yet been worthily presented in a really handsome library form.

The collection comprises all the minor writings it was Mr. Dickens's wish to preserve.

SKETCHES BY "BOZ." With 40 Illustrations by GEORGE CRUIKSHANK.
PICKWICK PAPERS. 2 vols. With 42 Illustrations by PHIZ.
OLIVER TWIST. With 24 Illustrations by CRUIKSHANK.
NICHOLAS NICKLEBY. 2 vols. With 40 Illustrations by PHIZ.
OLD CURIOSITY SHOP AND REPRINTED PIECES. 2 vols. With Illustrations by CATTERMOLE, &c.
BARNABY RUDGE AND HARD TIMES. 2 vols. With Illustrations by CATTERMOLE, &c.
MARTIN CHUZZLEWIT. 2 vols. With 40 Illustrations by PHIZ.
AMERICAN NOTES AND PICTURES FROM ITALY. 1 vol. With 8 Illusts.
DOMBEY AND SON. 2 vols. With 40 Illustrations by PHIZ.
DAVID COPPERFIELD. 2 vols. With 40 Illustrations by PHIZ.

BLEAK HOUSE. 2 vols. With 40 Illustrations by PHIZ.
LITTLE DORRIT. 2 vols. With 40 Illustrations by PHIZ.
A TALE OF TWO CITIES. With 16 Illustrations by PHIZ.
THE UNCOMMERCIAL TRAVELLER. With 8 Illustrations by MARCUS STONE.
GREAT EXPECTATIONS. With 8 Illustrations by MARCUS STONE.
OUR MUTUAL FRIEND. 2 vols. With 40 Illustrations by MARCUS STONE.
CHRISTMAS BOOKS. With 17 Illustrations by Sir EDWIN LANDSEER, R.A., MACLISE, R.A., &c., &c.
HISTORY OF ENGLAND. With 8 Illustrations by MARCUS STONE.
CHRISTMAS STORIES. (From "Household Words" and "All the Year Round.") With 14 Illustrations.
EDWIN DROOD AND OTHER STORIES. With 12 Illustrations by S. L. FILDES.

Uniform with above.

LIFE OF CHARLES DICKENS. By JOHN FORSTER. With Portraits. 2 vols.

HOUSEHOLD EDITION.

(WITH LIFE.)

In 22 Volumes. Crown 4to., cloth, £4 8s. 6d.

MARTIN CHUZZLEWIT. With 59 Illustrations, 5s.
DAVID COPPERFIELD. With 60 Illustrations and a Portrait, 5s.
BLEAK HOUSE. With 61 Illustrations, 5s.
LITTLE DORRIT. With 58 Illus., 5s.
PICKWICK PAPERS. With 56 Illus., 5s.
OUR MUTUAL FRIEND. With 58 Illustrations, 5s.
NICHOLAS NICKLEBY. With 59 Illustrations, 5s.
DOMBEY AND SON. With 61 Illus., 5s.
EDWIN DROOD; REPRINTED PIECES; and other Stories, with 30 Illustrations, 5s.
THE LIFE OF DICKENS. By JOHN FORSTER. With 40 Illustrations, 5s.
BARNABY RUDGE. With 46 Illus., 4s.

OLD CURIOSITY SHOP. With 32 Illustrations, 4s.
CHRISTMAS STORIES. With 23 Illustrations, 4s.
OLIVER TWIST. With 28 Illus., 3s.
GREAT EXPECTATIONS. With 26 Illustrations, 3s.
SKETCHES BY "BOZ." With 36 Illus. 3s.
UNCOMMERCIAL TRAVELLER. With 26 Illustrations, 3s.
CHRISTMAS BOOKS. With 28 Illus., 3s.
THE HISTORY OF ENGLAND. With 15 Illustrations, 3s.
AMERICAN NOTES AND PICTURES FROM ITALY. With 18 Illus., 3s.
A TALE OF TWO CITIES. With 25 Illustrations, 3s.
HARD TIMES. With 20 Illus., 2s. 6d.

CHARLES DICKENS'S WORKS—*Continued.*

THE CROWN EDITION,

Complete in 17 vols. Containing all the Original Illustrations; and the Letterpress is printed from Type expressly cast for this Edition. Large Crown 8vo. Price Five Shillings each.

THE PICKWICK PAPERS. With Forty-three Illustrations by SEYMOUR and PHIZ.
NICHOLAS NICKLEBY. With Forty Illustrations by PHIZ.
DOMBEY AND SON. With Forty Illustrations by PHIZ.
DAVID COPPERFIELD. With Forty Illustrations by PHIZ.
SKETCHES BY "BOZ." With Forty Illustrations by GEO. CRUIKSHANK.
MARTIN CHUZZLEWIT. With Forty Illustrations by PHIZ.
THE OLD CURIOSITY SHOP. With Seventy-five Illustrations by GEORGE CATTERMOLE and H. K. BROWNE.
BARNABY RUDGE: a Tale of the Riots of 'Eighty. With Seventy-eight Illustrations by GEORGE CATTERMOLE and H. K. BROWNE.
OLIVER TWIST and A TALE OF TWO CITIES. With Twenty-four Illustrations by CRUIKSHANK and Sixteen by PHIZ.
BLEAK HOUSE. With Forty Illustrations by PHIZ.

LITTLE DORRIT. With Forty Illustrations by PHIZ.
OUR MUTUAL FRIEND. With Forty Illustrations by MARCUS STONE.
AMERICAN NOTES; PICTURES FROM ITALY; and A CHILD'S HISTORY OF ENGLAND. With Sixteen Illustrations by MARCUS STONE.
CHIRSTMAS BOOKS AND HARD TIMES. With Illustrations by LANDSEER, MACLISE, STANFIELD, LEECH, DOYLE, F. WALKER, etc.
CHRISTMAS STORIES AND OTHER STORIES, including HUMPHREY'S CLOCK. With Illustrations by DALZIEL, CHARLES GREEN, MAHONEY, PHIZ, CATTERMOLE, etc.
GREAT EXPECTATIONS. UNCOMMERCIAL TRAVELLER. With Sixteen Illustrations by MARCUS STONE.
EDWIN DROOD and REPRINTED PIECES. With Sixteen Illustrations by LUKE FILDES and F. WALKER.

Uniform with the above.

THE LIFE OF CHARLES DICKENS. By JOHN FORSTER. With Portraits and Illustrations. Will be added at the request of numerous Subscribers.
THE DICKENS DICTIONARY. A Key to the Characters and Principal Incidents in the Tales of Charles Dickens. By GILBERT PIERCE, with additions by WILLIAM A. WHEELER.
THE LAZY TOUR OF TWO IDLE APPRENTICES; NO THOROUGHFARE; THE PERILS OF CERTAIN ENGLISH PRISONERS. By CHARLES DICKENS and WILKIE COLLINS. With Illustrations. Crown 8vo., 5s.

** These Stories are now reprinted in complete form for the first time.

CHARLES DICKENS'S CHRISTMAS BOOKS.
REPRINTED FROM THE ORIGINAL PLATES.

Illustrated by JOHN LEECH, D. MACLISE, R.A., R. DOYLE, C. STANFIELD, R.A., *etc.*
Fcap. cloth, 1s. *each.* *Complete in a case*, 5s.

A CHRISTMAS CAROL IN PROSE.
THE CHIMES: A GOBLIN STORY.
THE CRICKET ON THE HEARTH: A FAIRY TALE OF HOME.
THE BATTLE OF LIFE. A LOVE STORY.
THE HAUNTED MAN AND THE GHOST'S STORY.

SIXPENNY REPRINTS of DICKENS'S WORKS.

OLIVER TWIST. With 28 Illustrations by J. MAHONEY. Medium 8vo.
READINGS FROM THE WORKS OF CHARLES DICKENS. As selected and read by himself, and now published for the first time. Illustrated.
A CHRISTMAS CAROL AND THE HAUNTED MAN. Illustrated.
THE CHIMES: A GOBLIN STORY, AND THE CRICKET ON THE HEARTH. Illustrated.
THE BATTLE OF LIFE: A LOVE STORY, HUNTED DOWN, AND A HOLIDAY ROMANCE. Illustrated.

CHARLES DICKENS'S WORKS—*Continued.*

THE CABINET EDITION.

In 32 vols., small fcap. 8vo., Marble Paper Sides, Cloth Backs, with uncut edges, price Eighteenpence each. Each Volume contains Eight Illustrations reproduced from the Originals. In Sets only, bound in blue and red cloth, with cut edges, £2 8s.

CHRISTMAS BOOKS.
MARTIN CHUZZLEWIT, 2 vols.
DAVID COPPERFIELD, 2 vols.
OLIVER TWIST.
GREAT EXPECTATIONS.
NICHOLAS NICKLEBY, 2 vols.
SKETCHES BY "BOZ."
CHRISTMAS STORIES.
THE PICKWICK PAPERS, 2 vols.
BARNABY RUDGE, 2 vols.
BLEAK HOUSE, 2 vols.

AMERICAN NOTES AND PICTURES FROM ITALY.
EDWIN DROOD; & OTHER STORIES.
THE OLD CURIOSITY SHOP, 2 vols.
A CHILD'S HISTORY OF ENGLAND.
DOMBEY AND SON, 2 vols.
A TALE OF TWO CITIES.
LITTLE DORRIT, 2 vols.
MUTUAL FRIEND, 2 vols.
HARD TIMES.
UNCOMMERCIAL TRAVELLER.
REPRINTED PIECES.

THE PICTORIAL EDITION.

CONTAINING UPWARDS OF NINE HUNDRED ENGRAVINGS.

Complete in 17 vols. Royal 8vo., 3s. 6d. each.

DOMBEY AND SON. With 62 Illustrations by F. BARNARD.
DAVID COPPERFIELD. With 61 Illustrations by F. BARNARD.
NICHOLAS NICKLEBY. With 59 Illustrations by F. BARNARD.
BARNABY RUDGE. With 46 Illustrations by F. BARNARD.
OLD CURIOSITY SHOP. With 39 Illustrations by CHARLES GREEN.
MARTIN CHUZZLEWIT. With 59 Illustrations by F. BARNARD.
OLIVER TWIST AND A TALE OF TWO CITIES. With 53 Illustrations by J. MAHONEY and F. BARNARD.
OUR MUTUAL FRIEND. With 58 Illustrations by J. MAHONEY.
BLEAK HOUSE. With 61 Illustrations by F. BARNARD.
PICKWICK PAPERS. With 57 Illustrations by PHIZ.

LITTLE DORRIT. With 58 Illustrations by J. MAHONEY.
GREAT EXPECTATIONS AND HARD TIMES. With 50 Illustrations by J. A. FRASER and H. FRENCH.
AMERICAN NOTES, PICTURES FROM ITALY, AND A CHILD'S HISTORY OF ENGLAND. With 33 Illustrations by FROST, GORDON, THOMSON, and RALSTON.
SKETCHES BY "BOZ" AND CHRISTMAS BOOKS. With 62 Illustrations by F. BARNARD.
CHRISTMAS STORIES AND UNCOMMERCIAL TRAVELLER. With 49 Illustrations by E. G. DALZIEL.
EDWIN DROOD, REPRINTED PIECES, AND OTHER STORIES. With 30 Illustrations by L. FILDES, E. G. DALZIEL, and F. BARNARD.
THE LIFE OF CHARLES DICKENS. By JOHN FORSTER. With 40 Illustrations by F. BARNARD and others.

THE TWO - SHILLING EDITION.

Each Volume contains a Frontispiece. Crown 8vo., 2s.

DOMBEY AND SON.
MARTIN CHUZZLEWIT.
THE PICKWICK PAPERS.
BLEAK HOUSE.
OLD CURIOSITY SHOP.
BARNABY RUDGE.
DAVID COPPERFIELD.
NICHOLAS NICKLEBY.
CHRISTMAS STORIES.
AMERICAN NOTES.
HARD TIMES AND PICTURES FROM ITALY.

GREAT EXPECTATIONS.
OUR MUTUAL FRIEND.
CHRISTMAS BOOKS.
OLIVER TWIST.
LITTLE DORRIT.
TALE OF TWO CITIES.
UNCOMMERCIAL TRAVELLER.
SKETCHES BY "BOZ."
A CHILD'S HISTORY OF ENGLAND.
EDWIN DROOD AND OTHER STORIES.

The Fortnightly Review.

EDITED BY W. L. COURTNEY.

PRICE TWO SHILLINGS AND SIXPENCE.

The FORTNIGHTLY REVIEW is published Monthly.

A VOLUME IS COMPLETED EVERY SIX MONTHS.

The following are among the Contributors:—

ADMIRAL LORD ALCESTER.
SIR RUTHERFORD ALCOCK.
PROFESSOR BAIN.
SIR SAMUEL BAKER.
SIR R. BALL, F.R.S.
PROFESSOR BEESLY.
PAUL BOURGET.
DR. BRIDGES.
HON. GEORGE C. BRODRICK.
FERDINAND BRUNETIERE.
JAMES BRYCE, M.P.
EMILIO CASTELAR.
RT. HON. J. CHAMBERLAIN, M.P.
PROFESSOR SIDNEY COLVIN.
THE EARL COMPTON.
MONTAGUE CRACKENTHORPE, Q.C.
L. H. COURTNEY, M.P.
G. H. DARWIN.
PROFESSOR A. V. DICEY.
SIR CHAS. DILKE, BART.
PROFESSOR DOWDEN.
M. E. GRANT DUFF.
ARCHDEACON FARRAR.
EDWARD A. FREEMAN.
J. A. FROUDE.
MRS. GARRET-ANDERSON, M.D.
J. W. L. GLAISHER, F.R.S.
SIR J. E. GORST, Q.C., M.P.
THOMAS HARE.
FREDERIC HARRISON.
ADMIRAL SIR G. P. HORNBY.
LORD HOUGHTON.
PROFESSOR HUXLEY.
PROFESSOR R. C. JEBB.
LADY JEUNE.
LORD KELVIN, P.R.S.
ANDREW LANG.
E. B. LANIN.
EMILE DE LAVELEYE.
W. E. H. LECKY.
T. E. CLIFFE LESLIE.
W. S. LILLY.
MARQUIS OF LORNE.
PIERRE LOTI.

SIR JOHN LUBBOCK, BART., M.P.
W. H. MALLOCK.
DR. MAUDSLEY.
PROFESSOR MAX MULLER.
GEORGE MEREDITH.
G. OSBORNE MORGAN, Q.C., M.P.
JOHN MORLEY, M.P.
WILLIAM MORRIS.
PROFESSOR H. N. MOSELEY.
F. W. H. MYERS.
F. W. NEWMAN.
PROFESSOR JOHN NICHOL.
W. G. PALGRAVE.
WALTER H. PATER.
LYON PLAYFAIR, M.P.
SIR HENRY POTTINGER, BART.
T. E. REDMOND, M.P.
PROFESSOR SAYCE.
PROFESSOR J. R. SEELEY.
LORD SHERBROOKE.
PROFESSOR SIDGWICK.
HERBERT SPENCER.
M. JULES SIMON.
HON. E. L. STANLEY.
SIR J. FITZJAMES STEPHEN, Q.C.
LESLIE STEPHEN.
J. HUTCHISON STIRLING.
A. C. SWINBURNE.
DR. VON SYBEL.
J. A. SYMONDS.
SIR THOMAS SYMONDS.
THE REV. EDWARD F. TALBOT.
SIR RICHARD TEMPLE, BART.
HON. LIONEL A. TOLLEMACHE.
COUNT LEO TOLSTOI.
H. D. TRAILL.
PROFESSOR TYNDALL.
ALFRED RUSSELL WALLACE.
SIDNEY WEBB.
A. J. WILSON.
GEN. VISCOUNT WOLSELEY.
GEN. SIR EVELYN WOOD.
THE EDITOR.
ETC., ETC., ETC.

**CHAPMAN & HALL, LD., 11, HENRIETTA STREET,
COVENT GARDEN, W.C.**

www.ingramcontent.com/pod-product-compliance
Lightning Source LLC
Chambersburg PA
CBHW031733230426
43669CB00007B/343